Further Praise for *Reading My Father*

"Fascinating and deeply moving."

—*San Francisco Chronicle*

"By turns brilliant and shocking . . . Alexandra Styron's account of 'the whole crazy-town scene in which I was raised,' and of the slow dawning of the severity of her father's condition, is handled with great skill."

—James Campbell, *The New York Times Book Review*

"Alexandra Styron is a natural writer, fluid, and engaging."

—Eric Liebetrau, *The Boston Globe*

"Riveting and heart-rending."

—Gail Caldwell, *Los Angeles Times*

"Alexandra Styron's beautifully honest memoir . . . gives us a multi-dimensional, continually fascinating portrait of William Styron's life."

—Heller McAlpin, *The Washington Post*

"A candid, compelling account, by turns heartwarming and heartbreaking . . . Vividly re-creates the delights of life as the child of a cultural icon."

—NPR.org

"A harrowing and at times darkly funny tale of towering successes . . . Gallant and unflinchingly honest."

—*The Atlanta Journal-Constitution*

"Styron . . . tells this harrowing, Icarus-like tale beautifully."

—*The Palm Beach Post*

"Fascinating and painful in what it reveals."

—*The Washington Times*

"Told with straightforward candor, remarkable objectivity, and the elegance of a well-honed craft . . . Alexandra Styron offers every privileged bit of information you've wondered and wanted to know about the inner workings and private family dynamic of an iconic writer."

—*The Martha's Vineyard Times*

"One of the finest, most lyrical, somewhat painful, terribly revealing books I've read in years. Styron is definitely the inheritor of her father's touch with prose."

—*Tallahassee Democrat*

"Utterly beautiful, clear-eyed, and poignant . . . Told respectfully and well."

—*San Antonio Express-News*

"Alexandra Styron is a gifted storyteller. . . . Her writing is crisp, direct, and, above all else, honest. . . . Despite the unpleasant revelations, Alexandra Styron's portrait of her father is nuanced, even tender."

—*Ottawa Citizen*

"Intelligent and compelling."

—*Library Journal*

"A magnificent book—clear-eyed, unsentimental, beautifully conceived and wrought, a picture of heady, long-gone literary times and a story as much about Styron herself as her illustrious and often disturbing father."

—*The Buffalo News*

"Enthralling storytelling . . . An abundance of humor, affection, and keen appreciation."

— *The Santa Fe New Mexican*

"Blended with skill, and driven by urgent, devoted, compassionate curiosity . . . [A] brave and unflinching book."

— *The Daily Telegraph* (UK)

"*Reading My Father* is the memoir of a childhood in an intellectually glittering, artistically engaged, and emotionally precarious household. In this portrait, by turns tender and unsparing, we meet William Styron, the charming bon vivant undone by depression, the gifted and prolific writer whose long struggle to finish his final novel may have imperiled his sanity. Fluid and fascinating, dark and funny, Alexandra Styron's book brings her father before us in all of his complexity, a literary lion, roaring his way through America's postwar landscape."

— **Geraldine Brooks, author of *March* and *People of the Book***

"A gene has been passed from father to daughter. Alexandra Styron, a born writer, tells the story of her father and the price he and his wife and children paid for his gift. Hers is a shocking book, painful in its truthfulness and moving in the love that holds this remarkable family together as depression and darkness claim the great man who is the center of their lives."

— **Mike Nichols**

"With great sympathy and bracing humor, Alexandra Styron tells the story of the development and maturation of William Styron's singular artistic talent, and of the tragic drowning of that talent—and of the man himself—in an inexorable tide of chronic depression. *Reading My Father* is a beautiful, utterly absorbing portrait of the artist, and moving proof of how his youngest daughter grew up to become a writer who would make her father proud."

—**John Burnham Schwartz, author of** *The Commoner* **and**
Reservation Road

"William Styron's autobiographical writings were both candid and withholding, and this penetrating memoir shines light on what they left out; it does so with tenderness and compassion. This would be a bracing examination of the father-daughter relationship even if its suffering hero were not famous."

—**Andrew Solomon, National Book Award–winning author of**
The Noonday Demon

"Alexandra Styron's account of her father is clear-eyed, frightening, and compassionate: an often lyrical view of Styron's struggle with despair, writing, and living. She is unsentimental about the toll his depression and alcoholism took on his work, and even less sentimental about the damage it did to his family. William Styron was a great writer and complex person; his daughter does him justice."

—**Kay Redfield Jamison, Ph.D., Professor of Psychiatry, The**
Johns Hopkins University School of Medicine,
and author of *An Unquiet Mind* **and**
Nothing Was the Same

ALSO BY ALEXANDRA STYRON

All the Finest Girls

Reading
My Father

A Memoir

Alexandra Styron

Scribner

NEW YORK   LONDON   TORONTO   SYDNEY   NEW DELHI

SCRIBNER
A Division of Simon & Schuster, Inc.
1230 Avenue of the Americas
New York, NY 10020

First Scribner trade paperback edition March 2012

SCRIBNER and design are registered trademarks of The Gale Group, Inc.,
used under license by Simon & Schuster, Inc., the publisher of this work.

For information about special discounts for bulk purchases, please contact
Simon & Schuster Special Sales at 1-866-506-1949
or business@simonandschuster.com.

The Simon & Schuster Speakers Bureau can bring authors to your
live event. For more information or to book an event, contact
the Simon & Schuster Speakers Bureau at 1-866-248-3049
or visit our website at www.simonspeakers.com.

Designed by Paul Dippolito

Manufactured in the United States of America

1   3   5   7   9   10   8   6   4   2

Library of Congress Control Number: 2010049145

ISBN 978-1-4165-9179-5
ISBN 978-1-4165-9181-8 (pbk)
ISBN 978-1-4165-9506-9 (ebook)

for Ed

and for Huck and Martha

I came to explore the wreck.
The words are purposes.
The words are maps.
I came to see the damage that was done
and the treasures that prevail.

—ADRIENNE RICH, "DIVING INTO THE WRECK"

Reading
My Father

One

After the funeral, walking home

WE BURIED MY father on a remarkably mild morning in November 2006. From our family's house on Martha's Vineyard to the small graveyard is less than a quarter mile, so we walked along the road, where, it being off-season, not a single car disturbed our quiet formation. Beneath the shade of a tall pin oak, we gathered around the grave site. Joining us were a dozen or so of my parents' closest friends. The ceremony had been planned the way we thought he'd have liked it—short on pomp, and shorter still on religion. A couple of people spoke; my father's friend Peter Matthiessen, a Zen priest, performed a simple blessing; and, as a family, we read the Emily Dickinson poem that my father had quoted at the end of his novel *Sophie's Choice.*

Ample make this bed.
Make this bed with awe;
In it wait till judgment break
Excellent and fair.

Be its mattress straight,
Be its pillow round;
Let no sunrise' yellow noise
Interrupt this ground.

My father had been a Marine, so the local VA offered us a full military funeral. Mindful of his sensibilities, we declined the chaplain. We also nixed the three-volley salute. But we were sure Daddy would have been pleased by the six local honor guards who folded the flag for my mother, and the lone bugler who played taps before we dispersed. Of military service, my father once wrote, "It was an experience I would not care to miss, if only because of the way it tested my endurance and my capacity for sheer misery, physical and of the spirit." The bugler, then, had honored another of my father's quirks: his penchant for a good metaphor.

A year and a half later, I was walking across the West Campus Quad of Duke University, my father's alma mater. Passing beneath the chapel's Gothic spire, I opened the heavy doors of Perkins Library and headed for the Rare Book, Manuscript, and Special Collections Library. It is there that the William Styron Papers, 22,500 items pertaining to his life and work, are housed. I was at the end of my third trip to North Carolina in as many months. Before I flew home to New York that afternoon, there were two big boxes I still hoped to get a look through.

In 1952, when he was twenty-six, my father published his first novel, *Lie Down in Darkness*. The book was an immediate success, and he was soon hailed as one of the great literary voices of his generation. Descendants of the so-called Lost Generation, my father and his crowd, including Norman Mailer, James Jones, and Irwin Shaw, embraced their roles as Big Male Writers. For years they perpetuated, without apology, the cliché of the gifted, hard-drinking, bellicose writer that gave so much of twentieth-century literature a muscular, glamorous aura. In 1967, after the disappointing reception of his second novel, *Set This House on Fire,* my father published *The Confessions of Nat Turner.* It became a number one bestseller, helped fuel the tense national debate over race, and provoked another one regarding the boundaries of artistic license. *Sophie's Choice,* published in 1979, won him critical and popular success around the world. Three years later, with the release of the film adaptation starring Meryl Streep and Kevin Kline, that story also brought him an extraliterary measure of fame. Winner of the Prix de Rome, American Book Award, Pulitzer Prize, the Howells Medal from the American Academy of Arts and Letters, and France's Légion d'Honneur, my father was considered one of the finest novelists of his time. He was also praised, perhaps by an even larger readership, for *Darkness Visible,* his frank account of battling, in 1985, with major clinical depression. A tale of descent and recovery, the book brought tremendous hope to fellow sufferers and their families. His eloquent prose dissuaded legions of would-be suicides and gave him an unlikely second act as the public face of unipolar depression.

As it turned out, the illness wasn't finished with my father. I think we all recognized, in the aftermath of his cataclysmic breakdown, that Bill Styron had *always* been depressed. A serious drinker, he relied on alcohol not only to self-medicate but to charm the considerable powers of his creative muse. When, at sixty, liquor began to disagree with him, he was surprised to find himself thoroughly unmanned. For many years after his '85 episode, he maintained a fragile equilibrium. But the scars were deep, and left him profoundly changed. He was stalked by feelings of guilt and shame. Several setbacks, mini major depressions, humbled him further and wore a still deeper cavity in the underpinnings of his confidence.

It seems that my father's Get out of Jail Free card had been unceremoniously revoked. And though he went about his business, he'd become a man both hunted and haunted.

*   *   *

ONE DAY WHEN I was still a baby, not yet old enough to walk, my mother went out, leaving me in the care of my seven-year-old brother, Tommy, and nine-year-old sister, Polly. Before she left, my mother placed me in my walker. For a while, Polly, Tommy, and the two friends they had over played on the ground floor of our house while I gummed my hands and tooled around the kitchen island. Then, one by one, the older kids drifted outside. Maybe a half hour later, they found themselves together at Carl Carlson's farm stand at the bottom of our hill. On the makeshift counter of his small shed, Carl sold penny candy; no one could resist a visit on the couple of days a week he was open. It took a little while, scrabbling over bubble gum and fireballs, before, with a sickening feeling, my siblings realized that nobody was watching the Baby. Racing back up the hill, Polly burst into the kitchen but couldn't find me. After a minute or so, she heard a small moaning sound and followed it to the basement door. I was still strapped in my walker, but upside down on the concrete floor at the bottom of the rickety wood stairs. My forehead had swelled into a grotesque mound. My eyes were glassy and still. Cradling me, Polly and Tommy passed another stricken, terrified hour before my mother got home and rushed me to the hospital.

I've known this famous family story for as long as I can remember. But I was in my thirties before Polly confessed a detail I'd never known: our father was upstairs napping the whole time. Afraid for her own life as much as for mine, she couldn't bring herself to wake him.

Until 1985, my father's tempestuous spirit ruled our family's private life as surely as his eminence defined the more public one.

At times querulous and taciturn, cutting and remote, melancholy when he was sober and rageful when in his cups, he inspired fear and loathing in us a good deal more often than it feels comfortable to admit. But the same malaise that so decimated my father's equanimity when he was depressed also quelled his inner storm when he recovered. In my adult years, he became remarkably mellow. A lion in winter, he drank less and relaxed more. He showed some patience, was mild, and expressed flashes of great tenderness for his children, his growing tribe of grandchildren, and, most especially, his wife.

He also managed, for the first time, to access some of his childhood's unexamined but corrosive sorrows. In 1987 my father wrote "A Tidewater Morning," a short story in which he delivered a poignant chronicle of his mother's death from cancer when he was thirteen. The story would become the title of a collection of short fiction, published in 1993, that centered on the most significant themes of his youth. During these years he also wrote several essays for *The New Yorker, Esquire, The New York Times, Newsweek,* and other magazines. He published a clutch of editorials; wrote thirty some odd speeches, commencement addresses, eulogies, and tributes; and traveled frequently to speak on the subject of mental illness.

As for long fiction, it was less clear what he was doing. (If there was a golden rule in our house when I was growing up, it was, unequivocally, "Don't ask Daddy about his work.") First and foremost, my father was a novelist. "A high priest at the altar of fiction," as Carlos Fuentes describes him, he consecrated himself to the Novel. He wrote in order to explore the sorts of grand and sometimes existential themes whose complexity and scope are best served by long fiction. With a kind of sacred devotion, he kept at it, maintaining his belief in the narrative powers of a great story—and he suffered accordingly in the process. His prose, laid down in an elegant hand on yellow legal pads with Venus Velvet No. 2 pencils, came at a trickle. He labored over every word, editing as he went, to produce manuscripts that, when he placed the final period, needed very little in the way of revision. But, even at the height of his powers, this meant sometimes a decade or more between major works. Like that of a marathoner running in the dark, my father's path was sometimes as murky as it was long.

*   *   *

THE AIR-CONDITIONED HUSH of the Duke library was, as always, a relief to me. Zach, my favorite student employee, gave me his familiar smile and nod, then passed a small lock across the circulation desk. If you've ever spent time in a rare book library, you know that the system for protecting its contents can be a little intimidating. You may not bring coats or hats, purses or bags of any kind into the reading room. No snacks or drinks, including water. Pencils only. And notebooks, but preferably without the complicated pockets or linings that might abet an act of smuggling, were you so inclined. White cotton gloves are provided for handling photographs. And at Duke, anyway, they'll give you a sheet of laminated paper to use as a place marker, plus a folder for transferring documents up to the copier. When you leave, you're subject to inspection. Notebooks are riffled, papers are stamped. It's a polite but mandatory ritual, necessary for the safekeeping of all that is unique and fragile under the institution's custodial care. When I started spending time at the library, I was struck by how curiously familiar it all was to me. Then I had a good laugh when I realized why: it's a lot like the routines of a psychiatric hospital.

Taking a spot at one of the long wood tables, I flipped through the inventory list for the call numbers of the boxes I would need that morning. Up until then, I'd spent most of my time at Duke reading my father's correspondence, trying to shake loose some memories of this man I'd rather impetuously agreed to write a book about. Somehow, in the time since his death, I'd mentally misplaced him. I thought if I heard his voice, sifted through his epistolary remains, he'd resurface—which he did, and then some. Not only had I begun to remember the father I'd known but I became acquainted with the son, mentor, and friend he was to others. In addition to the letters, I'd trolled through scrapbooks, magazine essays, interview transcripts, journals, audiocassettes, and all sorts of other ephemera. Being neither a scholar nor a critic, I'd written off my list the enormous cache of typescripts, proofs, and fragmentary monographic work that had been published before. After several months of work, there were only a couple more boxes of curiosity to me: "WS16: Speeches Subseries, 1942–1996," and "WS17: Unfinished Work Subseries, 1970–1990s and undated."

* * *

IN THE EARLY 1970s, shortly after the publication of *The Confessions of Nat Turner,* my father began work on a new novel. *The Way of the Warrior,* its title taken from the Japanese *Bushido,* or samurai code of conduct, was a World War II story. In it he hoped to explore the military mind-set, and his own ambivalence about the glory and honor associated with patriotic service. Just as the civil rights movement echoed in the themes of *Nat Turner,* my father's new book, conceived during the Vietnam conflict, would, he hoped, gather force from the timeliness of its subject. But the central elements of the story failed to coalesce, and Daddy grew discouraged. Then, in 1973, he awoke from a powerful dream about a woman, a Holocaust survivor, he'd encountered while living in Brooklyn as a young man. Putting aside *The Way of the Warrior,* he quickly began work on his new idea. Six years later, Random House published *Sophie's Choice.*

Just as some people can tag a family event by remembering what bank Dad was indentured to that year or which shift Mom worked, each phase of my youth is joined in my mind to the novel my father was writing at the time. I was twelve years old when *Sophie's Choice* came out. Newly arrived on the shores of adolescence, I was acutely conscious of myself and my family's place in the world. It seemed I'd been waiting my entire life for my father to *finish what-*

ever he was doing. With only the vaguest memory of *Nat Turner,* I'd begun to seriously doubt my father did anything really except sleep all morning and spend the rest of the day stomping in and out through his study door. So it was a huge personal relief to me when *Sophie's Choice* was completed at last, validating my father's years of work and, in the process, me.

If the story of Sophie played in the background of my schoolgirl years, my father's book about the Marines set the mood through my teens. In the early eighties, after the hullabaloo surrounding *Sophie* had died down, he returned to *The Way of the Warrior* with renewed vigor. The project, his Next Big Book, took on a kind of stolid permanence in our home, like a sofa around which we were subconsciously arrayed. About this time, I left home, as my siblings had before me, for boarding school. And though I knew little about what my father was writing, it was useful to have the title. For the part of myself defined by his profession—and for anyone who asked—it was enough.

In its 1985 summer reading issue, *Esquire* magazine published "Love Day," billing it as an excerpt from his long-awaited novel. My father was showered with mail, from friends and fans alike, the reaction immediate and overwhelmingly positive. The world had been put on alert. Bill Styron was at it again; great American literature would live to see another day.

And then he cracked up.

These days, the characterization of my father's illness would be readily identifiable. But this was back in the Stone Age of clinical depression. The mid-eighties was not only a pre-Prozac world but one without any of the edifying voices that would cry out from the wilderness in the years ahead. There was no Kay Jamison, no Andrew Solomon, and, of course, no Bill Styron—no one yet back from the fresh hell of depression with any cogent field notes. So, like everybody else around my father, our family was mystified by his sudden spiral. By his paralytic anxiety, his numb affect, his rambling, suicidal ideation. He had everything going for him, didn't he? Loving family, towering talent, money, friends. When, just before Christmas, my mother admitted him with his consent to the psychiatric ward of Yale–New Haven Hospital, we had absolutely no idea what would become of him. When he emerged two months later, declaring himself cured, we were just as quick as he was to embrace the diagnosis.

For the third time, he returned to *The Way of the Warrior*. I don't know for how long he worked at it this go-round. Away at college by then, I was not only uninterested in my father but determinedly on the run from him, from my mother, from the whole crazy-town scene in which I was raised. Fulfilling my long-standing efforts to grow up as fast as I could, I'd moved with my much older boyfriend into a stodgy building where I lived like someone three times my age. Like someone who neither had, nor needed, parents, especially ones as nutty as mine.

What remained between my father and me was our enduring common ground, and practically the only place we ever met: our shared sense of humor. The youngest of my parents' four children by a wide margin, I was known, long past the time it was seemly, as the Baby. As a girl, I often found myself home alone with him. My sisters and brother were all gone by the time I was in fourth grade; my mother, escaping the tinderbox her marriage had become, had begun traveling constantly by the time I was five. The house where we spent most of the year, a creaky old Connecticut farmhouse bound by woods, was scary. My father was scarier. I survived by employing a child's best instinct for getting what she needs. I didn't whine, I didn't demand, and I hid my multiple failings and fears behind a smooth and carefully cultivated mask of self-sufficiency. But, above all, I soothed my father's savage breast by making him laugh—and standing up to even the most extreme of his humor in kind.

After *Darkness Visible,* my father was inundated by mail. Not simple fan letters but the raw outpourings of depression's many victims—breathless fellow escapees; those still in its clutches; the grief-struck mothers, husbands, and daughters of the countless suicides who simply could not live with the pain one more day. Occasionally, his readers breached the boundaries of letter writing. People accosted him on the street, at parties, when he lectured. They spoke to him as though he were, at the very least, a supremely trained doctor, if not some divine medium who might heal them with empathy. More than once, he got a late-night call from the police. Someone somewhere was intent on committing suicide, but they kept mentioning Bill Styron. Was it possible he might try talking the poor fellow down?

My father devoted an enormous amount of time, time that might otherwise have been spent on his own work, reacting to his readers. He talked and wrote, listened and opined. Of course, not everyone who reached out to him was a fan. The day's post often included missives from disgruntled readers who didn't think much of his opinions on mental health, or who urged him to consider their own protocols for recovery and happy living. And some were just plain bananas (which came as no surprise to him—my father was the first to admit he himself had, during his depressive episode, been totally off his rocker). He'd always received mail from cranks and kooks— writing about slavery and the Holocaust *will* bring them out of the woodwork—but never as many as after *Darkness Visible*.

During my visits to Duke, I read through scores of these letters. Most of them are intimate, confessional, harrowing, and occasionally inspiring. Taken collectively, they are a stunning testament to the power of my father's memoir. But they're also completely overwhelming, a kind of paper Babel from which even the most patient psychiatrist might flee in search of quiet and sanity. As I flipped through them, I began to imagine all this material peck-peck-pecking away at my father's still fragile psyche. Every day, year after year. I also thought, not for the first time, of the exquisite irony embedded in my father's relationship with his readers, an irony I was still trying to reconcile as I worked to make sense of the man after his death: how could a guy whose thoughts elicit this much pathos have been, for so many years, such a monumental asshole to the people closest to him?

I felt like picking the letters up by the fistful and shouting into the silence of the library, *PEOPLE! Do you have ANY idea who you are dealing with here?*

In the spring of 2000, fifteen years after his first depression, my father once again heard "the wind of the wing of madness."* Swiftly, he succumbed to a depression easily as fierce as his 1985 episode. In June, Mum admitted him to the Yale Psychiatric Institute. Thrown again into triage mode, all of us gathered around. We took turns sitting with him, monitoring his bouts of psychosis, consulting with his doctors, and walking him along the fluorescent-lit corridors of the ward. When the four kids—Susanna, Polly, Tom, and me, now adults—were alone together, we fretted and laughed and traded "you won't believe what happened today" stories. And each of us, pushing the mute button on our ambivalent feelings, willed our father onward in the hope that he'd achieve the same kind of recovery he'd had before. Not this time. Our father left YPI later that summer, sprung by our mother after a frightful and chaotic two months, in which any improvement in his mood was entirely undone by his physical deterioration. He came home to the Vineyard, ragged, out of his mind, patched together with psychopharmacological tape and thread. And then the shit really hit the fan. Though he would live another six years, the summer of 2000 undisputedly marked the beginning of the end.

*　*　*

A COUPLE OF years before my father's death, I caught a glimpse of his last manuscript. It was September, and my husband and I

---

*William Styron, *Darkness Visible* (New York: Random House, 1990), p. 46, quoting Baudelaire.

had taken our son up to the house in Connecticut, which had for months been uninhabitable. The prior spring, in a perfect metaphoric act, a prolonged stretch of rain had caused the living room floor to collapse. Inspections revealed not only water damage but termites, a dodgy foundation, and a fireplace hearth of highly questionable integrity. My mother relocated to the Vineyard place, from which my father came and went on what had become a merry-go-round of hospital stays. A crew spent the summer propping up and patching the Connecticut house, while in Massachusetts our family continued a similar project on Daddy. No one, except maybe our unrestrainedly optimistic mother, expected him to write again.

I'd been wandering around the house, checking on the state of things, when I walked into my sister Polly's old bedroom, where, when all the kids had grown, my father had chosen to write. A thin layer of dust covered his tilt-top desk. But everything else was laid out just so, as if he'd stepped out for lunch and might come back to work any minute. On the right side of the desk lay a thick wedge of yellow legal paper, filled with my father's script. And on top of that was a sheaf of yellowing stationery with an envelope paper-clipped to it, postmarked 1914.

"Dear Eunice," it began. I scanned the letter, picking up phrases. "I went down to Goldsboro that Sunday expecting to see you and to hear your voice 'for old time's sake' . . . my mind and soul tortured by the ghosts of former days, my conscience tortured by the might have beens . . . I can hardly say the words—your approaching wedding. . . . I can only hold your friendship in the shrine of memory."

The letter, which struck me as unbearably poignant, had been written by my grandfather William Clark Styron, Sr. Though I'd never read it, I knew what it was and why it was on my father's desk. For a while, he had worked on a novel loosely based on the life of his father, a marine engineer whose singular character had done more than anything else to mold my father's own. I knew of this book only vaguely, having heard my mother talk about it once and maybe having read something of it in an interview my father had given some years before. As always, it was to be a "Big Book," about the skeins of troubled history running through the American South in which he was raised. It was about War and Race. And, at its heart, it was to be a love story. I remember, when I first heard the idea, thinking of García Márquez's *Love in the Time of Cholera,* and how much more I would enjoy a tale of romance than the war story Daddy seemed forever bent on. That day in his study, I leaned in and began to read the manuscript's opening paragraph, my guilt for snooping so deeply ingrained I didn't allow myself even to follow the last sentence onto the next page. Somewhere in the basement, I could hear drills and nail guns. And suddenly I thought, *This thing is just sitting here. What if someone steals it? What if the house goes up in flames? Someone ought to take better care of this stuff.*

Several days later, on a fiercely rainy day, I carried the manuscript in a pink Jill Stuart shopping bag up to the offices of Random House and my father's editor, Bob Loomis. I deposited the bag on Bob's desk, wiping the edges with the sleeve of my shirt. We chatted for a bit about my father's health, about our families, and about the upcoming tribute to my father being hosted by *The Paris Review.* Getting him there was going to be a challenge. We'd probably have to spring him from Mass General, his residence of the moment, and hire a car or something to bring him down. But then again, I said, who knew where he'd be several weeks on? He might be fine by November.

Well, not fine. Or I wouldn't have been standing there. For what Bob and I were tacitly acknowledging, with that bag on the table, was that my father would never be fine again.

*　　*　　*

THE BOX OF speeches in the Duke library turned out to be much more interesting than I'd expected. There were nearly fifty compositions inside, including the commencement address my father had given at my high school graduation, a great recounting of how he missed out on a Rhodes scholarship, and a college address that fascinated me because, from its date, I knew he was in the midst of a depression when he delivered it. With no more than a half hour before I had to leave to catch my flight home, I finally opened the last box, that of his unfinished work.

Several fat folders dominated the box. Flipping them open, I found that the contents of each one was prefaced by an explanatory note from the man who had been my father's Boswell of sorts, James West. Having spent a decade on his 1998 authorized biography, *William Styron: A Life*, Jim had gone on to become a crucial figure in the preservation of my father's legacy. He frequently served as a conduit for the donations to Duke. And, in my father's final years, he had begun the complex task of organizing and editing material that my father no longer had the strength for and that would, more than likely, be published after he was gone.

"THE WAY OF THE WARRIOR," began the first note, in caps. And then it continued, "The Material in this folder appears to be part of the first effort Styron made to write a novel under this title." Jim added some information about the material in general, concluding with qualifying testimony. "I cannot absolutely vouch for the fact that these materials are part of the first effort on *Warrior*," he wrote, "but I think I've made the identifications correctly."

I looked at the manuscript but found that the first page was page 5 and began in the middle of a sentence. The second page was page 11, after which the manuscript moved on sequentially till page 33. The page after that was 39, and then the numbers began to run backward, then forward again. 22, 199, 68 twice. Four different pages numbered 74. 77, 70, 1, 3, 173.

On and on it went like this. Hundreds of pages jumbled, others omitted entirely. In the order they were in, the manuscript made no sense at all, though I had little doubt that Jim and everyone at Duke had taken exquisite care of these documents, as they had with all the archives. I opened the second *Warrior* folder. It was much the same, except bigger—maybe 90,000 or 100,000 words of prose—and, if possible, even more disorganized. The first page was 105, the last 211. The third folder was, blessedly, organized, pages 1 to 159, and included a short note from Daddy to the library's curator of manuscripts. It was dated February 2, 1985.

I sat for a while, trying to understand what I was looking at. What the hell had happened? Looking through the folders again, I could see it wasn't just a matter of putting the pages in order. Even when I held up two pages so the numbers followed sequentially, the sentence fragments didn't flow. It was like someone had taken a cabinet full of puzzles, tossed a bunch of pieces into two boxes, and thrown the rest out. Nothing fit. More unnerving still was the sheer volume. This World War II story, whatever it was, he ran at it again and again. Two hundred fifty thousand, maybe 300,000 words. Crafted sentences, polished, honed. Avenues of thought, narrative built on mountains of research. Great, long loops of memory and emotion. The edifice of a story, constructed, deconstructed, and constructed again and again over the course of years. Images of Daddy clicked through my head, a slide show cascading suddenly as urgent and disordered as the pile of prose before me. My head reeled. Was it any wonder he was depressed?

I turned back to the box, which contained several more folders. My eyesight telescoped as I began flipping through the material, a kind of fuzziness taking over the outer edges of my vision. I could actually feel all my other body functions slowing down in the service of my brain and its need to absorb the information before me. Could it be? There was not one, as I had thought, but *four* other books my father had started on over the years. The folder tabs, marked "Father," "Grandfather," "Nicaragua," "Hospital," hinted at the contents. Some of the manuscripts were thick, some thin, all of them produced on Daddy's signature legal-length paper, his carefully wrought hand covering the pages from margin to margin. These, too, were disordered, filled with stops and starts, the page numbers suggestive of chunks missing, or thrown away. The whole huge pile vibrated with the strength of his effort. And with a certain madness.

I went outside to get some air. Under practically every willow oak lining the quad stood flocks of prospective students and their parents. Their young guides gestured animatedly, mouths shaping words I couldn't hear. The sun was blazing. I wandered around the corner to the shelter of a magnolia and called Susanna on my cell phone. Though she is the eldest of my siblings, and there are twelve years between us, it is Susanna to whom I've grown closest over the years. We speak frequently; on that day, she knew where I was and what I was doing.

"Hi," she answered, seeing my number on her screen.

"Holy shit," I said.

"What?"

"I don't know," I replied, pacing, sucking in the dense Southern heat. "It's like *A Beautiful Mind* in there. There are all these manuscripts. A whole bunch of them. And none of the pages follow each other. It's bizarre. And kind of horrible. Did you know about them?"

She did not. But, in talking to me, she put words to what I was thinking.

"Wow," she said, after a bit. "Perfect metaphor, huh?"

"Yeah," I replied. "But was he depressed, and then he couldn't write? Or was he unable to write? And it drove him completely mad."

Two

The family. Newsweek *photo shoot, 1967. That's me
at the center, poised to vandalize Polly's homework.*

I USED TO THINK my father looked like Desi Arnaz. Anyone
who ever met Bill Styron, or has seen a picture of him, knows this
is crazy. My father looked about as much like Desi as he looked
like Lucy. His complexion was Scotch-Irish fair, his thin lips were
peaked by a faint cupid's bow, and his expressive eyes lay tucked
behind sloping, hooded lids that lent him a permanent look of
world-weariness. As for the way Daddy put himself together, he
didn't. He wore the same clothes day after day, shambled about in
whatever worn and homely shoes would accommodate his troublesome feet, and let his hair take the attitude it struck when he awoke
that day. As Mike Nichols said of him at his memorial service, "Bill
had a great sense of style. He never had any idea what he was wearing." My father's resemblance, then, to the slick Cuban crooner

with full mouth and limpid gaze began and ended with the color—
brown—of his eyes and hair.

I thought he looked like Desi Arnaz because I watched a lot of
television. Most American kids growing up in the seventies and
eighties watched too much TV. I watched more. Returning home
at the end of the day, I could run through the kitchen, drop my
book bag, and twist the knob on our Zenith in less time than it took
whoever had picked me up that day to shut the car door I'd probably left open. And there I would sit, like some doped-up zombie,
till it was time for bed. My brother watched, too. Racing me to
the TV room, he'd grab the best seat, then tee up a butch menu—
Emergency!, *Adam-12*, *Mission: Impossible*—that I endured like
any kid sister, glad enough to be allowed to breathe the same air.
Eventually Tommy wandered off, on to girls and Bob Dylan and
dabbling in the silver market, and I had the joint to myself. I ate
my dinner in front of the TV. I did my homework (or didn't) in the
same spot, with the television on. And on weekends I fell asleep
there, to the laugh track of *The Carol Burnett Show* (or the famous
theme to *The Twilight Zone*, if I was sugared up enough to last
that long). Between kindergarten and tenth grade, I suppose I saw
every episode of every popular television show broadcast between
4:30 and 9:00 P.M. Eastern Standard Time. *I Love Lucy*, on nightly
in reruns, inveigled its way into my spongy mind.

Most of the time, no one bothered me about my despicable
habit. My father was oblivious. And Mum, a great believer in the
value of fun, would have let me set my hair on fire if I told her
that I wanted to. Also, they were busy. In addition to the house on
the Vineyard, my parents kept a small apartment in Manhattan, a
two-hour drive away. My mother, in particular, spent a lot of time
there. In the early seventies, she took up the cause of human rights,
which, along with her poetry and love of travel, absorbed her more
and more over the years. Sometimes several times a week, she went
"into town" for work as well as pleasure. There were board meetings and benefits, marches and symposiums, early-morning flights

to Eastern Bloc countries, and dinners that went too late to make the long drive home. Sometimes, she came in the door just in time to see me off to school. With the old name tag still on her jacket, she'd be gone again by afternoon.

When they were home together, my parents ate at nine or so, European-style, after the house had calmed down and the children were out of their hair. As often as not, this didn't go so well. Mum would get on the phone and forget about the stove. Smoke drifted into the TV room like some cartoon cloud, oozing down the hall-way, where it would soon deliver the bad news to my father: dinner was ruined. Mum chatted, the steak burned. I pulled up tight on the couch and waited for the ax to fall. *Rose! Jesus fucking Christ! . . . I'm sorry, sweetheart, I just turned my back a second. . . . Well, look, it's totally ruined! . . . No, no, I can fix it. Look. . . . Just forget it! I'm not hungry!* On better nights, usually just as I was getting ready for bed, Daddy would call to me. "Albert! You want to get us some wine?" Screwing up my courage, I'd head for the base-ment. I had no memory of my infamous tumble. But beneath the kitchen was a dark and musty netherworld, mysterious holes in the rock foundation tunneling back into oblivion, and it terrified me. Still, I took my job seriously and did it with pride. Scurrying back upstairs with a nice bottle of cabernet, I'd hoist myself up on the counter, where I could get some leverage on the corkscrew, and tug till I got the clean *pop.* "Thank *you,*" Daddy would say, reaching out for the handoff. Then I'd beat a hasty retreat, while Mum ran things back and forth to the table. My father was already plunging into his meal.

Occasionally, they drove to the city together. A book party, an opening, or an event at which my father was being honored would coax him out of his Wallabees and into a blue blazer. While he paced back and forth through the TV room, periodically shouting up the stairs, *Goddamn it, Rose! We've got to leave NOW!,* I'd pry myself off the couch and reach up to dust the dandruff from his lapels. "How do I look?" he might say. "Groovy," I might reply ironically, returning to my spot like a dog to her bed. I'd listen over the laugh track to the *clatter clatter* of shoes down the stairs and *Just one more thing* and *Well, I'm going out to the car! I'm going without you!* and *I'm coming, darling,* and then they were gone.

I wasn't usually alone. Help of every description came and went at our house. Ethel and James Terry, a couple whom my parents had hired when my sisters were small, were for years the rock foundation of our family. Ettie, as we called her, was a big woman with the wide-planed face of her Native American people. She cooked, did laundry, and babysat. Terry (always just "Terry"), about the only black man in Litchfield County, was handyman, gardener, and driver. He was also Tommy's godfather and, along with Lillian Hellman, the dedicatee of *The Confessions of Nat Turner.* They lived in New Milford, a short drive away. When they weren't at our house, Terry ran a little car repair outfit from the back of his house, for which Ettie (Terry could not read or write) tended the books. Early in the morning, they would drive over the hill to Roxbury in time to get us ready for school.

"You had a good home, but you wouldn't stay there!" Terry would holler, standing over my bed. Years after he'd moved north, his South Carolina drawl remained thick as mud. I sometimes had no idea what he was talking about; phrases picked up on the cotton farm where he was raised, and from his years in the Army, studded his conversation. But I couldn't miss the intent. If his voice didn't roust you, you'd get a cold washcloth. After that, it was a glass of water.

"Come on, Toolum!" he'd roar as the cold splash hit my face. "We gots to get goin'! There's more snow out there than Cotta [Cotter? Carter?] got oats!"

Sometimes, when Ettie made me turn the TV off, I'd hitch a ride around the lawn on Terry's mower. Or I'd sit with him in the converted chicken coop that was his toolshed and all-around clubhouse. The place reeked of gasoline, Newport cigarettes, and the charred embers of the wood-burning stove. Along with the feel of his flannel shirt against my cheek, the aroma of Terry's shed was the essence of comfort and permanence.

When I was still small, diabetes began to slow Ettie down. After I was about seven, we saw little of her. Terry continued on at my parents' house for a couple of years after that, but his hours got shorter as he grew dotty and less reliable. In his final years, after Ettie had died, Terry's mind collapsed on him completely. One day when I was about twelve and on a visit, I walked into his living room. All around his sectional couch, he'd opened and propped magazines. The faces of my parents' many famous friends—Ted Kennedy, Frank Sinatra, Joan Baez, people Terry had met and many times served—stared out from each one.

"The Kennedys, they've been here for days," he said, his eyes tired and anxious. "I've been taking care of them, but they won't leave."

My parents placed Terry in a minimum-care assisted living facility—more like a bed-and-breakfast for the aged—but he kept wandering off. One day, his sister, a craven woman who'd never before shown much interest in her brother, came up from Washington and took Terry, and his savings, away. Tommy went to D.C. a couple of times to visit; seeing Terry in the grim environs of his sister's apartment was awful. None of the rest of us ever saw him again.

In between, after, and all along the way, dozens of other faces peopled the landscape. Mavis was my baby nurse, and she stayed till I was two. Marjorie lived with us when I was four and five. So did Nicky, the daughter of one of Daddy's old girlfriends, until her bizarre behavior—coming in at 3:00 A.M. and running full speed, Mrs. Rochester–like, up to the attic; hiding out in the laundry room eating dog bones—made her a liability. Local girls like Katie, Stacey, and Sandy from the dairy farm down the hill picked me up at school, made me dinner, and went home. Bertha Jackson cleaned the house. Larry Schmidtheimie, who chewed a stub of a fat cigar and looked not unlike Santa Claus, maintained the yard after Terry left (he also drove me to my first day of college and moved me into my dorm; my parents were, I think, on the Vineyard). Eventually Daphne Lewis arrived, though everyone, including Daphne herself, has a different opinion about *when.* Shuttling back and forth from her nurse's aide job in Toronto, Daphne lived with us for a few months at a stretch, cooking for my parents and watching after me. She helped look after my grandfather in his final years, and my father in his.

Under the feet of this human parade was a smaller but no less constant stream of animals. Newfoundlands and Labradors; domestic cats and mangy strays; lovebirds, until they were eaten by the cats; mice, until they were fed to the snakes; hamsters, squirrels, guinea pigs, lizards. We had a goat named Feather, who wore out her welcome when she got in bed with my father one morning. And a pony named Gino, kept down in Carl Carlson's pasture, who liked to turn back to the barn at a full gallop, then throw me headfirst through the doorway.

My parents also had a huge circle of friends. Philip Roth, Dick and Jean Widmark, Arthur Miller and Inge Morath, Mike and Annabelle Nichols, Lewis and Jay Allen, Francine and Cleve Gray. When my parents arrived in 1954, Litchfield County was still a remote and relatively untrammeled corner of Connecticut. But, over the years, dozens of urban refugees arrived, drawn by the tranquil beauty of the area and the proximity to New York. By the time I was born, it was all rather Chekhovian, with its countrified intellectuals, rambling dachas, and loops of important conversation unfolding on walks through the green, birch-studded hills. Thanks to Daddy's star power and Mum's charm, my parents were very much at the center of this world. People came from great distances for an evening at the Styrons'. Their dinners were magical, the candlelit table groaning with food, great, running rivers of alcohol, and guest lists that were rarely less than Olympian. Our Christmas party was not to be missed—Leonard Bernstein on the piano, presents for everyone—and even the flimsier holidays got a goosing from my mother until they erupted into crowded, merry festivals. By the ends of these galas, my father was usually in a mellow mood. Kicked back in his favorite yellow chair, with a Scotch and cigar, he would amiably steer the conversation around the tent poles of his desiring—politics, literature, money, high-end gossip. Urgent voices responded in kind, swelled by laughter, profanity, complex movements of thought. The music of a great night rose and fell in our living room, and no one wanted to leave. All of this delighted my mother, for whom a house full of people was the greatest pleasure, a reward for all the dark days she endured in between.

*   *   *

WHEN I WAS born, my father was poised on one of his life's great precipices. He was forty-one years old. Fifteen years had passed since *Lie Down in Darkness* heralded him as a wunderkind, and six since the publication of *Set This House on Fire.* Having set a punishing schedule for himself, he spent the intervening years transforming exhaustive research into a stirring 200,000-word narrative that was about to become *The Confessions of Nat Turner.* As always, his work was at the center of our family's existence, playing like a constant drumbeat under everything we did—whether we were strictly conscious of it or not. On the evening of January 22, 1967, Daddy walked down the hill from his study to find his family assembled in the kitchen. Mum was at the stove; Susanna, Polly, and Tommy were all sitting down waiting for dinner. Eleven weeks old, I was in a bouncy seat on top of the kitchen table, working my pacifier.

"Well, I've finished," Daddy said, weary but triumphant.

On cue, before anyone else had made a sound, I popped the pacifier out of my mouth like a cork from a bottle of champagne.

And so the late sixties were marked in our family by twin births, *Nat* and me, each making our own noise. The novel arrived in bookstores in October '67. The week of my first birthday, Daddy was on the cover of *Newsweek.* With a few exceptions, *The Confessions of Nat Turner* drew rave reviews. Philip Rahv, in *The New*

York Review of Books, called it a "a first-rate novel, the best William Styron has ever written and the best by an American writer that has appeared in some years." "A new peak in the literature of the South," said *Time* magazine; "a dazzling shaft of light . . . a triumph," said *The New York Times.* In November, my father received an honorary degree from Wilberforce University, America's oldest private all-black university, in Wilberforce, Ohio. It was an immensely gratifying experience for him. The risk he'd taken—fictively embodying a rebel slave, a black icon, in order to produce what he called a "meditation on history"—not only had paid off but was being embraced by the people whose acceptance he wished most to gain. In a 1992 essay for *American Heritage,* my father described the event. "There was much applause," he wrote. "George Shirley, a Wilberforce alumnus who was the leading tenor with the Metropolitan Opera, gave a spine-chilling rendition of the Battle Hymn of the Republic, in which the audience joined together, singing with great emotion. Standing in that auditorium, I was moved by a feeling of oneness with these people. I felt gratitude at their acceptance of me . . . as if my literary labors and my plunge into history had helped dissolve many of the preconceptions about race that had been my birthright as a Southerner and allowed me to better understand the forces that had shaped our common destiny. For me it was a moment of intense warmth and brotherhood."

It was also a moment that wouldn't last. My father, like many first-rate artists, had a cunning sense of history. He knew there is a time, of urgency and relevance, for certain books, and that hitting that moment right can transform one's words from a pretty bit of business into a profound testament to humanity with a history-enhancing power all its own. Indeed, with a touch of Icarus about him, my father seemed interested almost exclusively in this kind of luminous flight. It was no coincidence that *Nat Turner* came to life in the crucible of the civil rights movement. Likewise, I doubt my father could have been surprised that a high-profile novel about race would provoke some of the same convulsive and polarizing feelings that characterized the era. Many years later, in a documentary about Daddy, the eminent African American scholar (and friend to my father) Henry Louis Gates, Jr., talked about the firestorm of controversy that ultimately erupted around the book. In the era of Huey Newton and the Black Panther culture, he said, my father's decision to conceive of Nat as a man who not only lusts after white women but also has homosexual feelings was bound to provoke outrage. My father's Nat Turner "was at odds with the kind of black man necessary for the times," he said. Daddy "*had* to know he was setting himself up as a sacrificial lamb," said Gates, adding with a sympathetic chuckle, "as we like to say, 'Nigga *please.*'"

And yet, my father was deeply upset by the controversy. In 1968 our household began to resemble a roiling little microcosm of the drama unfolding all across America. Scathing attacks on *Nat Turner* appeared in *The New Republic, The Yale Review, The Kenyon Review,* and *The Journal of Negro History,* to name a few. The Marxist historian Herbert Aptheker excoriated my father in *The Nation,* a situation Daddy inflamed when he took the bait and responded in a subsequent issue. Soon the Aptheker-Styron feud was national news. A planned film adaptation of the book was derailed by an organization calling itself the Black Anti-Defamation Association, created by Ossie Davis and Ruby Dee with the express purpose of shutting down the film project. And during two conferences my father participated in, at Harvard and at the Southern Historical Association, he was hectored by the same man, dressed in a dashiki and intent on proving he was a "liar."

In May 1968, just weeks after Martin Luther King's assassination, *The Confessions of Nat Turner* was awarded the Pulitzer Prize. In June, my father served as an honorary pallbearer at Bobby Kennedy's funeral. Two months later, while Daddy was at the Democratic convention in Chicago witnessing firsthand a nation on the brink of anarchy, Beacon Press published *William Styron's Nat Turner: Ten Black Writers Respond.* A compendium of essays edited by a history teacher named John Henrik Clarke, the book is a roundhouse assault on *Nat Turner,* deriding my father's "vile racist imagination," accusing him of "destroying [Nat] as a man and a leader," and, by extension, implicating him in losses more recent and raw. "Black Brothers and Sisters," urged John Oliver Killens in his essay "The Confessions of Willie Styron," "be not deceived by the obscene weeping and gnashing of teeth by white America over the assassination of our great black brother and Messiah, Martin Luther King. They loved him not . . . they understood him not. Our Martin was a revolutionary, and they did not dig him; therefore they destroyed him."

All through this period, my father was receiving reams of mail, both positive and negative. Some of the letters, from blacks and whites alike, were truly menacing. They unnerved him with increasing frequency. One afternoon while Mum was spending the night in New York and Daddy couldn't reach her, he completely panicked. Jumping in the car without a belt or socks on, he drove to New York and frantically called around the city from my mother's empty hotel room. When she at last turned up—she'd been collaborating with some Russian poets on translations of their work and hadn't thought to call—Daddy was beside himself. For a long while after this incident, he would require my mother to check in with him at regular intervals.

Bumbling along in the pre-memory phase of life, I don't have any concrete recollections of the *Nat Turner* years. What remains is a feeling of foreboding that, in my unformed mind, emanated entirely from the building we called the "little house." A converted barn, the two-bedroom cottage lay just twenty yards up our hill, separated from the main house by a stone walkway covered with a tangled arbor of grape. When my parents first came to Connecticut, they lived in the little house. Two years later, after renovating the main house, they moved down the hill. The little house became my father's study. Cool and dark, with a high-ceilinged living room anchored by an enormous stone fireplace, the little house was, to me, eternally spooky. I always feared someone, or something, would reach out for me from the shadows. Every movement set off a chorus of dust dancing in the scant sunlight. And, though small, the house had dozens of fathomless corners. Next to the chimney there hung a large pen-and-ink print that must have been a tie-in to the publication of *Nat Turner.* About the size of a movie poster, it depicted a wild-eyed "negro" in tattered garments gesturing to two other shabby-looking black men, who are crouched but attentive to the ravings of the man beside them. In the background are the squalid effects of what one assumes are slave quarters. The picture, along with the unpainted wallboards, the gloomy downstairs bedroom, and the squirrels gamboling in the rafters, gave the whole place a thoroughly haunted vibe.

Sometimes there were guests in the little house. It was they, perhaps more than the décor, who account for the confusing ideas I possessed before I had much of a grasp on logic. In 1961, just as Daddy was beginning *Nat Turner,* he and my mother invited James Baldwin to live in the little house. Jimmy was short on funds and trying to finish a novel he was calling *Another Country.* Though he stayed for only a few months, my father took a great deal away from the arrangement; the friendship the two men developed and their many long, late-night conversations had a deep impact on my father's novel. Inevitably, and especially during the most tumultuous time in the book's reception, Jimmy became part of the narrative of *Nat Turner*'s rise and fall. He alone among prominent black writers came to my father's defense. The paperback version of the book still bears Jimmy's oft-cited quotation about my father: "He has begun the common history—ours."

Somehow, in my dim little mind, I conflated the talk of Jimmy Baldwin, Daddy's black friend, and Nat Turner, the raving madman. Matters were tangled further with the arrival of a music teacher, who lived one season in the little house in exchange for teaching my siblings the piano. For a time, I possessed the bizarre idea that some unhinged friend of my father's was going to come over and either teach my sisters scales or murder me with an ax. I lived in a state of constant suspense and hid whenever the piano cover was lifted.

For years this strange memory lay at the farthest reaches of my mind. I left it there like a furry carcass you've seen in the corner of the garage, one you'd rather ignore for a bit than get up close and inspect. Then, a decade ago, the mystery unraveled. One day, when I was living on the Upper West Side of Manhattan, I took my Labrador for her daily trek through Riverside Park. While Wally was being cheerfully harassed by an animated terrier, I struck up a conversation with the dog's owner. A nattily dressed older man, he revealed a few benign details about his life, and I responded with a few of my own. Charles Turner was the man's name. And what was mine?

"Styron?" he replied, surprised. "You're not Bill Styron's daughter, are you? I lived in your family's little house one year." *Turner*, I thought. *Duh. Turner.* "I taught you, or perhaps it was your sisters, the piano."

*   *   *

THE HOUSE IN Connecticut was, once upon a time, part of a gentleman's farm. The half dozen acres purchased by my mother and father include a traditional nineteenth-century colonial, the little house cottage, and several smaller buildings, all set into a gentle slope in the state's western hills. The improvements they made to the big house included the addition of what we still call the "new" or "big living room" (to distinguish it from the "old living room" near the front door). Built from reclaimed wood and surfaced with rough stucco, the high-ceilinged room is light filled and rustically elegant. A series of glass doors runs along one wall. An oversize fireplace is flanked by bookshelves, and a built-in bar, made of soft pine, dominates one corner. The big living room was Daddy's domain. Here he read, watched the news, clinked the ice around in his Scotch glass, and hid from the rest of us. During the day, he wrote in his study in the little house. But when evening came, he'd set his manuscript pages up at the bar and pace the gold shag carpet, making revisions to the day's work with Mozart blaring on the hi-fi.

Around the corner, the TV room was a passageway of sorts. Littered with toys and pet hair, it connected, via an elbowed hallway, to the kitchen. Most days, I saw little of Daddy. Before school, I was careful not to wake him. Nor would I have dreamt of disturbing him in the afternoon. So it was sometimes not until he came out to prepare dinner or sharpen his pencils that I ever got a glimpse of him. First came the tinny *click* of the living room door latch, which let me know he was coming. Then a multipart glottal clearing (my father's chronic ear, nose, and throat problems caused him habitual congestion; the noises he made to clear them were grotesque, and constant). Finally, his profile, hoving into view just about parallel to the television.

"Albert," he'd say, if he was in the mood to linger for a moment, "have you heard about the Man?"

This was one of Daddy's stories. He didn't really talk to me much, like a regular person might. But he had a few stories, and he liked to watch my reaction when he told them. The Man, according to Daddy, was some sort of homicidal maniac. He roamed New York City, killing innocent people—parents, children, the occasional fluffy dog—and then he chopped them up, stuffing their parts into big green garbage bags. With sacks on his back, he made the ninety-mile trip to Roxbury, Connecticut, on foot. Then he stored his victims' remains in the attic of our house. "It's true," Daddy would say, passing back the other way while I tried, aggressively, to ignore him. "They're looking for him. I just saw it on the news."

It wasn't clear to me why the Man chose Lone Spruce Farm, as our place was once called, as his boneyard. Maybe the Man was related to the Farmer's Son. Maybe they were just friends, drawn together by their horrible fetishes. The Farmer's Son, another stone-cold killer my father knew all about, had grown up in our house. Evil to his marrow, the boy (and in my mind he remained a boy) liked to torture animals. Squirrels, cats, chickens, small things you'd find on a place like ours. After they were dead, he too kept and stored his quarry. But the Farmer's Son didn't use the attic, which could be reached only by a set of stairs that began just outside my bedroom door. Instead, he favored the dreaded basement. Naturally, my big brother liked to get in on this act. He was always convincing me I needed to go down to the bowels of the house, where we had an extra fridge and an old Ping-Pong table our mother used to wrap presents on. *Mum left you a toy. That thing you really wanted. I swear!* Tommy would say. Then he'd slam the door and turn the lights off, just to listen to me scream.

Beyond our house, the countryside pulsed with plenty of other dangers. Not five miles away, in a bedlam that filled my worst dreams, lived hundreds of residents of the Southbury Training School, a state institution for the mentally retarded. I'd never actually been inside. And I'd only ever seen a few of the inhabitants. But their asymmetrical faces and helter-skelter movements gave me some particular ideas about life inside the big brick buildings up on the hill. When we drove by the rolling campus, I gripped the door handle, or pushed myself back into the car seat. "Some of the really dangerous ones," Daddy liked to tell me, "they escape and do *vile* things." I watched the men and women ("retards," we cheerfully called them) crossing the campus's green lawn, scattering the geese that hung around near the pond at the edge of the road. "They can't help it," my father continued, a trace of a smile forming around the edges of his mouth. "They're imbeciles. *Deranged.*"

I didn't really believe in the Man. And the Farmer's Son seemed like a bit of a stretch, too. But I couldn't be sure. Uneasiness was the name of the game, especially when my mother was away. Daddy's stories had a way of taking root then, fed by everything else that was *not right,* till my fears had grown into jungle weed. In my bed at night, I lay paralyzed, listening. The banging shut of the storm door below me. The screeching of the little house door up the hill. The rumble and click of a dying car engine drifted in from the road, followed by a smart closing of a car door and footfalls. The Man and his carnage menaced, then receded, replaced by a truer sound. A Woman, her voice captured in the cold, still air, and my father's whiskey-tongued welcome. With a pillow over my head, I squeezed my eyes shut, the week's rages—*I can't stand it anymore. Oh, Bill, please don't be that way. Fuck you! I'm leaving. No, please don't*—filling the void of sound. Lifting my head and sucking air, I searched the cerulean underside of my canopy bed for a spot to drift into, a place to take me away. The hours ground on until the car on the road pulled away in the dawn.

*　　*　　*

LIKE LOTS OF girls, I had a passion for horses. No amount of bucking and tossing from Gino, the pony I inherited from Polly, could dampen my enthusiasm. When I was about seven, Gino was moved from the pasture at the bottom of our hill to a proper horse farm, and I was dropped there after school, on weekends, and nearly every day during vacations. As I got older, I took the sport to another level. Honing my skills with one trainer and then another, I spent the weekends competing, kept an eye on my ranking, and hung my ribbons in row after row around my room. I loved horses, plain and simple. I loved hanging around their stalls, talking to them as I brushed the burrs from their fuzzy coats, loved nuzzling my face into their chests, braiding their manes, and picking the dirt from their hooves. I loved riding bareback down to the river and easing in for a cold swim; loved trail rides, and picnics, and sitting on the fence watching the horses kick up their heels when you let them loose after a night in the barn. I loved the lessons, the sweat, the competition, even the fear. But most of all, I loved life at the barn. The places I rode weren't fancy. Our corner of Connecticut was, back then, a simple place. It was rural and largely middle class; the farms were not manicured, nor had they yet been sold off to sate the coming craving for McMansions. My best friend, Laura, was also a rider. Together, we'd exercise our horses, then exercise a half dozen others. We mucked out stalls, groomed and swept, cleaned our tack and hauled down hay bales, shared our lunch with the dogs, and played practical jokes on our teachers. Everything I longed for—camaraderie and ease, rituals, simplicity—came together on long days at the barn. Going home was a crapshoot. I never knew what I'd find.

My father didn't like horses much. And he really didn't like his children riding them. My mother always said this was why he didn't come to my horse shows more often—it frightened him to watch me flying over huge fences on the back of an eight-hundred-pound animal. It was also why, she said, he wouldn't buy me a better horse, though the problem with the one I had was his tendency to try to kill me. The logic here was not something Daddy was interested in. And his distaste for the whole enterprise might have sown the seed for the story of his I remember best. I was eight. Daddy called me into the kitchen. We were alone in the house, and, having just made himself a late lunch, he sat with his burger and beer, reading *The New York Times*.

"Al," he said, head still in the paper. "Do you know who Ella Grasso is?"

"Yes," I replied, standing at attention, a little blossom of pride blooming within me. "She's the new governor."

Daddy nodded thoughtfully.

"Well, I've just read something terrible. It seems that Governor Grasso has banned horses in the state of Connecticut."

The beat that followed was long enough for him to silently recheck the facts of the article. He put the paper down and tendered a look of paternal sympathy. "I'm afraid we're going to have to sell your pony to the glue factory."

I remember a tingling around my lips. My legs wobbled. I waited for him to laugh.

"Come on, Daddy," I blurted. "That's not true."

"Yes, it most certainly is," he replied.

"That's so stupid," I pushed on, grinning dumbly.

"Well, I'm sorry, Al, but that's how it is."

Playful and bold, I grabbed for the newspaper. "Lemme see."

"No," he growled. "Now cut it out. Get out of here."

I went back to the TV room, curled up on the couch, and looked at the screen. Later, when Daddy passed through, I tried one more time to draw out a retraction from him. There might have been humor in his eyes, but I couldn't be sure, and I didn't press it. I knew only that the game, or whatever it was, was over.

*   *   *

WHEN I GOT older, Daddy's stories became my own. I took the Man and the Farmer's Son and Ella Grasso's injunction against horses and made them into little set pieces. And I dined out on them frequently. In dorm rooms, at dinner parties, on dates, this ghoulish scenario seemed to satisfy the question *So what was it like having William Styron for a father?*, which often hovered when I got to know new people. The Great Man at home, then, was eccentric, dark, and cruelly funny. His transgressive behavior and his wicked imagination shocked people. But they also stoked a romantic idea about the private lives of famous writers in general, and Bill Styron in particular.

The last time I told my father's ghost stories was at his memorial service, February 2, 2007. His death, when it happened, had been a long time coming; I'm not ashamed to say that when he breathed his last, it was a relief. Still, I was surprised by how shaken I was, at the graveyard, watching my brother lower the box of ashes into its small, deep hole. And I sobbed while that soldier played taps. But, within days, our family had begun to plan a celebration of Daddy's life, a party to which my mother could at last invite *everyone*. I knew without a doubt that I wanted to write something. It seemed natural, since writing is what I do. It would be an opportunity for closure, as they say in griefspeak. And then I would be really, seriously free from this whole freaking deal.

On a messy, sleet-drenched day, more than eight hundred people filed into St. Bartholomew's Church in Manhattan. President Clinton, Senator Kennedy, Mike Nichols, Carlos Fuentes, and Bob Loomis would be offering remembrances. Daddy's best friend, Peter Matthiessen, was delivering the eulogy. Meryl Streep and Mia Farrow were among the readers of Daddy's work, and my siblings had chosen works by Rumi, Faulkner, and Mary Oliver. I'd spent a week or so fussing over my words, but through all the revisions my first line remained the same.

"My father used to scare the crap out of me," I declared. The lurid stories I chose that day were selective (omitting a couple that my husband, Ed, thought were actually too awful to get a laugh). And after I told them, I wondered aloud *why* he had done it. Why would a grown man scare his children so completely? (He had told similar tales to each of my siblings, and every one of them had a different twist.) Was it catharsis? Was he blowing off steam after a day grappling with all those barbarous slavers and Nazis who inhabited his books—real-life maniacs on the loose inside his head? Or was it a ham-fisted attempt at fatherhood? Was he just a dad with a faulty radar trying to make a connection? The answer that I settled on reflected what I believed was a deeper truth. Whether he meant to or not, Daddy taught us the lesson—a lesson which tested him hard at the end of his days—that life requires courage, and a sense of humor.

Now that he was gone, I had to wonder not why my father told those stories but why *I* told them. Why was this narrative—as hokey as a fifties TV show—the one that I was stuck on? There was something disingenuous about it. These hoaxes, and the way I described them, implied that a certain lightheartedness ruled the day in our house. That it was a Roald Dahl sort of place, and that Daddy, curmudgeonly and outrageous, was still at the core a comic figure. Which really couldn't have been further from the truth.

Even before *Darkness Visible* opened a window onto my father's personal history, I encountered people who appeared to know more. Strangers often seemed hip to some broad and unsavory secret, though they never said it outright. *It must have been hard,* they would say vaguely, putting a physical ellipsis to the conversation by rhythmically, knowingly nodding their heads. *It must have been hard dot dot dot.* Or they would laugh a little too loudly and maybe touch my shoulder, smile, and shake their heads. Sympathetic gestures all, but they often hit quite wide of the mark. Retelling Daddy's stories was, I guess, my way of managing that false intimacy by providing satisfying tidbits. They kept me from heading into territory I didn't want to explore. And they preserved a myth I was obviously as invested in as anyone.

Three

Billy and Pauline, circa 1926

ON CHRISTMAS DAY 1939, my father received a Wanamaker Diary from his mother's old friend "Auntie" Elmer Holmes. Elmer (her father had wanted a boy) lived in Philadelphia with her husband, Lynwood, and, having no children of her own, took a special interest in Daddy. She started him on stamp collecting and promoted the hobby by writing him letters tucked inside prized first day cover envelopes. My father wrote back chatty thank-you notes, dappled with purple prose and five-dollar words, that show the effort of a boy grateful for the keen attentions of an adult. The year before, just after my father's thirteenth birthday, Elmer and Lynwood had invited him up from Virginia for his first-ever trip, alone, to a Northern city. In anticipation of his departure, he wrote to Elmer with his itinerary. "At 6:56pm, I will alight for the Day

Coach at Broad Street Station, Philadelphia, PA." He wanted her to know he was "tickled sky blue pink" by the invitation and was certain it would be a "splendiferous" experience. It was.

Daddy spent six days with the Holmeses, visiting the city's big attractions—Independence Hall, the Liberty Bell, the Fels Planetarium—and passed the quiet hours in a guest room, happily perusing maps and reading the encyclopedia. So when Elmer was picking out a Christmas present for my father the following year, I suspect his visit must have played a role in her choosing. Wanamaker's, the famous emporium across from City Hall, would have been right on the sightseeing route they traveled. Straddling a city block, the store, the first shopping mecca of its kind, featured a soaring, marble-walled Grand Court and the biggest pipe organ in the world, with 28,482 pipes. It was a tourist destination all its own; the store's daily planners were for a long time popular souvenirs. Whether Daddy ever got inside Wanamaker's or just passed its imposing façade, the gift would surely have evoked happy memories of his Philadelphia adventure.

I found the little cloth-bound book at Duke. My father really took to it, recording in brief detail his activities nearly every day of 1940, from New Year's until September, when he left for boarding school. The entries draw a portrait of American boyhood during the Depression that could practically stand alone in a time capsule from the era. Daddy and his friends Carl, Bozo, Knocky, Leon, Buddy, Scutter, and Pete alternately "fooled around," "loafed around," "piddled around," and "loafed around" some more. My father had a job ("Got up and toted papers for Old Man Adams"), went to Sunday school, did his homework, and squired a few girls around town. ("Dick O. and I both had dates. I had Peggy Barbor, he had Jean.") School wasn't much of a priority at fourteen, and, either through shiftlessness ("got kicked out of history class") or absenteeism ("home sick again with earache"), he seems to have had plenty of idle time. He and the guys were always playing chess or cards, going "up to the stores" in Hilton Village to loiter, gathering around the radio for *Amos 'n' Andy,* or heading for a swim off the pier, a favorite destination Daddy once described as "my second summer home, my hangout, my club, my Riviera, my salvation." Like most families, the Styrons were in tough financial straits. But, in the spring, Grandpop scraped together ten dollars to buy my father a little, beat-up sailboat. It had been dry-docked for ages in a nearby shed, and, with the help of his older cousin Hugh, Daddy spent weeks making the boat seaworthy. He loved the shoddy old skiff, but after enduring a few hairy trials—swampings, lost tillers, squalls—he lost some of his enthusiasm and decided to keep his water activities closer to shore.

If one thing remained a constant in my father's life in 1940, it was the picture show. These were fine years for filmmaking, considered by many the Golden Age of movies. In 1939 alone Hollywood produced, among other classics, *Gone With the Wind, The Wizard of Oz, Ninotchka, Mr. Smith Goes to Washington,* and *Stagecoach.* After a decade of ironing out the glitches wrought by the advent of sound, film was suddenly a polished, modern medium, and filmmakers were working hard to satisfy a nation in need of amusement. During the half dozen years before World War II, the eight major studios made an average of 350 films a year. Daddy would probably have seen them all if he could. For the better part of 1940, he went to the movies almost every night, then came home and recorded terse critiques in his diary. It was the year of *Fantasia, Pinocchio, His Girl Friday,* and *The Grapes of Wrath.* Charlie Chaplin released his first "talkie," *The Great Dictator,* and the Hope-Crosby road movie franchise took off with *Road to Singapore.* Tex Avery's third Bugs Bunny cartoon, *A Wild Hare,* introduced the "wascally wabbit" to Elmer Fudd, provoking for the first time the immortal query "Eh, what's up, Doc?" *Rebecca* took the Oscar for Best Film, and Jimmy Stewart won in the Best Actor category for *The Philadelphia Story.* My father enjoyed many of the year's big pictures, including *Gone With the Wind,* which he and Leon took the train to Richmond to see. But he also lazed happily through dozens and dozens of more minor entertainments. In one week, as he noted in his diary, he caught "Muni in *We Are Not Alone*," "Sonja Henie in *Everything Happens at Night*," "Edward G. Robinson in *Blackmail*," and *The Hunchback of Notre Dame*.

Forty-eight years later, in the spring of '88, my father spoke about the Wanamaker Diary, which he'd recently been perusing, in a commencement address at Claremont McKenna College. It was a time of great uncertainty for him. With his first depression only two years past, he was still struggling to find his confidence again. The current iteration of *Way of the Warrior*, now called *Marriott the Marine*, wasn't working. And though the laurels being bestowed upon him—the Légion d'Honneur in '87, the MacDowell Medal in '88—were pleasing, they also ramped up the pressure to justify such lionization. His childhood, and the forces that shaped it, had been on his mind a lot. He'd just written "A Tidewater Morning" for *Esquire*, and the idea of a book about Grandpop was in its beginning stages. So my father was already in a vulnerable state when, shortly before his trip to California, he began to lose sensation in his right hand, the result of a neck injury he'd suffered while on a training run during the Korean War. Tremendously anxious about impending surgery, he found himself unable to sleep. A doctor prescribed Halcion for relief, and, just as it had in '85 (though he wouldn't piece it together for several more years), the sleeping aid wreaked havoc on his mind. Unable to stem the sudden tide of depression, he tried to back out of his commitments at Claremont (where he'd also agreed to teach a class). But it was too late. Accompanied by my mother, he flew out west in a state of abject terror. "There in that sunny landscape," he wrote later, "I was all but totally consumed by thoughts of suicide that were like a form of lust. . . . I kept constant schemes in mind to have my wife lured away so I could secrete myself in a closet and end it all with a plastic bag."*

---

*William Styron, "Prozac Days, Halcion Nights," *Nation*, January 4/11, 1993.

Somehow, my father made it to graduation day. Probably betraying little of his mood, he stood at the lectern and struck a humorously self-deprecating tone. He spoke about how startled he was by the teenage portrait of himself that emerged from the diary. "I searched," he said,

> for the tiniest fragment of introspection, of romantic agony, the Weltschmerz, the self-lacerating moonings expected of an incipient novelist. There are no meditations on Nature, on God, or our moral existence; there are not even any girls. Instead there are only movies—once, twice, even three times a day.
>
> A rough count would indicate that during this particular summer I went to close to fifty movies. . . . There is no indication that during the summer I ever read a single book. No books at all.

There is also no indication that the boy disappearing all day and night into the dark of a theater and the world of celluloid fantasy had just, a few months before, buried his mother. No indication of why "Pop didn't feel so good" on more than one occasion. And no indication of how it came to be that, on a February evening, Daddy was in a position to remark: "After supper, Pop went out to the hospital for a few weeks rest and Jim, Spotty, Bud and I played cards over at the Hayes'. I'm spending nights there now."

*   *   *

MY FATHER WAS born on June 11, 1925, at the Buxton Hospital on Chesapeake Avenue in Newport News, Virginia. Delivered by Dr. Buxton himself, Daddy came into the world cheerful, chubby, and blond. Billy, as they called him, was a miracle baby for his parents, Pauline and William Clark Styron, Sr., who, at thirty-seven and thirty-five respectively, were old to be first-time parents. Aside from frequent and painful earaches, my father was a healthy boy.

Doted upon by Bill and Pauline, he developed an early gift for language, loved books, and by first grade was testing at a seventh-grade reading level.

When my father was six, the Styrons moved to 56 Hopkins Street in Hilton Village, a leafy neighborhood on the outskirts of the city. Their modest stucco cottage, like all the other houses in the neighborhood, had been built in the early years of World War I for employees of the Newport News Shipbuilding and Drydock Company (NNS), for which Grandpop worked as a marine engineer. It was the first federal war-housing project of its kind. The five hundred houses of Hilton Village, built in fourteen different styles, were laid out on a hundred acres of cleared woodlands, which, before the Civil War, had been a part of the Hilton Homestead. The neighborhood included four churches, a library, a firehouse, a commercial area, and an elementary school. At the edge of town lay a park, a beach, and a fishing pier that jutted out into the wide, estuarial plains of the James River. In 1922, the shipyard's owner, Henry E. Huntington, purchased the development from the U.S. government and made it possible for NNS employees to buy their homes from the corporation outright. It was a nice place to raise children. The streets were safe and quiet, the neighborhood psychically bound together by the twin forces of Southern culture and hard, inherently patriotic work.

My father had a lot of happy memories of Hilton Village. In interviews over the years, he recalled his life there as "pleasant," even "idyllic." But there was a deep current of isolation running through much of his family's experiences, and it affected all of them to varying degrees. In my father, the solitary aspect began with his status as an only child. And though it nurtured the writer's gaze in him, it set him up for a kind of chronic loneliness.

"The village had many children," my father writes in "A Tidewater Morning." "It was a place and an era of busy procreation. The houses of the village, small-scale as they appeared, were swollen with vigorous, rowdy families, and my friends all had siblings I envied for the very fact of their being—splendid older brothers, sensible younger sisters; even the little runny-nosed brats at the bottom of the family chain I would have loved to cuddle and protect. . . . In my room I felt as alone as if I were in a dungeon."

His parents grappled with their own respective feelings of alienation, though theirs had a complicated network of roots.

In my grandparents' day, Newport News was a company town. Collis P. Huntington had practically built the city single-handedly when he extended his Central Pacific Railroad from Richmond down to Hampton Roads. By 1881, bituminous coal moved unabated from the black hills of West Virginia to the busy shipping lanes along the Virginia Tidewater. Huntington went on to develop the shipyard and agitated for the incorporation of Newport News as an independent city. After his death, in 1900, Collis's stepson, Archer Huntington, and nephew, Henry Huntington, inherited the industrialist's financial interests as well as his influence in the region. Newport News grew into a thriving small city, its purse strings tied to the resources Huntington had so cannily promoted. Like other Southern cities, it developed its own caste system. At the top of that ladder were many of the shipyard's senior executives. They lived over in Huntington Heights, drove fancy cars, and enjoyed lazy Sundays with their families at the James River Country Club. Firmly entrenched in the South of their forefathers, they maintained the front office from a place of entitlement and authority.

At the other end of the shipyard, and the culture of the town, were the shipbuilders. Thousands of men, white and black, pulled long shifts to construct the great leviathans of the sea. Many were unskilled and uneducated and were put to all manner of grunt work. Others made up the artisan class of carpenters, welders, riveters, and boilermakers essential to maritime industry. Newport News Shipbuilding was a busy hive, even during the Depression. Though salaries and positions were greatly reduced, production puttered along. From 1907 to 1923, Newport News built six of the U.S. Navy's twenty-two dreadnoughts, twenty-five naval destroyers, and seven of the sixteen battleships that became known as the

"Great White Fleet," commissioned by Theodore Roosevelt to circumnavigate the globe. My grandfather was a proud member of the engineering team that conceived the world's first purpose-built aircraft carrier, the USS *Ranger*. On the day it launched, February 25, 1933, Daddy stood beside his father, awestruck, as Mrs. Herbert Hoover struck the ship's prow with a benedictory bottle of champagne. The *Ranger* was one of a dozen military vessels built at NNS in the thirties and forties, including the *Yorktown*, the *Enterprise*, the *Hornet*, the *Essex*, and the now famous aircraft museum that berths at Pier 86 in Manhattan, the USS *Intrepid*. By the end of World War II, NNS had branched out to the manufacture of cruisers and Liberty ships. At the time of my grandfather's retirement, in 1955, NNS was developing propulsion systems that would eventually power a newer instrument of war: the nuclear submarine.

For Grandpop and his colleagues, shipyard work was a great blessing. Times were hard, particularly between the wars, and there was heavy competition for remunerative gigs guaranteed by the U.S. government. At night, most of the men packed into sprawling barracks that had sprung up around the port, buildings that made an already industrial city look even more makeshift and unsightly. But for some, like the skilled Scots, Welshmen, and Irish whose specialized talents earned them a better wage, the move to Hilton Village gained them a toehold on the American dream. Their children, often born in profusion from Catholic households, were the boys and girls my father grew up so longingly beside.

It was a symbiotic environment at NNS, with clubby circles among every financial, ethnic, and racial bracket. But somewhere uncomfortably outside all of them moved my grandfather. Like many of the company's administrators, Grandpop was a native of the region, having grown up about a hundred miles south, in the town of Washington, North Carolina (or "Little Washington," as it is affectionately known). His father, Alpheus Whitehurst Styron, had been a wheel-boat captain, shipbuilder, and cigarette manufacturer before the Duke brothers put small tobacco operators like him out of business. His mother, Marianna Clark, from a venerable Carolina family, had passed her childhood on a vast plantation along the Pungo River but had suffered terrible privations when her home was ransacked by Union soldiers during the Civil War. (My father's imagination, as well as his storytelling gifts, got a good stoking from Marianna, who often described how her family and their slaves nearly starved in the assault's aftermath.) Alpheus and Marianna had eight children. Six survived, and Grandpop, born in 1889, fell in the middle of the pack. His childhood was pleasant, if not grand. A sharp student, he showed a passion for poetry and an early flair for writing. But his father's downward financial course extinguished his potential literary dreams, and, at seventeen, Grandpop entered the North Carolina College of Agriculture and Mechanic Arts (now North Carolina State) on full scholarship. After a brief stint at sea, he moved to Newport News and began his lifelong career as a mechanical draftsman.

My grandfather had a fine mind. Intellectually, he might have found kinship with some of the fellows in management, graduates of Mr. Jefferson's university, or even the more freethinking of the Annapolis men. But he had no patience for the culture of the local patriarchy. Nor had he the money for those kinds of associations even if he wanted them. Philosophically and politically, Grandpop aligned himself much more closely with the Hilton Villagers among whom he lived. He supported the local unions, though he didn't belong. And, like much of his precinct, he voted along Democratic lines. But even among his working-class friends, Grandpop was always an awkward fit. Caught between his humanism—with a special sympathy for the Negro cause—and his ingrained identification as a Southerner, he was a fundamentally conflicted man. Though extremely mild mannered, he could be drawn into arguments over politics, once coming to blows with an Irishman who ran his mouth about the character of the local whites and the region's history in general. What's more, Grandpop had refined sensibilities. Unusually cultured for a man of his time and place, he could quote long passages of Tennyson and Shakespeare, was well versed in classical music, and attended church as much for the transportive power of the hymns as for the service itself. In fact, it was through music that, as a lonely twenty-nine-year-old bachelor, he connected with his wife to be, Pauline Abraham.

For a woman of her era, my grandmother had already lived a pretty full life before finding herself in Virginia. Born in 1888 in Uniontown, Pennsylvania, and descended from Quaker colonists, she grew up a child of privilege. Her father, Enoch, was a supervisor for Henry Clay Frick before striking out with partners to form the Newcomer Coke Company. Having absorbed some of Frick's key philosophies—antilabor sentiment chief among them—he operated a successful business, human cost secondary to the eternal chase for profits. When his Eastern European workforce went on strike, Enoch sent for Southern Negroes to take their place. When riots broke out across racial lines, he expressed little sympathy for either side. It was a kind of xenophobia and passive bigotry, subtly taught by Enoch to Pauline and her three siblings, and it played in the background of their lives even if it mattered little in their blinkered, everyday experience.

Pauline's oldest brother, Clyde, went to West Point and rose to the rank of brigadier general. Harold served in World War I but soon after returning became plagued by hallucinations and thoughts of suicide. Given an official diagnosis of "shell shock," he spent most of the rest of his life in a Maryland VA hospital. The two girls, Pauline and her sister, Edith, attended the private Mount Pleasant Institute, where they both showed an aptitude for music. After graduation, Enoch paid for them to go to Europe, where they could take in the culture and continue their training. My grandmother toured London, Rome, Paris, Amsterdam, Brussels, and Florence. But it was in Vienna that, as a vocalist, she hit her artistic stride, honing her beautiful contralto under the tutelage of Maestro Theodor Leschetizky. The Austrian capital was also where Pauline always felt the best years of her life had been spent.

It's difficult to have an idea what my grandmother was really like. Not much evidence remains of her. After Europe, Pauline returned home, staying for almost three years while, all around her, girls (Edith included) were getting married and moving on. Her father had died, and she lived with her mother, earning a small income giving voice lessons to children in the neighborhood. On Sundays, she performed as a soloist at the Presbyterian church. In 1914, perhaps considering that life might pass her by in Uniontown, she enrolled at the University of Pittsburgh. After graduating two years later with a certificate in public school music, she taught first in Pittsburgh and then in Pueblo, Colorado. In 1917, when she was twenty-nine years old, America entered World War I. Pauline decided to join the war effort. Alone, and thoroughly independent, she moved to Newport News to take a position at the shipyard YMCA.

* * *

I WAS FIVE the first time I had a thought of Pauline. It was 1971, around the time of my grandfather's third marriage. I was, I suppose, just old enough to understand the rudiments of progenitorship, but not sufficiently sophisticated to plumb the mysteries of loss. Considering the woman Grandpop was to marry, it suddenly occurred to me that my father's *real* mother was a blank to me. My mother's father was dead. I knew that. She had a picture of him. And there were many more at Nana's house in Baltimore. But my father's mother? I had never heard anyone mention her. Never seen a picture, or any evidence that she existed. *He MUST have a mommy,* I thought. *Or he HAD a mommy.* Over the years, I absorbed errant details. *Pauline. Dead. Cancer.* But, having been disappeared by Daddy and Grandpop, she was nothing more than a name in my head. Not until my father gave her an afterlife in the fiction of his later years did she take on any real dimensions for me. And still she was not *animate*, she did not breathe. Then I found her voice at Duke.

Dear Elmer—

Well, the boy got home all safe and sound—the very
happiest child I have ever seen! You will never know how
grateful I am to you for opening up a new world to Billy.
You remember I told you how enthusiastic he was at the
prospect of a trip to [Philadelphia]. When I asked him if it
was as grand as he thought it would be his eyes popped and
from his heart he said: "O, ten thousand times better than I
ever dreamed it could be!"

Pauline's letters (there are no more than a half dozen at the library) were a total revelation to me. From them, she bursts forth a warm, winning, even exuberant figure. She is thoroughly engaged in her environment, penning descriptive passages on the day's weather, the state of the garden, and the comings and goings in her household while always stopping short of what her intended reader might find tedious or overly informational. She's solicitous of her friends' well-being, charmingly frank about her own health, and proudly maternal. "In some ways he is so child-like—" she continues in her thank-you letter to Elmer after Daddy's trip to Philadelphia, "and then again I am struck by his—shall I say intelligence? And then he is sweet—"

Instantly, and unshakably, Pauline reminded me of my mother-in-law, Ann Beason. Ann grew up in an antebellum Greek Revival house on a three-hundred-acre farm in LaGrange, Georgia. After years in New York, New Jersey, and Louisiana, she and my father-in-law, Ted, have returned to live in the house in which Ann was raised. Maybe it's the Southern climate and the rhythms of the day that draw out a similar writing style. Or maybe it's the simple act of writing itself. Ann writes to me, Ed, and our children regularly, for no other purpose than to say hello and fill us in on her day or week. She tells us about the new puppy, and her artwork, the church picnic, and what the magnolia trees are doing. She lets us know how much she misses us, and what she's looking forward to doing with us on our next visit. She sends hugs and asks for pictures of the kids. It's of course what people used to do all the time, keep up correspondence. But I don't receive letters from anyone but Ann anymore. When I got down to Duke, I was out of the habit of "hearing" someone else's voice on paper. In Pauline's description of her jonquils, and demonstrable love for her boy, I found unmistakable echoes of Ann's steady, lively affection.

It's not at all what I expected. Until recently, I'd known only one photograph of my grandmother. It's a formal mother-and-child portrait, in which my father appears to be about two years old. Fair and round, he's dressed in a neat white romper, hair freshly cut, and stands on something to put him at eye level with his mother. Pauline, holding him about the waist, gazes at his face with a look of attentive pride. But though she must be only in her late thirties, she appears decades older. Even in black and white, it's obvious that her carefully marcelled hair is steel gray, and she wears quintessential "granny glasses" on her prominent beak. Her prim blouse and jacket, though entirely appropriate for the time, add to a schoolmarmish effect, and I now realize that for years I've been confusing her with another picture I've seen somewhere else of my legitimately aged *great*-grandmother. Inasmuch as I ever thought about Pauline, she was colorless, a pinched and faded daguerreotype who must have been bypassed entirely by youth or radiance.

But it wasn't just her elderly look. My father's depiction of her in the stories of *A Tidewater Morning,* and even fleetingly in *Sophie's Choice,* limn the portrait of a cross, pedagogic, humorless soul swamped by disappointment and bereft of whimsy. I can see how, through the fire of his experience, Daddy would have forged this image of her. About the same time that photograph was taken, Pauline was diagnosed with breast cancer. She underwent the common treatment of the day, a radical mastectomy of both breasts, which sent the disease into a brief remission. But it soon returned, this time in her bones, and for the next decade continued to metastasize through the rest of her body. It invaded her arms and legs, and the lining of her scalp. Her hair fell out. She had difficulty keeping her balance. After she broke her leg in a fall, she had to be fitted with a metal brace, "a gruesome contraption of steel and leather straps" was how my father remembered it. Her bones refused to knit again and she was compelled to wear the uncomfortable, restrictive apparatus the rest of her life. It not only caused her "wicked distress" but made it impossible for her to fold her legs at the piano bench. At the time when she probably needed it most, Pauline was unable to seek refuge in the comfort of music.

She was in terrible pain. All the time. It would have been hard to think straight, and harder still to keep up with an active little boy. At the onset of her cancer, Daddy was too young to understand what was happening. As the years, and the disease, progressed, no one talked with him about his mother's health, placated his fears, or solicited his feelings. My grandparents simply pulled the veil more tightly around their already stifled existence. Bill and Pauline attended Sunday service at the Presbyterian church and were faithful patrons of a local classical music concert series. But beyond that, they had very little social interaction. The Victrola warbled, and conversation batted about, but for the most part 56 Hopkins Street was a sepulchrally quiet place. Daddy was encouraged to read, or go out and play, but not to be a bother to his mother. The house's glum tone acted as a powerful agent on my father's memory, coloring his perception of Pauline then, and his vision of her later.

Further darkening my father's picture was the tension at 56 Hopkins Street, which often ran high, particularly in Pauline's last years. My grandfather doted on his wife and, by every indication, worked ceaselessly to ease her strain. But he was also trying to manage his own terrific concerns. The Depression was on, money was very tight, and, as the medical bills mounted, so too did his grief for himself and anxiety for his family. The whole business was destined to bubble over into a cold, black river. The couple bickered more and more, exposing a rift that made a strong impression on Daddy.

Despite their common cultural leanings, Bill and Pauline came at the world from very different angles. She was a Northerner, raised with money, nurtured in a conservative household. He was a prideful Southerner, mistrustful of Big Business, a lonely white progressive in a Jim Crow world. I don't think Daddy ever believed his mother was a bigot, but the picture he drew, in his fiction anyway, was of a woman ill at ease with the overwhelming "blackness" of her adopted land. She was neither passively accepting of the racial inequality all around her nor interested in integrating herself more thoroughly. But if she found it hard to relate to the Negroes, she found it harder still to countenance the whites, who bored her. Turning to the music she loved—Brahms, Bach, Wagner—and memories of Europe, she came to appear haughty and out of touch. Familiar with this idea of her, I was surprised to find in her letters so much stoicism and self-deprecating humor. After Grandpop's altercation with the Irishman, which resulted in a dislocated shoulder, Pauline gave Elmer a visual of mornings on Hopkins Street. "We are a scream when we start out together—" she wrote, "one armless and the other legless! Ho-hum." Maybe Pauline expressed herself best with people like Elmer, who'd known her in the flush of youth. But if she was ever playful at home, my father's renderings consistently belie it.

What Daddy seems to have remembered best is a suffocating air of defeat about him, of being foundered, for which his own overweening ambitions became a counterpoint. In "A Tidewater Morning," the narrator, Paul Whitehurst, recalls a long-ago argument between his mother, Adelaide, and father, Jefferson. Adelaide has labeled as a drunk one of the only local men Jeff feels he can talk to. Stung, Jeff calls his wife a snob. In a controlled fit of pique, Adelaide counters,

> . . . if you and I were simply divided over politics, there would be no problem. It's this whole community, these dull-

as-dishwater people, who couldn't be nicer, couldn't be more bighearted, you understand, but whom I have nothing in common with whatsoever. They've helped drive the wedge between us. For years I've tried to understand southerners, to get along with them, but I've been finally defeated by a kind of provinciality and cultural blindness unequaled anywhere in the world. Isn't it H. L. Mencken, whom you so idolize, who calls the South, correctly, the Sahara of the Bozart? If I didn't have my music I'd go insane!

Jeff's response distills Grandpop's fundamental conundrum.

Then I'm sorry you settled for so little, Adelaide. I never promised you riches. You knew that wasn't my style. The compact we made was for a home and love and companionship. I would be incapable of lavishing luxury on you, or myself, even if I cared to accumulate the money to make it possible. I've always admired much in you. But I can't admire your inability to understand that my own passions are not of tangible objects, but, if you'll pardon my saying so, of the spirit and intellect. . . . That is why I am and doubtless always will be a humble drone earning humble wages in a job I don't much care for.

My father obviously felt that both of his parents were lost in their own peculiar ways. That they each got off at the wrong station and, having no ticket out, muddled on together. Had they lived in New York, for instance, or even Atlanta, things might have turned out better for them. If anything bound them together, it was a determination for their only son to escape the same fate. My father handily synthesized the attitudes of both his parents, and took what he needed from each. Like Grandpop, Daddy became a proud progressive and a champion of civil rights. Through both his writing and his activism, he did his part to drag the South into the twentieth century. But he did so from exile, up North, having tired himself of the provincialism in which he was raised.

In the spring of 1939, when my father was fourteen, Pauline's cancer made a rapid advance. Daddy was sent to stay with cousins for several weeks down near Little Washington. Coming home, he found his mother in terrible shape: bedridden, skeletal, in exquisite agony. Dr. Russell Buxton, son of the man who had delivered Daddy, attended to her daily, prescribing the maximum dosage of morphine several times a day. But no palliative seemed to put a dent in her pain. By July, it was obvious the end was near. In their small house, Daddy lay in his room at night under the weak breath of a fan, choking on the summer heat and his unmitigated fear. In "A Tidewater Morning," Paul Whitehurst recollects:

> Suddenly my mother screamed—a scream, long and hopeless, containing a note of anguish like nothing I had ever heard before. It was a shriek that swept up and down my naked body like a flame. It was an alien sound, which is to say unexpectedly beyond my sense of logic and my experience, so that for the barest instant it had the effect of something histrionic, out of the movies, a Frankenstein-Dracula film in which a bad actress emoted implausible terror. But it was real, and I plunged my face into my pillow, wrapping it about my head like a humid caul. I tried to shut out the scream. Deaf, in darkness, I sought to think of anything but that scream.

I have no idea what last words were exchanged between mother and son. Daddy never could recall much about that time. Toward the very end, he was sent to his friend Buddy Hayes's house. Buddy's mother, Sally, a former teacher, ran a tight ship, but she took good care of my father. When, on the evening of July 20, 1939, Pauline finally passed away, Sally broke the news gently. Daddy was upstairs at the Hayeses', in a room by himself, reading. "Billy, your mother is no longer with us," Daddy remembered her saying. He also remembered that he didn't cry.

*   *   *

THE WANAMAKER DIARY got to Daddy, eventually. Though he would spend the rest of his life implicating exterior forces—Halcion, alcohol withdrawal, inept doctors—for his depressions, he must have detected the same repressed grief in that journal that I did twenty years later. It disturbed him, and it gave him pause. In the year after his panic attack at Claremont McKenna, he began writing a series of nonfiction pieces about his depression, which would culminate in 1990 with *Darkness Visible*. He began to recognize the heavy impact his parents' plight had on him—emotionally, genetically—and, though he couldn't seem to fix it, he could at least put his experiences into some knowable context.

After Pauline's death, Grandpop was in a bad state. Grieving and agitated, he spent more and more time at work, leaving my father to his own devices. When he was home, the stress he was under showed itself in frightening and unexpected bursts. In his biography, Jim West relates a story my father told him. It was a Sunday some months after his mother died, and my father was upstairs, reading. Down below, Grandpop was tuned in to the weekly radio broadcast of the NBC Symphony, performing Ravel's *Bolero*. Suddenly my father heard a loud crash. When he came downstairs, he found Grandpop standing over the radio, the one he and Pauline had so often listened to, which was now lying cracked on the floor. The repetitive thumping of the orchestral piece had apparently made Grandpop snap, and he'd tossed the radio to the floor. My father remembered this story all his life because it showed a kind of sudden rage that was totally unlike Grandpop. Daddy, by contrast, behaved that way *all the time.* His anger often erupted without any warning, the irrationality of it as frightening as the actions that accompanied it. A toy left in his path, a pencil with no point, a departure delayed by some bit of domestic business. These were the kinds of catalysts that could suddenly pull the pin on my father's temper. He'd lob his invective into the room, storm away, and leave everything behind him in flames. If he ever recognized in himself the same mismanagement of emotions that preceded Grandpop's breakdown, he certainly never let on to any of us.

In February 1940, Grandpop spent three weeks in the hospital, having succumbed to what was then called "nervous exhaustion." My father moved back to the Hayeses', where he remained well into April. While his father was convalescing, Daddy muddled through the school year, visited his mother's kin in Pennsylvania, learned how to drive, and endured the steadying hand of Buddy's mother. ("She is so hard to get along with. Kinda old fashioned. I love her a lot, but, ohmigosh!") It was during this time that a new character appeared in my father's journal, Dr. Russell Buxton's unmarried sister, Elizabeth. Referred to by Daddy as "Miss Elizabeth Buxton," "Miss Buxton," "Lizzie Buxton," and "Lizzie Bux," Elizabeth was an accomplished forty-year-old woman, born into a family of medical practitioners, who probably would have become a doctor herself in another era. Instead she went into nursing, rising to the top position of the Virginia State Board of Nurse Examiners. Unattached and inclined to ministration, she drew close to Grandpop in his vulnerable period and became an increasingly common presence in the life of the Styron men. Soon the three of them were sharing meals, going to movies, and taking Sunday drives. Or Grandpop and Elizabeth were keeping company, and my father was on his own.

Sometime that summer, the decision was made that my father should go to boarding school. His academic record was a huge disappointment to Grandpop, especially given his son's tremendous intellectual capacity. He wanted more for my father than what Newport News had to offer. And he knew that, as a hardworking widower, he couldn't make up for all the deficits my father faced. What role Elizabeth played in Daddy going away is unclear. She and my grandfather entered into a rather sober engagement—she wouldn't marry him until her ailing father had passed away—and her feelings for her future stepson were never warm. Over time, Elizabeth developed into a kind of caricature of a bad stepmother—cruel, withholding, judgmental—and my father would come to loathe her, not only for her condemnation of him but for cutting him off from his father and the last vestiges of his childhood. In the end, perhaps Elizabeth saved Grandpop from his own now obvious undiagnosed depression. But she had an insidious influence on his sensitive son. Rather than reaching out to him as well, she helped shepherd his feelings where they didn't belong: underground.

Four

The young Marine, 1944

IN THE FALL of 1982, I was a crummy student at the Taft School, a boarding school in Watertown, Connecticut. I hadn't had a very impressive academic career since fifth grade. My orgiastic television watching had not done much for my study skills. Since first grade, which I was advanced enough to skip, I'd been on a steady downward course toward the lower middle of my class, buoyed above the complete bottom only by a genetic facility for English and the abundance of remedial students at the weird grade school I attended. My brother had gone to Taft, which is probably why they accepted me despite my mediocrity. But by eleventh grade I was a pitiful student, and the school stewards informed my parents that I would be either held back or kicked out. There was a meeting, my mother worked some magic, and I avoided both fates. The message, though, stuck. I holed up in my dorm room, and, despite an adolescent resentment of every grown-up in my orbit, I knuckled down. By senior year, I'd pulled my grade point average high enough to consider colleges more competitive than the list put together for me by the Taft admissions counselor, which included some schools I'd never even heard of. That's when my father, in a rare spasm of parental engagement, took me down to North Carolina to look at Duke.

I'm not sure how or why this exercise began. At sixteen, I was fully intent on becoming an actor and living, as my siblings did, in New York City. There was nothing about Duke—location, emphasis on the sciences, preeminent sports programs—that appealed to me. I was a black-turtleneck-wearing, cigarette-smoking chatterbox who passed the time in biology class writing Joni Mitchell lyrics in the margins of my textbook. What the hell would I do in Durham? But off I went, probably to curry favor with my father and harboring the hope that, if I was accepted at no other university in America, thanks to Daddy's legacy, I might at least have a shot at Duke. My siblings, smarter and better than me in most respects, had gone to Yale, Brown, and Columbia. It was my fondest wish to follow my brother on to Morningside Heights, though I understood why the college counselor kept rolling her eyes at me. The trip to Raleigh-Durham was an odd detour in every way. With Mum along for the ride, we set off in a typical formation that was totally atypical for us. The nuclear family on a college visit.

At the time, my father was among Duke's most illustrious living alumni, and he was treated accordingly when he came to visit. Our first night, we were invited to dine with Terry Sanford, the former governor of North Carolina and future U.S. senator who was then president of the university. We sat in the gracious living room of his residence, where I pretended to be excited by what Duke had to offer, and he, under the illusion that I was halfway qualified, expressed the school's certain desire to have me. The following day, we were given a private, red-carpet tour of the university. After a classroom visit, and a look at a couple of dorms, we ended our walk at the library, where Daddy and I were expected for a very special appointment.

In 1969, Grandpop had donated to the Duke library several scrapbooks and more than a hundred letters my father had written him. Soon my father started adding to the collection with correspondence, manuscript drafts, research files, and page proofs for all his published work. Some of the archives dated back to the early fifties, when he had the foresight to begin collecting his personal records. Ever frugal, he chose to donate the original, completed manuscripts of each of his books to the Library of Congress, a gift for which the government offered a modest tax deduction. But everything else went to Duke at regular intervals. Three years after the publication of *Sophie's Choice*, the William Styron Papers had taken on considerable size and significance.

Passing through a series of heavy wooden doors, we entered the Rare Book, Manuscript, and Special Collections Library. Inside was very, well, libraryish, and I remember feeling my head go numb with instant boredom and the desire to find a corner in which to take a small nap. Indifferent to books, I didn't enter a library unless I had to, nor did I want to talk with any *librarians* about my *father*, which was what I was about to do. Robert Byrd, the manuscripts librarian, was on hand, as were much of the other staff, and they gave us the most exuberant sort of a welcome one could hope for in a place where silence reigns. The Duke library is home to many unique collections, including a wealth of Greek papyri and several original Walt Whitman manuscripts. But unlike most of the other authors represented, my father was alive. He was also at the height of his literary celebrity, and so the papers were, for the time being anyway, the jewel in the Perkins Library crown. I felt like the dauphin dropping in on the gardeners at Versailles.

Bob Byrd, a kind and reserved young man, took us back into the closed stacks of the manuscript department. With quiet efficiency but also vested pride, he pointed out the many shelves of archival Styronalia. Daddy asked a few polite questions—*So these are the manuscripts here? And these are the letters?*—rocked back on his heels, and generally beamed at the sight. Row upon row of brown boxes, stacked in a windowless room in a North Carolina library. I couldn't get over how sleepy I felt. From within a dedicated, oversize box, Bob removed one of several large scrapbooks my grandfather had created. He placed it on a nearby wooden table and opened for us the decaying, umber-colored cover.

I have no memory of what I saw that day. I know that my father was immensely enthusiastic about showing the book to me. His eagerness wasn't immodest, just sweet, and I marshaled my attention for his sake as well as for the nice man who was custodian of all the yellowing paper around us. I have the feeling that someone took a photograph of us standing over the scrapbook, but it might be a trick of memory. It may just have been me, making a mental photograph from a proximal distance. Famous Writer Shows Daughter Evidence of His Early Days. Daughter Feigns Interest in This and Entire, Alien Southern Experience.

After saying our good-byes, Daddy and I left the library and stood beneath the university's soaring cathedral tower.

"What do you think, Albert?" he asked, cuffing me on the back. "Is it a groove and a gas?" *A groove and a gas* was one of the dopey phrases he and I liked to work into our conversations with each other.

"Yeah, Pops. Definitely." I nodded, wilting in the dense September heat. "A groove and a gas."

The boy in my father was an elusive animal. There was his wicked sense of humor, which could always be easily tapped. And a playfulness that popped up sometimes like a sprightly daisy in a field of ash. But mostly he presented himself as a Grown-up, and a crosspatch. That day on West Campus stands out in my mind for the glow my father flashed, like light from a long-ago star. A man of unqualified success, he was tickled now to be Big Man on Campus. He also seemed nostalgic, the way a person gets walking around old haunts, a nostalgia layered with the particular wistfulness reserved for parents showing their alma maters to college-bound children. My father had entered college an unfocused boy. He'd emerged not only a man but a writer of gargantuan ambition and a soldier who, though he never saw combat, came home whipped by the winds of violence.

I didn't get into Duke. Or rather I did, with some strange back-door contingency that involved me going to summer school to make up for my abysmal math and science grades. But by then I'd been accepted at Barnard College, where black turtlenecks were practically mandatory and they apparently didn't care that, if the math portion of my SATs was any indicator, I might be half an idiot. I felt bad about letting my father down, though I don't think he ever really believed I'd embrace the Southern option. As always, I was also ashamed of my shoddy scholarship. Why I was the most dunderheaded member of my family I couldn't figure out. But no matter. I'd gotten lucky. In the fall, I gleefully moved to Manhattan and the campus of Columbia's sister school. There I continued my campaign of academic incompetence and plotted my future as a star of stage and screen.

*   *   *

MY FATHER WAS sixteen and a half when the United States entered World War II. In a commencement address he delivered in 1974 at his old boarding school, Christchurch, he recalled the Day That Will Live in Infamy as it unfolded for a couple of prep school boys in Middlesex County, Virginia. Having scored a borrowed Ford V-8, he and his pal Mick Bowman left campus and were on the prowl for fun. They got their hands on a bagful of cheap, lousy beer and picked up two girls they knew in nearby Urbanna. The afternoon wore on, and, finding themselves in West Point, they pulled into a divey café and ordered burgers. As they were enjoying their food, and sipping beers on the sly, the waitress came over with news she'd just heard on the radio.

"I'll never forget her homely face," he wrote, "which was like a slab of pale pine with two small holes bored in it, nor her voice which had all the sad languor of the upper Pamunkey River. 'The Japanese,' she said, 'they done bombed Pearl Harbor.' Her expression contained a certain real fear. 'God help us,' she went on, 'it's so close. Imagine them gettin' all the way to South Carolina.'"

The transformation of life for my father and his classmates was instantaneous. Yesterday sheltered and callow ("That woman's knowledge of geography," Daddy wrote of the waitress, "was only a little less informed than our own"), today off to war. Virtually the entire Christchurch class of '42 served in Europe or the Pacific. Many saw action, some did not make it home alive. Still a year from being drafted, my father would go to college, though the list of schools approved by my grandfather was disappointingly short. Hampden-Sydney, a small school in mid-Virginia, was Grandpop's first choice for his son. But my father begged not to be consigned to somewhere so remote. So the two men compromised and, in the summer of '42, Daddy enrolled at Davidson College in Davidson, North Carolina, where he began an accelerated program for future enlistees.

"The most miserable freshman in the state of North Carolina" was how my father would one day describe himself during his compressed year at Davidson. At the time a strict and sober-minded Presbyterian institution, the school was a poor fit for my antiauthoritarian father. He would come up against the Court of Control, a black-robed student tribunal, several times, for crimes such as "disrespect for upperclassmen" and not wearing a freshman beanie. He was further penalized for dragging in late to Bible class, a course requirement he loathed, and he performed with aggressive mediocrity in every other academic subject. Writing for the college humor magazine gave him some amusement, and he managed to shed his virginity, as he recalled, "for two dollars in a walk-up hotel room in Charlotte, North Carolina." He also joined a fraternity, Phi Delta Theta, where he drank a lot of (forbidden) beer and picked up what would become a decades-long cigarette smoking habit. (Shortly before my marriage, Daddy and Ed, another malcontented product of Southern academe, discovered their unlikely Greek brotherhood and often amused each other with a series of hieroglyphic Phi Delt hand gestures.)

Whatever else inspired my father's knavery, he was unquestionably distracted by the war and the dust storm it was kicking up around campus. In the winter, a rumor circulated that the entire freshman and sophomore classes would be transferred to another college to make room for more trainees. Anticipating his fate, Daddy joined the Marine Corps Reserve in March. Two weeks later, on a Sunday night, he wrote to Grandpop:

> *Dear Pop,*
>
> *Everything around here sure is in turmoil. About 115 boys left yesterday. Another dormitory, West, was evacuated, to provide for accommodations for more than 250 Air Cadets. People are being drafted right and left. At present there are only about 225 boys left in school, which is quite a decimation, what? The morale is really quite awful. No one is studying much, and activities are at a minimum.*

The tension would break soon enough for Daddy. On June 11, 1943, he celebrated his eighteenth birthday. After enrolling in the V-12 Navy College Training Program, through which future officers combined academics and military training, he was ordered to report to Duke University. The academic picture didn't get any rosier in Durham: C+ in Political Science, D+ in French. But in many other ways he came alive in the fresh setting. The large university, with a newly completed Gothic-style campus on its western flank, was lovely, diverse, and, blessedly, coed. He made new friends, got up to some off-campus mischief, and began to enjoy the carnal pleasures of young adulthood. Eventually he met a pretty coed from Cambridge, Massachusetts, named Barbara Taeusch, "Bobbie," to whom he found himself enormously attracted. A botany major, Bobbie was also literary-minded, clever, and good company. She and my father began a romance that would last beyond college.

V-12 students were required to carry seventeen credit hours and nine and a half physical training hours per week. It was a rigorous and often exhausting program. "We're studying boxing, wrestling, and jiu-jitsu," my father wrote to Pop. "They're all very educational—especially jiu-jitsu. My partner is the son of a Marine officer who was stationed in Japan before the war—just my luck! I'm continually being thrown on my can." But Daddy seemed to adapt quickly and felt confident he would advance to Officer Candidate School in good time.

Most significant, my father became a serious reader at Duke and began to find his voice as a writer. His letters to my grandfather started as a trickle of perfunctory reports from Davidson but swelled to a steady effluence by the end of his first year at Duke. They chart his dismal progress in the subjects that left him cold ("That Physics course sure is tough," he writes, rationalizing his latest blunder—"The whole class average is about a D") but also reveal his growing confidence in, and excitement about, his literary skills. The dejected and defensive boy who only the year before was compelled to write to his father from Davidson, "I . . . realize you have expended a lot of money to keep your worthless son in school. The only consolation I have is that I have made no academic failing large enough to actually 'flunk me out' of school," was now about to have his second story published in the Duke literary magazine and could cheerfully relay comments written to him by his creative writing professor: "I take great pride in your progress this term. While I don't usually urge undergraduates to make writing their livelihood, you are definitely one to be encouraged."

Indeed, it was just such praise, honestly and laboriously earned from this exacting professor, that transformed my father's collegiate experience and very likely his entire future. Dr. William Blackburn was, at first blush, an unlikely literary mentor. When my father got to Duke, Blackburn was idling in the English Department, still an associate professor after almost twenty years at the university. A Rhodes scholar, with a B.A. and M.A. from Oxford, he was nevertheless a literary man, not an academic, and hadn't bothered to acquire a Ph.D. until Duke urged him to take a leave of absence to do so. Returning from New Haven in 1943, he resumed his duties, teaching among other courses a dynamic and inspirational class in "literary composition." But, continuing to feel devalued by an administration that didn't yet consider creative writing a valid academic pursuit, he grew taciturn and remote. Of his early days in Blackburn's class, my father once wrote, "Only a remarkably gentle South Carolina voice softened my initial feeling that he was filled with bone-hard melancholy and quiet desperation. For several weeks it seemed to me impossible that one could ever draw close—or be drawn close—to such a despondent, distant man."

The professor found in my father a kindred spirit, and drew him into a rare communion, from which my father benefited enormously. Blackburn was a brilliant teacher, coaxing his students to realize their best work by tasking them to seriousness and carefully reserving praise. My father's first submission to him was an essay in which he endeavored to describe a Tidewater river scene. The fishnet stakes, he wrote, stood in the gray water "looking stark and mute." The effort garnered him a D-, a lesson in pathetic fallacy ("Mute?" commented Blackburn. "Did those stakes *ever* say anything?"), and the newfound desire to earn the approbation of a teacher from whom he had much to learn. Eventually my father and Blackburn developed a strong bond. Daddy "sweated like a coolie" over his writing for Blackburn, until his "splintered syntax and humpbacked prose achieved a measure of clarity and grace." In turn, Blackburn threw Daddy the periodic "Nice!" or "Fine touch!" He instructed his pupil to read and also told him *what* to read (Thomas Mann, Proust, the Russians, Shakespeare), a directive Daddy responded to with gusto, plowing through great literature during his every waking hour. Blackburn invited my father to his home, where they shared their mutual interest in classical music. And, when my father found himself marooned in Durham over Christmas break (Thanksgiving with his stepmother, Elizabeth, had been enough holiday at home for the year), he welcomed Daddy to pass the day with his wife and children.

By the close of his first year at Duke, my father was in the midst of a true intellectual awakening. He'd fallen in love with Thomas Wolfe, discovered Balzac, Joyce, Poe, Maupassant, Dos Passos, Hemingway, and Faulkner. He'd completed several fine short stories and even made a stab at a first novel. At nineteen, he knew he wanted to be a writer. When his call-up finally came, in October '44, he made his good-byes to Blackburn and Bobbie, loaded up a stackful of books, and bravely boarded a train for Parris Island, South Carolina.

*   *   *

BORN WITH A cataract in his right eye, my father might have been excused from service altogether. But, like lots of boys his age, he wanted to serve and was crafty enough to memorize the eye chart while waiting to have his vision tested. After landing on Parris Island, he was subjected to a battery of other tests, including a routine blood screening. Each examiner waved him on until finally, uniformed and given a number, Private W. C. Styron had officially become a Marine. His days were soon a typical slog of drills and classes, marching and rifle mechanics, falling out and falling in, all broken up by a rare hour or two of recreation at the club set up for enlisted men. With his imperfect vision, my father gave a terrible performance on the rifle range. And, as usual, he bristled at authority, as well as the endless physical and mental trials of military training. But still, he liked the esprit de corps. And he was lured by the "fatal glamour," as he would one day describe it, personified by the battle-scarred officers who strode the camp like giants.

In November, three weeks into boot camp, my father heard his name summoning him out of training exercises. He was told to report to the naval hospital's urological ward. Once there, he was promptly informed that he had syphilis. A Kahn test, he was told, had revealed blood serum lousy with telltale spirochetes; my father was to remain in semiquarantine indefinitely. The news stunned and terrified him. He was just nineteen, and since his first virginal encounter, he had "known" only two other women, including a lusty girl from Queens whom he dated before meeting Bobbie. Confined to the "Clap Shack" and separated from the swaggering and mostly older population whose disease, gonorrhea, had given rise to the ward's nickname, Daddy passed several miserable weeks. The chief of urology, a "threatening"-looking man named Dr. Klotz, offered him no solace. Repeated Kahn tests showed little improvement in his condition. "Suspended in a monotony of fear," as he would one day describe it, he ruminated on his fate and revisited memories of his uncle Harold, who, as Daddy knew, had died not of "shell shock" but of syphilis-related madness and the attendant physical complications.

After writing to Grandpop and Elizabeth to tell them he'd been sidelined by "a little blood problem," Daddy looked for a reply that could offer a dose of sympathetic cheer. Instead he received a frosty advisory that only intensified his despair. Elizabeth, with her nursing experience, had immediately gleaned the true nature of Daddy's problem. He recalled the letter like this: "How appalled she and my father were, she wrote, at the terrible news. . . . She had no intention of judging me, she announced (pointing out that there was, of course, a Higher Judge), but then she asked me to look back at my recent way of life and ponder whether my self-indulgent behavior had not led to this—the words remain ineffaceable to this day—'awful moment of truth.'"

My father revisited this episode in his writing at least twice. In 1972, after publishing the excerpt from *The Way of the Warrior* in *Esquire,* he put the novel aside and wrote a play called *In the Clap Shack.* A mixed reception at the Yale Rep the following winter scuttled any hopes for a New York production, but the themes he cultivated from the experience remained relevant in his mind. In 1995, with the AIDS crisis still leading the evening news, my father sat down and wrote an essay about America's long history of stigmatizing sufferers of sexually transmitted illness and the spurious rectitude of a culture that perpetrates the idea of God visiting such trouble on those who "deserve" it. "A Case of the Great Pox" was published in *The New Yorker* in the fall of 1995. The piece explicitly addresses the feelings of personal failure that illness manifested in him at the time. But, coming a decade after his first major depression, it also limns the chronic and unmanageable fear of death that would stay with him all his life. Echoing the suicidal reveries he rendered so clearly in *Darkness Visible,* Daddy describes his internment in the Clap Shack: "At night, after lights-out, I began to prowl the ward, padding about in anxiety until, returning to the stool, I would sit and stare at the expanse of water, dim in the starlight, and seemingly frozen solid. What a blessed relief it would be, I thought, to lie down and be encased in that overcoat of ice, motionless, without sensation and, finally, without care, gazing up at the indifferent stars."

These frightful days marked my father's first brush with true depression. Fortunately, the resilience of youth, and an almost comical reversal of fortune, broke the mood's siege. While he was quartered in the ward, Daddy's gums, which had been bothering him for some time, began to bleed quite seriously. The hospital dentist, "a dour man, trapped in routine," responded with a certificate of indifference in the form of a prescription for gentian violet. It was left to the chief pharmacist's mate, following a curious hunch, to draw the scientific connection. My father didn't have syphilis, he was told days before Christmas, but rather Vincent's infection—trench mouth. His mistake had not been unprotected sex with three women of questionable morals but eating off unsanitary trays at the Duke University mess hall. Under a microscope, Vincent's and syphilis looked nearly identical. If Daddy's gums hadn't bled, who knows how long it would have taken for Klotz to recognize his error?

My father left the hospital later that afternoon, returning to the drill field with all the grateful enthusiasm of a man just given a stay of execution. On his way, he stopped at the PX for cigarettes and candy bars. A postcard, depicting a phalanx of Marines engaged in calisthenics, caught his eye. "Greetings from Parris Island," the banner read. "Toward Christmas," Daddy recalled, "I addressed it to my stepmother, and scribbled":

Dear Old Girl,
My frantic, obsessive copulations produced not syphilis
but trench mouth. (Escaped from the Clap Shack in time to
celebrate the birth of our Lord and Savior.)
Much love, Bill

In March 1945, Daddy at last received, as he had so hoped, his officer's commission and was transferred to Camp Lejeune. There he began, with other officer candidates, to prepare for what was becoming inevitable, an assault on mainland Japan. In May, he received orders for Quantico, and, in late July, Daddy made preparations to ship west. The Allied victory on Okinawa in June had at last cleared the way for a full-scale invasion, which was to begin with the capture of Kyūshū. Certain to be shipped out to the front lines imminently, my father quivered with anticipation as well as "gut-heaving frights." But his day never came. On August 15, Emperor Hirohito announced his country's acceptance of the Potsdam Declaration. The war was over; my father and his comrades would soon be discharged. They were, to a man, overwhelmed by their good fortune. "Death had seemed such a certainty that my very *aliveness* had become a recurrent marvel," my father wrote more than forty years later, in a thinly fictionalized account of the time. But it wasn't all joy. For the first time, but not the last, he felt the cold breath of mortality sidle up close, and it unsettled something deep inside him. After a short stint on Hart Island, where he was put in charge of the guard platoon at the naval prison, my father was discharged from the Marine Corps. When he returned to Duke, he was a man with a sudden seriousness of purpose and much to accomplish in his short earthly transit. "There are three things I wish you would try and find for me," he wrote his father. "First a desk lamp. . . . Also a record player, and a typewriter. I don't necessarily need the typewriter (for I can't type) but I do need the lamp."

Daddy never did master the typewriter. But with the aid of music and light, his life now began to revolve around literature. He submitted his fiction to *The Virginia Quarterly Review* and published several new stories in the *Duke Archive.* He acquired a circle of friends, including his fellow future writers Peter Maas, Guy Davenport, and Mac Hyman, who were also in Blackburn's class. And on Pub Row, the block of buildings where student publications were put together, he got to know Bob Loomis, who would one day be his editor at Random House. Bob's roommate was a young man named Clay Felker, until the future *Esquire* editor and founder of *New York* magazine got himself kicked out for eloping with his girlfriend, Leslie Blatt. Leslie, sexy and a terrific flirt, made a lasting impression on my father. His own girl, Bobbie Taeusch, had graduated by then and moved to New York for a job at Union Carbide.

Blackburn, meanwhile, was continuing to make an investment in his star pupil. Working his contacts in New York, he brought Daddy's writing to the attention of two editors: John Selby, at Rinehart, and Hiram Haydn, at Crown. Both men wrote encouragingly to my father and gave him confidence to start thinking beyond college. Ironically, he was at last getting some value out of his class time. In the autumn of '47, Daddy maintained a B average and rose, astonishingly, to the dean's list just in time to graduate that December. Without any other firm plan except to keep writing, he stuck around campus and enrolled in the graduate English program for the following semester. But March brought a change of heart, and, abruptly, Daddy dropped out. Among the ideas that were crystallizing into the formation of a lifelong sensibility: my father hated academia and everything associated with the scholastic structure.

* * *

IN LATE FALL of 2003, LaGrange College in Georgia, where my father-in-law is on the board, asked my father to come for their graduation the next spring and accept an honorary degree. In an increasingly fragile state, my father now made public appearances very rarely. He'd been in and out of hospitals a lot, sometimes compos mentis, sometimes not. When the request came, it was hard to know whether he'd even be walking by the time spring rolled around. It was testament to my father's affection for the Beasons, and I guess for me, that he accepted.

The journey began inauspiciously enough. Getting out of the car at LaGuardia, my father gave in to a full-scale panic attack and suddenly decided he couldn't make the trip. Which, frankly, was fine with me. Ed and I had arrived at the airport from Brooklyn with our six-month-old son. I hadn't seen my father in several weeks. Looking at him there on the curb, trying to put his foot back in the car while my mother pulled on his sleeve, didn't inspire a lot of confidence. He looked awful. Gaunt, ancient, his eyes practically spinning in his head, he was nearly as lunatic as I'd ever seen him. Disaster, it was obvious to me, loomed for everyone involved. But my mother, ever committed to staying positive and on the move, insisted we proceed. Alternately pushing and dragging, reasoning, cajoling, and forcing him, the three of us got Daddy on the flight. Meantime, I tried to tend to both our baby and the nauseating knot in my stomach. Ed, who looked like he wanted to die himself, tried his best to take care of all of us. Four anxiety-filled hours later, we arrived in Atlanta. Temporarily subdued by a narcotic-induced nap, Daddy shuffled off the plane and into a car headed to LaGrange.

The graduation ceremony, two days hence, held plenty of possibilities for trouble. Daddy could fall going up to the dais. Or he could pass out on the stage. Or he might just suffer the quiet indignity of knowing he looked like a man with one foot in the grave, inducing a deeper spiral (it had happened before when he was made conscious, in the mirror of an onlooker's eyes, of how badly he'd declined). But, for the most part, the conferring of this honorary degree wouldn't require much of him and was the lesser of my concerns. The much bigger deal was the luncheon, scheduled for the day after we arrived. It was there that my father was expected to give a speech. The morning of the event, sitting on the back deck of the house my father-in-law had procured for my parents, I couldn't begin to imagine how we were going to execute this plan. My father lay on a chaise, arms at his sides, his face a death mask turned up to the sun. The previous evening we'd had dinner at the Beasons', where Ed's ninety-five-year-old grandmother ran mental laps around Daddy while he sat, slumped and rheumy, in the seat of honor. *Well, I can always step in for him,* I thought. But had he even prepared anything to say? The pool shimmered, inviting me to chlorinated oblivion. I'd have given anything to be somewhere else.

The lunch went off, as such things do. The good people at our table smiled a lot and tried either to include my father in their conversation or to pay no mind when he completely checked out, disappearing behind the thick and strangely cloudy glasses he now wore. After he was introduced, a clatter of applause erupted in the windowed hall while my father, bent like a question mark, moved to the lectern with Ed at his elbow. I could feel the room fairly vibrate with sympathetic tension. Would he make it to the mike? Could the man talk? *Oh, God,* I thought, *please let's just get through this.* To tell the truth, I was less worried about my father's dignity at that point than that of my in-laws. Influential members of a smallish community, they were largely responsible for my father's presence that day. The local intelligentsia would not soon forget if their honored guest keeled over in medias res.

Gathering himself, Daddy began to speak. His voice was reedy and halting, a vague simulacrum of his old strong sound. In the winter of 1947, he said, when he was twenty-one, he came very close to becoming a Rhodes scholar. His mentor at Duke, William Blackburn, had urged him to enter the regional competition. A Rhodes scholar himself, the professor felt certain that, on the basis of my father's writing ability alone, he stood an excellent chance at being awarded the prestigious scholarship. Lured by the idea of two years at Oxford, with a stipend, and by romantic visions of punting down the Thames, Daddy agreed, submitting to the regional committee several short stories. To his astonishment, out of a field of twenty, he was one of two finalists chosen from the state of North Carolina. Several days later, he boarded a plane for Atlanta for the next level of competition. It was his first-ever nonmilitary flight.

My father had told this story before. "Almost a Rhodes Scholar" was originally a speech delivered to the South Atlantic Modern Language Association in 1979. It had then appeared as an essay in Daddy's collection *This Quiet Dust*. I wasn't, however, familiar with it. As his recollection wore on, and I watched Daddy shifting from foot to foot just as he always did when he gave a speech, I began to breathe again. He may have been tentative physically, but he was in complete command of his material. Of course he'd come prepared. And not only was he prepared but, I realized with mounting relief, he'd even chosen the right subject for the place and audience. When I graduated from Taft, in 1983, Daddy delivered the commencement speech. He'd instantly won over the student body by wearing a Grateful Dead pin I affixed to his robe. And he got a standing ovation by working a reference to the band into the body of his talk, fibbing adorably that it was his "favorite rock group." But my pride and self-satisfaction at our irreverent little prank turned quickly to horror when he began to lacerate Ronald Reagan in front of the large and mostly Republican crowd. I could hear the snickers, caught the flash of brick-red pants and Lilly Pulitzer dresses storming out of the courtyard, while Daddy basically called the sitting president an illiterate, warmongering fool intent on destroying our good capital in the world, not to mention the planet itself. The left-wing jeremiad he delivered that day—AIDS,

genocide, herpes, and the PLO were some of the topics he managed to touch on—might have gone over well at a banquet for *The
Nation.* But at this manicured redoubt of Connecticut WASPs, he
bombed. Had I been older, I probably would have been among the
few brave, mostly aging hippies who shouted "Right on!" from
the fringes of the affair. But I was a teenager, and my father had
thoroughly embarrassed me.

In LaGrange, something else happened. Eliding politics, Daddy
stuck to a script about academics and youth. After two days at the
Atlanta Biltmore, he said, where he was subjected to a battery of
interviews and intense scrutiny, after hours of fretting and fantasiz-
ing, he was passed over for the scholarship. The man who delivered
the news to him was kind. He let my father know it had been a very
difficult decision but assumed Daddy knew why he'd been rejected.
"My grades," my father replied, nodding. "Yes, to flunk physics
not just once but *four* times in a row. And that final exam grade,
the last semester: thirty-eight. We couldn't overlook that. . . . One
of the committee members said that you seemed to demonstrate a
'pertinacity in the desire to fail.'"

My father's audience lapped it up. The laughter and applause
carried him all the way back to his seat. They were amused and relieved both, I figured, just as I was. I looked over at Daddy's with-
ered countenance, from which still dimly flickered the rebel light.
The one that signaled his impatience for everything unimaginative
and doctrinaire, for physics and math and rubber chicken lunches,
for iced tea and academia and probably punting down the Thames.
For university gatherings and honors bestowed. I remember thinking, *How come I didn't know he was such a goddamn bad student?
Even I hadn't flunked physics four times.*

Five

*Back in class, Duke University. (Professor Blackburn
is on the far left, beaming at his former pupil.)*

IT SEEMED TO me that my father had been writing *Sophie's
Choice* all my life (which was true, more or less). In the spring of
1979, when I was twelve years old, a box filled with galley proofs
arrived at our house. At last it was done. Curious and proud, I
stuffed a copy in my book bag. My plan was to take the book to
school and read it between classes, attracting the maximum amount
of attention to me and what I believed was my father's Extremely
Important Achievement. Although Daddy had a reputation as a
man of accomplishment, nothing I'd ever seen him do qualified for
much of anything, never mind the sort of veneration that made him
so different from most of the other fathers I knew. I felt it incum-
bent upon me to somehow validate the rumors of his greatness.

I understood it was going to be a big book. During the previous

Christmas holiday, just a week after my father wrote the last page, we left for a Caribbean vacation with my parents' friends Bob and Norma, and their son, Danny. For much of the week, while we sailed through the Grenadines—Danny and I following the crew around, mocking their Australian accents, Tommy disappearing belowdecks with his French girlfriend, Monelle—the grown-ups sat in a quiet circle, passing the manuscript pages, hand to hand. Everyone agreed it was a masterpiece. Ever since, I'd heard talk around the house of book club rights and paperback rights and, finally, a sale to the movies. We were going to be rich, Daddy told me laughingly. I could see he was awfully pleased. So was I, for my father was in an excellent mood all winter long.

At school, I began my conspicuous project—placing the mint-green paperback on my desk at morning meeting, poking my nose in the pages before English class, studiously perusing it in the cookie line during recess. I eased off the act for fifth-period History, still smarting from an incident a few months before. Joan Baez, who was a friend of my mother's from their human rights work, had come to stay with us for a few days. No longer "Amazing Grace" and "We Shall Overcome" kind of famous, she was still a big celebrity. She was also wickedly funny, flirted with both my father and my brother, and generally knocked the socks off our entire family with her talent and charm. After staying up late while she played guitar for us, including a hilarious Bob Dylan imitation, I went to school still kind of bedazzled. It wasn't easy humping my books from class to class like it was any other day. Finally, I couldn't keep it to myself any longer.

"Hey, Mr. Spooner," I blurted as my history teacher came through the doorway. "Joan Baez was at my house last night."

A favorite teacher of mine, Rick Spooner often kidded around with me. Also, I knew he was a music buff, so I thought he'd get a particular kick out of my story. His indifferent response—"Oh, that's nice," I think he said—made me wonder if he'd even heard me. He had. Later that day, in the lunchroom, Mr. Spooner touched me on the shoulder as he walked to his table.

"Hey, Al," he said with a smile, barely breaking stride, "*Jaws* was in my bathtub last night."

I got the message, and was terribly ashamed for bragging. But still, deep in my academic doldrums, I craved recognition for *something*.

As it turned out, no one, least of all me, was the least bit interested in what I was doing. *Sophie's Choice* was, in my opinion, unbelievably boring. The difficult vocabulary and historical references kept eluding me until finally I began to let them sail on by, unchallenged.

Then I got to page 11. Recollecting his early days in New York City, the narrator, Stingo, describes the scene outside the window of his room at the University Residence Club. The meagerness of his lodgings (which "fell short of resemblance to a flophouse only by the most delicate of degrees") and the acuity of his multitudinous longings are brought into relief by the upscale garden across the fence, and its luscious proprietress. From his forlorn perch, Stingo invents an identity for his buxom neighbor and her "tweedy" husband. And then he spins his own "demented" imaginary narrative. "Gently my arms surrounded Mavis, and I cupped my hands under her full, free-floating, honeydew breasts. 'Is that you, Winston?' she whispered. 'No, it's I,' said I, her lover, in response, 'let me take you doggie fashion.' To which she invariably replied, 'Oh, darling yes—later.'"

I burned with embarrassment, and dread. *Calm down,* I told myself, *this is fiction. Daddy didn't actually* do *these things.* And yet everything about Stingo—his name, his literary aspirations, the rough contours of his biography—seemed perfectly, unadulteratedly true. My palms began to sweat. It occurred to me that I could probably get in trouble for reading this stuff at school. To my relief, things settled down a page or two later as Stingo, through a combination of impudence and myopia, loses his job and moves to Brooklyn. My father's description of 1940s Flatbush, the "pickle-fragrant air," the exotic crowds of mitteleuropean immigrants, piqued my interest the way a lively description of Marrakech or the bazaars of India might have. I started to enjoy Daddy's writing—the first I'd ever read—and to empathize with Stingo's feelings of homesickness, though I winced at the liberal sprinkling of words like *fucking* and *horny* and *lust*. I was a pretty sophisticated twelve-year-old, but even Stingo's satirical use of the phrase "pet to climax" raised a sumptuous blush to my cheek. It was, after all, my father's voice speaking the words into my reading ear.

I kept on through afternoon study hall and, just before the bell rang, reached page 47. Here, the narrator receives a letter from his father in Virginia, detailing the sad fate of a girl on whom he, Stingo, had had a youthful crush. Shocked by the news, he drinks himself into a heavy afternoon nap. In slumber, he says, "I was overtaken by the most ferociously erotic hallucination I had ever experienced." Bracing myself, I turned the page.

For now in some sunlit and serene pasture of the Tidewater, a secluded place hemmed around by undulant oak trees, my departed Maria was standing before me, with the abandon of a strumpet stripping down to the flesh—she who had never removed in my presence so much as her bobbysocks. Naked, peach-ripe, chestnut hair flowing across her creamy breasts, desirable beyond utterance, she approached me where I lay stiff as a dagger, importuning me with words delectably raunchy and lewd. "Stingo," she murmured. "Oh, Stingo, fuck me." A faint mist of perspiration clung to her skin like aphrodisia, little blisters of sweat adorned the dark hair of her mound. She wiggled toward me, a wanton nymph with moist and parted mouth, now bending down over my bare belly, crooning her glorious obscenities, prepared to take between those lips unkissed by my own the bone-rigid stalk of my passion.

Leaving study hall through the locker room, I stood on the back stairs that jutted out over the art room and tried not to throw up on my Bass Weejuns. After school, I quietly placed the galleys on the kitchen side table. I didn't return to *Sophie's Choice* for another twenty-five years.

❈   ❈   ❈

MY SUSPICIONS WERE all confirmed, eventually. The first fifty pages of *Sophie's Choice*, with their yearning and groping and coming-of-age misadventures, are in fact a pretty faithful portrait of my father's New York years. In March 1947, Stinky (as he was known at Davidson) arrived in Manhattan, hoping to make for himself a life in letters. With the help of Professor Blackburn's friend John Selby, he secured a junior editor position at McGraw-Hill's Whittlesey House imprint. And then he settled into a residence club in Greenwich Village where, like Stingo, he tried to make the best of an uninspiring situation. "I find my room on 11th Street a completely depressing affair," he wrote his father in May, describing plans to apartment-sit for a friend, "and I know I'd go mad if I had to stay pent up there for long." Alone a lot, he sought solace in books. The Viking Portable Library had just issued its edition of Faulkner, edited by Malcolm Cowley; Daddy found himself enraptured by his deep plunge into the mythic Yoknapatawpha County.

As usual, money was a worry. Even with the additional sum to which the G.I. Bill still entitled him, my father's salary didn't take him far. Cheap meals from cruddy places became the staples of his diet, and within a month he had come down with a case of food-borne hepatitis. He spent two weeks recovering on a bleak ward at the French Hospital on West Thirtieth Street, his boredom alleviated by a steady stream of manuscripts from McGraw-Hill and occasional visits by Bobbie Taeusch. Near the end of his convalescence, his stepmother wrote. She truly hoped he felt better. But, just as she'd pointed out when he was pent up in the Clap Shack, she also wished him to understand such illness was likely a result of his loose morals and questionable lifestyle. As ever, Elizabeth had found a way to kick my father when he was down. Still jaundiced and sufficiently reproved, he returned to work, where, yet within his grace period, he was welcomed back. At least for a little while.

Given my father's inability to conform, I suppose it was his destiny to fail at McGraw-Hill. For decades, the firm had been a leader in the trade publishing industry. The imprint at which my father had signed on, Whittlesey House, was little more than a boutique venue for the company, allowing it to keep a foot in the literary game. Still, most of the manuscripts that came to the door of their elaborate art deco headquarters had already been given a pass by the finer houses around town. And so my father, being the lowliest manuscript reader on a very low totem pole, had his work cut out for him. Each day, his gloom and frustration mounted. The rejection letters he crafted were thoughtful and kind, but his growing contempt for the tide of dreck that came his way made it hard to take much pride in the endeavor. Perhaps the only happy aspect to his drudgery was that, by contrast, it made his own work feel substantial, and promising. After three months on the job, he wrote to his father, "The novels I read remain uniformly bad or, at most, mediocre; and I am gaining comfort at least from the slightly invidious fact that I can do so much better than the majority of these *opera*."

One of the disappointing sagas that my father dispatched was a first-person account of an intrepid four-month-long expedition across the Pacific on a balsa-wood raft. The book, written by the Norwegian Thor Heyerdahl and named for the vessel that carried him, was, in my father's hoary opinion, not a bad idea. But Heyerdahl's manuscript was much too long and suffered from a severe case of humorlessness. Perhaps it would be suitable, in an abridged version, for a *National Geographic* issue. But not, my father advised, for Whittlesey House. When Rand McNally eventually published *Kon-Tiki* and Daddy stood by as it became one of the most treasured adventure tales of the twentieth century, he tried to comfort himself with the excuse that his employer had underpaid him into a dull-minded stupor.

Eventually, Daddy's lapses were more than ones of personal taste. Through the long, hot summer of 1947, he toiled with increasing lassitude, coming to work late, dozing through editorial meetings, and generally playing the flaneur who, by dint of native intelligence, managed to squeak by with only a scintilla of effort. In September, when Edward Aswell, who had once published Thomas Wolfe, was named editor in chief, Daddy grew momentarily optimistic. But he and "the Weasel," as he is called in *Sophie's Choice*, took an immediate dislike to each other. Daddy continued to hack around, and one fine autumn day, when he and his friend Didi Parker were caught blowing inflatable plasticine orbs—the sort that Wham-O would eventually market as Superelasticbubbleplastic—out the twentieth-floor window, the ax at last fell. My father's one and only proper job had lasted less than six months.

Necessity being the mother of invention, Daddy now set out in earnest to do the only thing he was evidently any good at. "Writing is a matter, really—that is, the *mechanics* of writing—of dogging both the idea and yourself to death," he wrote to Pop, divulging the news of his dismissal. He had other editing opportunities, he said, but had decided not to take them. At twenty-two, my father already understood the vagaries of the creative process and knew that to fully plumb the depths requires "pacing about the room until you've wrung every possible drop of richness out of your mind and into the story." He had a little money saved up, and would soon receive a felicitously timed bequest of a thousand dollars from his maternal grandmother's estate. Added to this figure were his VA benefits: twenty dollars every month and tuition money to pay for a writing workshop at the New School for Social Research. He was temporarily flush, and his dream didn't seem outlandish, or his reach beyond his grasp. "I'm going to try it honestly, even desperately," he wrote, "for I realize with a sort of blunt self-honesty that if I'm ever going to do anything with myself along literary lines I might as well start now while the trying is ripe. . . . If Hawthorne

could take 12 years to teach himself to write, I can certainly take a
year or so, or however long it will be."

*   *   *

AS A KID, I thought of my father's success as both unvarying and
eternal. It was one of the few seemingly simple facts I knew about
him. He had brown eyes, grew up in the South, and was *born* great.
It was an absurd and unfortunate notion. Besides the unrealistic
expectations it caused me to build for myself, it also obscured what
was probably the most useful lesson: without faith, talent is a fugi-
tive thing. My father's success came early, to be sure, but there was
nothing facile about it. *Lie Down in Darkness* was a three-and-
a-half-year gamble, fraught with all the setbacks, occlusions, and
long, dark nights of the soul that make up any great unmapped
venture. Had he been on a balsa-wood raft, he could hardly have
been more itinerant, or less certain of his journey's end.

It all started pretty well. Having made the decision to write
full-time, my father quickly went about getting himself organized.
With a friend from Duke named Ed Hatcher, he took a basement
apartment at Lexington and Ninety-fourth Street. He broke up
with Bobbie Taeusch, whom he was not ready to marry and didn't
want to string along. He got himself a cocker spaniel, named Mr.
Chips, for company. And then he began to pour his energy into
writing short stories. Hiram Haydn, whom Professor Blackburn
had introduced him to, was at the time running one of the most
rigorous and successful workshops in the country (over the course
of several years, one in every eight students went on to have novels
published). He was also an editor at Crown. Daddy was welcomed
into the class, where he found himself among a collection of interesting fellow writers and in the thrall of a new and influential
mentor.

Of all the students he got to know, Daddy struck up a particular friendship with a young woman named Sigrid de Lima. Sigrid's
mother, Agnes, was an education writer, and also the publicity

director at the New School. Already at work on her first novel, Sigrid provided my father with great encouragement when, toward the end of the fall semester, Haydn offered him a book contract—assuming a first chapter of some merit could be produced as testimony. It was an extraordinary piece of good fortune, Daddy knew, and he set out instantly to seize the opportunity.

The subject matter came to him swiftly. He had been brooding for some time already on his memories of several women from his youth. They were of a type, the twentieth-century Southern belle, and part of the middle-class country club culture, which both fascinated and repelled him. From his more modest Hilton Village perch, he'd observed that world for years, until at last he knew it like his own skin. Now, with Faulkner still coursing through his veins, my father began to conceive the story of beautiful, doomed Peyton Loftis. Dead by suicide at the book's outset, Peyton would come home to the Virginia Tidewater—and her fractured, grieving family—in a coffin. The train bearing her remains propels the narrative, and the reader is soon spirited into Peyton's past. Calling the book *Inheritance of Night,* my father planned a series of direct and interior monologues, including one from Peyton's simpleminded sister, Maudie. Reminiscent of Benjy Compson in *The Sound and the Fury,* Maudie's character was also drawn from that of Helen Buxton, his stepmother's handicapped sister. Alcohol, incest, and violence were, Daddy knew, the struts upon which the story's architecture would be built. The day after Christmas, while outside a record-breaking blizzard raged, he sat in his subterranean apartment and read the first chapter of Robert Penn Warren's *All the King's Men.* That same day he wrote the 128-word sentence that, almost word for word, would stand as the opening of *Lie Down in Darkness:*

Riding down to Port Warwick from Richmond the train begins to pick up speed on the outskirts of the city, past the tobacco factories with their ever-present, hovering haze of faintly acrid dust and past the rows of uniformly-brown, clapboard houses which stretch down the hilly streets for miles, it seems, the hundreds of rooftops all reflecting the pale light of dawn; past the suburban roads still sluggish and sleepy with early morning traffic, and rattling swiftly now over the long bridge which separates the last two hills where in the valley below you can see the James River winding beneath its acid-green, malignant crust of scum out past the chemical plants and more rows of uniformly-brown, clapboard houses and into the woods beyond.

Throughout the winter of '48, my father worked to produce the first fifty pages of *Inheritance of Night*. Haydn was pleased, furnishing him with a $250 advance and the high compliment that, so far, his novel stood up against "any contemporary American writer." But after an early surge of self-confidence, Daddy wasn't so sure he agreed. Taking a hard look at the manuscript, he concluded that only the first few pages were worthy of his ambitions. He'd been writing steadily for eight months; his timetable for the book now stretched out indefinitely. The pleasures, and suitability, of the empyrean city dwindled fast. So with Haydn's blessing, and the companionship of Mr. Chips, he headed back to Durham in hopes that the comforts of a familiar locale would make it easier to court his muse.

Daddy spent nine challenging months back in his college town. During that time, he and Blackburn forged a deeper, more equitable friendship. And my father squandered many pleasant evenings with a group of fellow alumni, including Ashbel Brice, Guy Davenport, and Bob Loomis, who jokingly referred to themselves as the East Durham Literary Society. But the writing got no better, nor did it come more quickly. "Every word I put down seems to be sheer pain," he told his father weeks after arriving. What's more, his financial outlook was no longer so rosy. He was finding it increasingly difficult to prove to the VA that he qualified for vocational benefits.

And the monthly installments from his grandmother's bequest would, he knew, soon come to an end. As he had done years before, Daddy was back to asking my grandfather for funds in nearly every communication. The situation obviously pained my father. Grandpop was not a rich man. Each dollar he gave his son came at the peril of his own future security. And yet, when Grandpop suggested sending him a monthly stipend of one hundred dollars, my father accepted it with alacrity. For beneath the quicksand in which my father appeared to be sinking, there began to arise an ever-widening plain of self-assurance from which he believed he could spring. It may have been counterintuitive, this fully fortified gut intuition, but it nevertheless became the bedrock on which he would build the next forty years of his career. He took his father's offer as "an informal sort of loan," swearing to repay it when he "made some money at this writing game. . . . That, of course, is a wild sort of statement," he continued, with the disingenuous modesty of a young man who clearly thinks there's nothing wild about it, "but in this miraculous country of ours anything can happen, so it's at least worth a try."

Still, in September, my father made a stab at diversifying his prospects. With an introduction from his friend Didi Parker, he wrote a letter to a young literary agent named Elizabeth McKee. He wondered if she might help him sell a few short stories while he continued to work on his novel. "I ain't no speedball," he admitted. Nor did he consciously write for "the slicks," as the big magazines were then called. "It's not pride," he said, "and Lord knows I could use the money. It's just that I don't know <u>how</u> to write a slick story." He was, however, willing to try, if McKee was willing to take him on. McKee accepted my father as a client, but over the next six months she had no luck selling anything he'd written. One story called "The Brothers," which he composed in a few weeks, was rejected by at least half a dozen magazines, including *The New Yorker, Harper's Bazaar,* and *The American Mercury.*

Meantime, he was getting nowhere with *Inheritance of Night.* During the winter of 1949, he produced no more than twenty new pages, very few of which he felt he could be proud of. "I'm terribly discouraged with the novel," he confessed to Grandpop, "and I suspect I'll have to consign what I've written to the fire." The prose was okay, he knew, but his characters were troublesome and elusive, refusing to carry their narrative forward. He sent the new section off to Haydn, appending it with some ideas for future chapters. "Or am I too far gone?" he concluded, bleakly. "Would like to write a war novel: These people give me the creeps."

A few weeks later, after some vigorous soul-searching and a momentous exchange of letters with Hiram Haydn, my father made a decision to put his novel aside. He was suffocating under the weight of his own expectations, and the deathly pace was just dragging him down deeper. He had another idea, about his stint as a military prison guard after the war. It would be "less ambiguous in conception," he told his father, "and perhaps less ambitious," but it would be manageable. Having made the decision, my father was flooded with relief. "It's actually what I should have started on a year ago," he wrote. Contingent on the new plan was another change: he would return to New York. "I guess I do need someone to throw a whip over me," he confessed, "someone like Haydn, until I get to the point of having enough confidence where I can wield the whip myself." But he assured his father, "It'll be the last move for some time for me."

At the end of April, my father packed up and took the train north again (this time without Mr. Chips, who turned out to be a bit of a pest and had to be given away to a philosophy professor). He had a line on an apartment on Grand Street, but when he arrived he discovered it had fallen through. Prevailing upon welcoming friends, my father passed his first few days back in New York on the de Limas' couch, during which time Agnes, who had taken a maternal interest in Daddy, helped him sort through the classifieds. He couldn't afford Manhattan after all. So he set out for Brooklyn—as he would one day put it, "another lean and lonesome young Southerner wandering amid the Kingdom of the Jews."

My father got a lot of mileage out of his Brooklyn experience. The house in which he lodged, a rambling clapboard on the southeastern edge of Prospect Park, became the model for Yetta Zimmerman's Pink Palace in *Sophie's Choice*. And the beautiful concentration camp survivor on the second floor would provide the outlines of perhaps his most enduring and indelible character. Now a Brooklyn resident myself, I was surprised recently to hear someone, unaware of my relationship to the subject, refer to Prospect Park South as "the *Sophie's Choice* neighborhood." But as closely identified as the book and, by extension, my father have become with the borough, the truth is he lasted there only two months. His two-room flat was comfortable enough (though he admitted to his father that he resented "not being able to settle down in a cozy Greenwich Village apartment"). And, except for the loud lovemaking of his upstairs neighbors, there was plenty of uninterrupted quiet. Indeed, during his brief Flatbush residency, my father began to feel quite comfortable in his solitude. Shortly after arriving, he wrote his father a long, self-examining letter. He had, he said, started the "New Novel" and felt, if "not exactly ecstatic about the world," then "very happy." He took measure of his Emersonian feelings of self-reliance and proudly noted that he needed neither company nor an excess of alcohol to maintain his focus or mood. What he *did* need, however, was a roommate to help pay the sixteen-dollar-a-week rent. When his friend Bob Loomis, with whom he'd expected to share the place, changed his plans, Daddy faced another reality: he would have to give up writing full-time and get himself a real job. In June, he wrote to Grandpop that he stood "a fair chance of getting a handyman's job in some publishing house." But the monthly check Grandpop provided was still crucial. "Without it," Daddy assured him, "I'd probably be working 10 hours a day in the subway."

Six

*One of many brooding portraits from
publicity for* Lie Down in Darkness

PROBING INTO MY father's early years, one would be forgiven
for thinking Bill Sr. was his only correspondent and writing his
only passion. I myself fell under the spell of that idea in the winter
of 2008, when Jim West sent me the galleys of a book he'd edited
called *Letters to My Father*, which was just about to be published
by LSU Press. Spanning the decade between my father's arrival at
Davidson in 1943 and his marriage to my mother in 1953, the book
is a collection of 103 letters from my father to his father. At the
back are three surviving letters written in the other direction, and
a few of my father's early stories gathered under the heading "Ap-
prentice Writing." Arriving as it did, just at the time I'd begun to
contemplate a memoir about Daddy, the manuscript was a welcome
surprise. I dove into the pages and made what felt like the first lap

across the sea of my father's years. Approaching him this way, in his verbal Sunday best ("Give my love to Eliza," "I certainly appreciate you and Eliza sending me the candy"), was a sweet experience. Unlike the ribald Stingo of my preadolescent encounter, Bill Jr. was earnest and chaste; he made me want to reach out and smooth his hair, or give him a little pat on the cheek. It was only a brief idyll—my father shorn of his libido wasn't, I knew, really my father at all—but the hours were a pleasant diversion, returning me to a state of ignorance I felt I deserved.

Ultimately, though, the full story—infinitely more interesting and true—beckoned. I began to pluck out details Daddy had written to his father and to cross-reference them with Jim's biography, my father's essays, and the various fictionalized narrators he'd fashioned for himself. In one letter, for instance, dated April 3, 1944, my father tells Grandpop about a trip he and a couple of pals took from Duke up to Danville to visit some young ladies at Averett College. "I have been dating this girl D— — S— — from Queens Village, L.I.," my father wrote. "She's 18 and very nice looking, intelligent, and her father is Sales Manager for National Distillers, Inc. (Old Granddad, Old Overholt, Wilson's, Black & White, etc.)!" The letter goes on to describe music at a Palm Sunday service he attended and that morning's difficult military training exercise. Nice-looking, intelligent D— — S— — gets no more play in my father's letters, nor do any girls specifically, until Bobbie after the war. But something about Queens had rung a bell for me. Thumbing through "A Case of the Great Pox," I found "ripe and lively" "Lisa Friedlaender,"* the coed from Kew Gardens who, at the time of my father's syphilis scare, had been second in his troika of sexual partners. Daddy had not told the dreaded Dr. Klotz (or his father, for that matter), but the reason for his multiple unprotected encounters with Lisa was embarrassingly simple: "we were fucking so continuously and furiously that I ran out of condoms."

---

*Daddy's pseudonym for her.

Down at Duke, my father's archives reveal a picture of him that is equally frank and forthcoming. Void of any obvious vanity, his uncensored correspondence lays bare a lot of his less attractive history: petty grievances, social misbehavior, flights of grandiosity, and grudges nursed beyond the point where anyone could reasonably be expected to remember how they'd begun. It is, with only the minimum accommodation for decorum, a very public display of his very private life as well. In a collection that spans seventy-two of my father's eighty-one years, there is only one box of restricted letters, which he requested no one open until ten years after his death. But everything else is up for grabs, including and most especially his personal memorabilia of the artist as a young man. That man, in the archives, is neither the virginal Bill Jr. from his letters to Grandpop nor the sexually frustrated Stingo of *Sophie's Choice*. He's a great deal more sophisticated than both. And more familiar, too. As always, my father was getting plenty of tail.

"My Darling." "Mon Petit Chou." "Dearest." So begin some of the dozens of billets-doux my father saved from his most ardent affair in the early fifties. She was married, and had a child, which may account for why she doesn't figure in his "official story" like Bobbie Taeusch and, later, Sigrid de Lima. It was, however, a significant relationship, beginning when they both worked at McGraw-Hill. Over the years, the affair managed to endure numerous separations, long and conflicting work spells, and, on both ends, romantic involvement with other people. Between 1949 and 1953, my father moved a dozen times. Daddy's lover wrote to him at every post, her letters crackling with humor, lust, and inevitable, heartache-tinged foreboding. To what degree her love was reciprocated is hard to know; his half of the correspondence does not survive. But there's no question that the connection was passionate and, at least for a time, something much more than physical. One night in 1951, after an explosive row with her husband, Daddy's girlfriend wrote him an agonizing letter, filled with longing for my father, despair at her predicament, and deep concern for her little boy. Around the same time, in a communication with Grandpop, my father confided somewhat vaguely, "I may get myself married sometime soon, to someone I think wonderful, but I'll let you know more about that when I see you." She and my father talked seriously about a future together, that much is clear. But there's little evidence that Daddy was ready for the responsibility, or that he truly encouraged her to get free. Instead they continued on, rendezvousing in Manhattan—and, later, Brooklyn—stealing long afternoons together, and writing constantly when they were apart. She angled for access to a side of him that remained elusive ("I shudder to think how great would be my joy if you ever really let me get close to you, spiritually"), while he kept one step ahead of a binding decision.

At the start of summer 1949, my father was happy to be back in New York. Hoping to hang on to his Brooklyn flat, he went into Manhattan to look for work and stopped by the de Limas' apartment for a visit. But when he told Agnes of his latest situation, she offered him another, enticing solution. She and Sigrid had a house in Valley Cottage, just up the Hudson. They both used it to write sometimes and went up frequently on weekends. The house wasn't big, but it had an extra bedroom and a vegetable garden that needed tending. If my father was willing to help around the house, said Agnes, he was welcome to spend the summer with them, rent-free.

Aggie's offer was hugely tempting. The house would not only mean peace, quiet, and a rest from his immediate money woes. It would offer something equally compelling for a lonely, displaced young man: female companionship of a familial sort. He felt loved by the de Limas, whom he would describe to his father as "two of the finest people in the world." If there were any unexamined feelings, any expectations that something might blossom between Sigrid and himself, he certainly wasn't addressing them. Instead, he gratefully accepted Agnes's offer. By the end of the month, he was contentedly ensconced in the pretty stone house up the Hudson, taking inspiration from Agnes's library of classical music and the dramatic greenery just then exploding all over the gentle Ramapo foothills.

My father ended up spending a year in Valley Cottage. Cleansed of his city concerns and fortified by the genial spirit of the women's home, he returned to the Peyton Loftis manuscript and at last broke the back of the story that had so bedeviled him. Occasionally, he went down to the city—the book party for Sigrid's novel *Captain's Beach* was a social highlight—but mostly he stayed still and wrote. By January, he had completed what he thought was half of the novel and expected to finish the entire manuscript by the following summer. "I feel as good about things at the moment as is possible in one so universally morose," he wrote his friend Leon Edwards, "so hooray!"

Romantically, however, he appears to have gotten himself in a pickle. When he eventually finished *Lie Down in Darkness,* my father would express his deep affection for Sigrid by placing her name alone on the dedication page. In Valley Cottage, they became very close, sharing meals and walks and long nights reading manuscript pages to each other, or talking of life and literature. They also shared a nickname—"Such a Dear Sweet Baby"—hailing each other with either the entire moniker or a shortened, initialed variation. In the spring of 1950, for instance, Sigrid signed off a letter:

This brings you all kinds of de Lima love starting with
Puppy Love on up and down in both directions.
Love, SB.

Plainly, Sigrid was besotted with my father. But once again, he seems to have felt something considerably less intense. His married girlfriend was still on the scene, and whatever intimacy he and Sigrid achieved—as momentary, occasional, or even frequent lovers—it certainly had none of the firepower of the more illicit relationship he continued to involve himself in. Sigrid was like a sister, and Daddy was very grateful to her. But her expectations for something deeper, and the inequity of the situation, became untenable for him. In June 1950, he left Valley Cottage and moved into an apartment on West Eighty-eighth Street in Manhattan. His leave-taking, he told Grandpop, was "not effected without a certain amount of regret on all sides." It also involved some delicate machinations, which left the dynamics of their relationship open and unresolved. My father soon had another girlfriend, an exotic Polish former model named Wanda Malinowska Montemora, and got up to plenty of other fun with his roommate Howard Hoffman. Sigrid meanwhile remained on standby, accepting her position as Daddy's dear "friend" but still signing her frequent letters, ever faithfully, "SB."

All summer, my father steamed toward the end of *Lie Down in Darkness.* Extending his work hours, he pushed on through the last third, hoping now to finish by the end of autumn. Much of the pressure he felt was financial. In July, Hiram Haydn informed my father that he was leaving Crown to become editor in chief of Bobbs-Merrill. Haydn could offer my father more money if he came with him, but he would need to finish the book to get the balance of his advance. The new contract was not, however, my father's greatest concern. On June 25, the Korean People's Army, 140,000 strong, crossed the Thirty-eighth Parallel into South Korea behind a barrage of artillery fire. Two days later, President Truman responded to the UN's call for intervention. America had entered the Korean War. My father, a Marine reserve, was quite literally under the gun, and he knew it.

"I almost faint with fright every time I see a brown envelope in the mailbox," Daddy wrote Bill Canine, a friend from Durham. He had good reason to worry. His decision to reenlist as a reserve just as he was leaving Duke in '47 had been foolish, a shortsighted impulse totally at odds with his peaceable nature. The idea was that it would allow him to hold on to his officer's status in the—highly unlikely—event that any major conflict would succeed the "war to end all wars." Now, my father was discovering that men of rank were being called up in abundance. His sole consolation was a relatively low serial number, which put him, for a while, toward the bottom of the hit list.

Throughout the fall, my father bore down on the penultimate section of the book. Playing Handel's *Messiah* on an almost endless phonographic loop, he wrote well into the evenings, delivering sections to Haydn as they came. He was by then so immersed in the world he'd created he could no longer imagine a life entirely beyond it. But still he pushed on, doggedly, until the January day when his dreaded call-up letter at last arrived. He was due at Camp Lejeune by March 3. "I've been walking around like a zombie," he wrote his father. Down at the Brooklyn Navy Yard, where he'd submitted to a physical, he met a handful of other officers who "all had the drugged look of men who are walking about in a nightmare. One fellow just had a new baby last week, has to close down his supply business in Jersey, and spent four years—besides all this—in the Pacific during the last war."

My father had only one hope for getting out of the service: the congenital cataract, which he'd so skillfully obscured to get *in* the first time around. A test at the navy yard determined vision in the eye to be 20–70, "half-blind," Daddy proclaimed acidly to Grandpop. "They're taking me anyway, and would have taken me, I fully believe, if I had walked in there with no arms." The twin specters of boot camp and war filled my father with unbearable gloom. But it was a darkness nearly superseded by despair over his work. The thought of having to abandon his manuscript so close to the finish line was intolerable. It was a situation that left him "about as shattered morally as it is possible to be."

Fortunately, others shared his concern. Calling on contacts at the Pentagon, Haydn was able to procure a brief deferment for my father. With the last section of the book still ahead of him, Daddy plunged in, writing Peyton's tormented interior monologue over the next few weeks in a physically punishing, headlong rush. Two months later, one hundred pages further along, and fifteen pounds lighter, he emerged with *Lie Down in Darkness* complete. After delivering the manuscript by train to Haydn's house in Westport, Connecticut, he returned to his apartment. Spent, and strangely sorrowful, he took to his bed and remained there for several days.

Dressed in his old uniform, Second Lieutenant William Styron reported to duty at Camp Lejeune on the first of May 1950. Up in New York, his first novel, so laboriously sweated over, was being prepared for galleys. The advance buzz was overwhelmingly excellent, giving my father the kind of boost that ought to have seen him through till publication. And yet, there he was, hundreds of miles away, a midlevel officer remanded to war, trudging through the bug-infested Carolina swamp. As he would later write, he couldn't help but fantasize about all the pleasures his bitter fate had stolen from him. He was meant to be "toast of the world, flattered and fussed over . . . plowing [his] way through galaxies of movie starlets and seraglios of wenchy Park Avenue matrons perishing with need of [his] favors." He knew his line of thinking was probably folly. But still, he wrote, "the contrast between this vision and the imminent reality—freezing on some bleak Korean tundra with the stench of cordite in my nostrils, and a heart congealed with terror—seemed to comprise an irony beyond all fathoming."

Seven

The Paris Review *gang at the magazine's twenty-fifth
anniversary party, 1978 (* left to right: *Bill Styron, Tom
Guinzburg, Peter Matthiessen, George Plimpton)*

IN THE SUMMER of 2008, shortly after a trip to Duke, I drove out
to the east end of Long Island. There, not far from the ocean, in a
comfortable shingled house, lives my father's closest friend, Peter
Matthiessen. For fifty-four years, until my father's death, Peter and
Daddy maintained a friendship that, if not always intimate, was
nevertheless abiding and true. The fellow writers with whom they
were so closely identified, (mostly) men with outsize ambition and
egos to match, were a contentious gang. Lots of relationships foundered over the years. But my father and Peter endured, despite (or
perhaps because of) their fundamental differences. Bill, the sensitive Tidewater Presbyterian turned prickly existentialist, with his
bumptious long-term marriage and high-profile social life. Peter, the
consummate Connecticut WASP whose route from CIA recruit to

Zen master ran through three wives, experiments in altered consciousness, and years of global wandering as the era's chronicler of dying ecosystems and cultures. Together, they had partied and traveled and joined forces against one political injustice or another. Both men lived to eulogize their mutual friends—Jim Jones, Terry Southern, Willie Morris, John Marquand, George Plimpton—and they stood together as the lights winked out, one by one, in their generation's dazzling firmament.

At Duke, I'd spent hours reading letters from Peter and the rest of their set, and found myself charmed and not a little envious. I'd always been entranced by the idea of them, ever since I was old enough to sit beneath the dining room table and listen to them carry on. I could imagine all those writers, chic and smart and full of promise, though by then they all had paunches—and the skirts they chased were two or three marriages in the past. The Americans in Paris in the fifties, like the Beats in Greenwich Village, or the Bloomsburyites of another era, were a rare flock, banded together by a kind of rebellion that, in a boundaryless world, seems harder to achieve now. As a whole they were greater than the sum of their parts. They took strength from their identification with one another, and the way they juxtaposed themselves against the rest of the world.

Perhaps nothing was as crucial to the longevity of their fellowship as the great and lost art of letter writing. My father and his friends wrote to one another constantly. No matter where they roamed, they kept open boisterous lines of communication, through marriage and divorce, success and failure, happiness and devastating sorrow. The letters crackle with the kind of sharp wit that their screenwriting peers worked into classic films of the era. And, like celluloid creations, even the ugliest bits are tempered by the artfulness of their presentation. Everyone had a nickname. Stybo, Jimbo, Guinzo. (Though Peter had his own nickname for Daddy: Porter.) Everyone drank. And everyone believed in the fundamental importance of their shared aspiration: literary sainthood. With each new book, they rooted for one another or, when warranted, delivered carefully worded criticism. Often separated by oceans, their accounts from the home front are newsy—

> *Madame Nabokov was here for two weeks and I skied with her, and she was very nice, although at night she had a tendency to dress like a female lion tamer.*[*]

and adolescent—

> *You'd love our apartment. I can stand in the window and piss in the Seine, but I don't.*[†]

absurd—

> *It was a great pleasure to see you last week. I am rather grateful you didn't join us later, since you would have seen me under the influence of my own liquor, bicycling Jane Lougee around the streets of Greenwich Village in a stolen Good Humor Vehicle.*[‡]

or advisory—

> *Dear Bill,*
> *Fuck them all!*[§]

And even at their most honest—anxiety about work, writer's block, and schadenfreude were common themes—they are rarely less than captivating. I envied the mystique of it all, even as I was aware of the damage—the alcoholism, depression, broken families—it covered for. But most of all, I coveted the part of my father that belonged to the rest of his crowd. Daddy, as it turns out, was a great friend. I knew this implicitly because he had so many friends.

---

[*] Irwin Shaw, The Klosters, March 6, 1955.

[†] James Jones, Paris, February 3, 1959.

[‡] Who else but George Plimpton? New York, February 18, 1959.

[§] George Mandel, in response to a bad *New York Times* review, June 4, 1960.

But I hadn't seen the evidence of all his kindnesses until I discovered, in his letters, the gratitude he inspired.

Among colleagues, he had been a patient, thoughtful, and enormously generous critic. Hundreds of writers, minor and major, benefited from his careful reading and the detailed notes he gave to manuscripts that used to come by the armful to my parents' door each day. When he thought writers worthy, my father went to enormous lengths to ensure they be considered for grants, awards, academic positions, and inclusion in various societies. He took people in when they were down on their luck, befriended jailhouse writers, bestowed gifts, and lifted flagging spirits. Financially, he was also unstinting. In the late fifties, Daddy was asked by his childhood friend Leon Edwards for a not insignificant loan to help get him and his young family through Leon's medical residency. Not only did my father make the loan but he did so without qualification or strings. A few years later, he wrote to Leon as he and my mother and siblings were about to embark on the SS *France* for its maiden voyage to Le Havre. He had just met with his lawyer and wanted to apprise Leon of some changes made to his estate: "In case one of the planes I will be flying on later should go down over Silesi and I should join bliss eternal, I want to inform you that I have made you the recipient, in my recently drawn-up will, of the note sum of $10,750."

This note may have been meant as a gentle reminder to Leon. But it also shows a generosity that on the surface seems at odds with my memories of Daddy and money. Whenever I had to ask him for a few bucks, the routine was the same. Slowly reaching into his pocket, he would open and expand the mouth of his billfold with a deliberateness that suggested there might not be anything in there to give. Which was never the case. He always carried a spectacular-looking wad of cash. "How much do you need?" he'd say, fingering the bills skeptically. Then he'd peel off a five and, before I skipped off, tell me to bring him the change. Looking back, I see that his thrift was probably a good thing. Given my mother's profligacy, I don't know how else I ever would have learned the value of a dollar. My father, by contrast, never lost his sense of wonder that he'd become a rich man. He liked having it but also took real pleasure in giving it away.

Leon, who became a successful surgeon, was deeply grateful to my father. The two of them kept up a warm and lengthy correspondence for many years. Eventually, Leon was able to pay back his debt to my father. But, ironically enough, it was he who died in a plane crash, when the private aircraft he was piloting went down in the early seventies. Leon's death came during a period when Daddy suffered a string of similar losses, and he drew closer to the old friends he still had.

When I arrived at the Matthiessens' house, Peter was in his study. I was greeted by Maria, Peter's third wife, who was outside dead-heading some rosebushes with her cheerful, gimpy dogs. When I was a little girl, Maria, to whom Peter has been married for almost forty years, frightened me. Beautiful and exotic, with a stripe of white running through her jet-black hair and the curious lilt of her Tanzanian upbringing, she'd march into our house and think nothing of giving me a dressing-down for, say, using too many paper towels. Or leaving my room a mess. As I grew up and began to go along on some of the bird-watching expeditions Peter led, I came to love Maria's shoot-from-the-hip style and her fierce honesty. Peter's second wife, Deborah, had died of cancer in 1972, leaving behind a daughter from her first marriage and the son she had with Peter, who at the time was just seven. With two small daughters of her own, Maria moved in and took care of the whole brood. Peter's work and his spiritual questing would continue to take him all over the world, often for months at a time. But Maria, from my point of view anyway, had anchored the wayward ship with a staunchness I deeply admired. It was, it seemed to me, almost the inverse of what I'd known growing up, with a father always at home upsetting the applecart and a mother who took every opportunity to run away.

Heading into the kitchen, Maria offered me some tea and asked eagerly after the progress of my research. She, like many of my parents' friends, had been full of enthusiasm about the book, and I found her no less so that day than when I'd seen her in New York some months before. But that didn't mean she wasn't chary. Listening as I described some of my ideas, she tipped the steaming kettle. When she was done, she turned to me and let forth a deep and genuine laugh. "Oh, Al, dear, you know it's just what we feared. That you'd all grow up and write books about us!"

Maria and I were still chatting quietly in the kitchen when Peter at last arrived. Handsome as ever, he gave me a kind, paternal welcome, and then I followed him out to Maria's garden. On the way to Sagaponack, I'd bought a tape recorder. Now I was fumbling about, trying to figure out how it worked and feeling a bit silly as I put it on the arm of his Adirondack chair, checking several times to make sure the light went on. I felt awkward, interviewing my father's friend. It was hard to shed my role as a child, and I wasn't even sure I wanted to. Did I need him revealing secrets? And would he, whether I wanted him to or not? Peter, far more comfortable in the interview dynamic than I, took the reins.

"Well," he said, as he lowered himself into his chair, "I'm not going to tell *that* story again."

That story was about the first time my father and Peter met. It was early May 1952, and Daddy had just arrived in Paris. With a letter of introduction from a mutual friend, he turned up at the studio apartment Peter shared with his first wife, Patsy, on the Rue Perceval. The three Americans hit it off right away, talking and boozing till at last the sun went down behind the Gare Montparnasse. Pleasantly lit, they all repaired to a local restaurant, Ti Jos, where they ordered oysters and kept on drinking. Toward the end of the meal, my father, who had been quite jolly all day, became suddenly and unaccountably maudlin. His subtle Southern accent grew almost comically heavy. Then Daddy—Peter usually tells this part in a deeply exaggerated cornpone way—swallowed his last oyster and declared dramatically, "Ahm goin' home to the Jay-mes Rivah to fahm peanuts! Ah ain't got no more resistance to chay-nge than a *snow*flake!"

In fact, my father's life had been nothing *but* change for the entire previous, head-spinning year. After only two months of officer training at Camp Lejeune, Daddy had been miraculously released from active duty. A dismal performance on the rifle range had sent him to the Marine hospital, where the ophthalmologist on duty reassessed his cataract and, in an instant, reversed his fate by declaring him 4F. He returned to New York toward the end of August. In September, just as he'd imagined, he awoke to find himself the new darling of the literary world. Reviewed in over a hundred news outlets, he was instantly, favorably compared to Faulkner and hailed as one of the finest new voices of his generation. Praised in *The Washington Post, The Boston Globe, The Nation,* and *The Atlantic Monthly,* he was singled out for the elegance of his prose, the vast and challenging scope of his narrative, and the strength of his moral vision. In the *Herald Tribune Book Review,* Howard Mumford Jones declared that "few [recent writers] have had the capacity to mingle beauty, wisdom and narrative art as he has done." Malcolm Cowley, writing in *The New Republic,* thought Peyton's final monologue outstripped the power of Quentin Compson's in *The Sound and the Fury.* Not all his reviews were positive—*Newsweek* found his prose "purple," *Time* thought his characters "spiritual leeches." And though much of his voluminous mail was complimentary, dozens of letters arrived from fainthearted readers and priggish scolds shocked by the book's grim subject matter and the rawness of the language. But for the most part there was a consensus that, with *Lie Down in Darkness,* a potent talent had arrived on the scene.

It was an exciting time, those early weeks after publication, and my father certainly savored the praise he'd worked so hard to earn. But there was one person whose pride would actually eclipse his own, and on whom the book's success was largely predicated: Bill

Styron, Sr. After all his promises, my father had done it. He'd made good. It was with a particular rush of pleasure that, having obtained an advance copy of his first review, Daddy could dash off this telegram on September 2, 1951:

WILLIAM STYRON

139 CHESAPEAKE AVE NEW PORT NEWS VIR

SATURDAY REVIEW SEPTEMBER EIGHTH QUOTE I
SHOULD SAY AT ONCE THAT LIE DOWN IN DARKNESS
IS A REMARKABLE AND FASCINATING NOVEL THE BEST
NOVEL OF THE YEAR BY MY STANDARDS IT IS PRACTI-
CALLY PERFECT UNQUOTE AM GLAD I AM YOUR SON

BILL

By the new year, it would seem my father had gotten a full dose of the beau monde. When he wasn't sifting through fan mail, signing contracts for foreign translations, sitting for interviews, or watching his book move up and down the bestseller list, he was rubbing elbows with the cream of New York society—and trying to figure out how to get his head screwed back on straight. Invited everywhere, he was meeting people—John Hersey, e. e. cummings, Bennett Cerf, Gore Vidal—whom previously he'd only read, and alongside whom he was suddenly treated as an equal. He spoke at forums with Herman Wouk and Malcolm Cowley, and was invited down to lecture graduate students at Johns Hopkins. Accompanied by his new friend "Jack" Marquand, son of the über-WASP writer John P. Marquand, he fell in with another New York crowd, clocking hours among the painters and poets at the Cedar Tavern. One evening, at Leo Lerman's apartment, he was introduced to Laurence Olivier, Vivian Leigh, Tennessee Williams, and Marlene Dietrich. Both Williams and Dietrich told him how much they'd enjoyed *Lie Down in Darkness.* Unconcealedly floored, he went home and straightaway wrote the news to his aunt Edith.

His achievement was also being measured that season by the cloak-and-dagger committees preparing to bestow the year's big literary awards. In the winter of '51, *Lie Down in Darkness* was sharing the spotlight with *The Catcher in the Rye, From Here to Eternity,* and *The Caine Mutiny.* For my father to be mentioned on any of the short lists was a real accomplishment. Through his editor, Daddy learned that he was in contention for the National Book Award as well as a new prize, administered by the American Academy of Arts and Letters, called the Prix de Rome. Later in the year he would also be in contention for the Pulitzer.

All of this glory and gallivanting certainly had its charms. But the more fun my father had, the less he wrote. And the longer he strayed from his desk, the more difficult it was to feel good. Adding to the endless distractions, his romance with his married lover had reached an emotional crescendo. With the whole world suddenly open to him, my father had to consider if now was the right time to be embroiled in this sort of drama. Did he really want to settle down, to become stepfather to a small child? An idea that had been organizing itself for some time began to take concrete shape. He would, he decided, go overseas for a while and get a fresh perspective. His British publishers had extended an invitation, and he had a few other introductions to explore. But mostly he wanted to see the world, and carve out some time to develop ideas for his second book. In February, he booked passage on the steamer *Ile de France,* bound for Southampton. That week, he wrote to his father, "I'm getting monstrous tired of cocktail parties, and I trust that in Europe I'll be shut of them, although at a recent one the scenery was graced by Messrs. Norman Mailer and James Jones, who are interesting characters and fun to talk to. Later, accompanied by some young ladies, we went uptown to a fancy café along with a movie actor, Montgomery Clift, and that Monty was along was a pity because he stole the show and was inundated by autograph hounds and even Jones went unnoticed. But it was fun."

Four days later, Daddy learned he'd been awarded the Prix de

Rome. A year to live, rent-free with a generous stipend, in the heart of Italy's capital, was in my father's estimation "truly the greatest honor that a young American artist can receive." Because the fellowship didn't begin until October, he would have six months to explore and enjoy Europe before he was expected in Rome.

On March 5, 1952, my father set sail in high spirits. After a pleasant transatlantic voyage (hobnobbing with Lena Horne and other guests up in first class), he put down in London, where he delivered to Grandpop a mixed report on "the land of my forefathers." England, he wrote, "combined a scene of dreariness with one of melancholy beauty." The food he judged "indescribably horrible." But he admired many of the people and the landscape of the countryside. Perhaps he'd have stayed on longer were it not for his reviews, some of which were published during his few short weeks in the country. Thin-skinned in the extreme, my father never took criticism well. He once said he could remember every single word of some of his bad reviews, though almost nothing from the raves. The British, with their near-mythical disinclination toward expansive emotion, weren't crazy for my father's florid style. *Lie Down in Darkness* would in fact be the first of many of his books to get a lukewarm reception in the United Kingdom. The English readers' indifference always rankled him. But no doubt it also burnished his affection for France, where Daddy arrived just in time for May Day celebrations.

"It was a wonderful summer," Peter said, his eyes twinkling with nostalgia as he recollected the events of '52, "but everybody drank too much." Whatever "too much" meant, that is, to a brotherhood of healthy young men suddenly free to pursue every appetite and idea that happened to seize them. Americans—novelists, poets, painters, ex-GIs as well as rich boys who'd been sheltered from the draft, come to hunt the ghosts of the Lost Generation—were streaming into Paris in the early fifties. Women arrived too, though in smaller numbers, and, for all of them, life proved surprisingly easy. Since the end of World War II, the battered French government had staged a strategic operation to lure wealthy tourists back to the City of Lights. Rules on black market currency were eased and tourist card requirements summarily repealed. But instead of big spenders, Paris got a flood of cash-strapped expats. My father arrived to a scene part Athens, part Woodstock, part Vincente Minnelli musical. Peter introduced him around town, and peanut farming, it seems, fell rather swiftly by the wayside.

It was with this new crowd that my father found himself cast in yet another unfamiliar role: éminence grise. The group—the writers John Train, Harold "Doc" Humes, and Terry Southern; the film director Aram "Al" Avakian; the artist William Pène du Bois; the publishing scions Cass Canfield and Tom Guinzburg—were all within a year or two of Daddy's age. But he was the only one with a novel already under his belt, and a measure of fame that had preceded him across the Atlantic. As such, he was quickly recruited to play an advisory role in the launch of a literary magazine that was just that summer coming together. Led by Matthiessen and Humes, *The Paris Review* founders—du Bois, Train, and Guinzburg rounded out the group—were working to fashion their mandate. The magazine, they believed, should promote the work of artists rather than criticize it, as was the fashion of the day. In addition to stories, poems, and sketches, each issue would include an in-depth interview with a novelist of stature. Rather than talk about it, *The Paris Review* would let creativity, every aspect, speak for itself. Train soon pressed his Harvard roommate Prince Sadruddin Aga Khan into the role of publisher. Peter enlisted another Harvard grad, his childhood pal George Plimpton, just then finishing studies at Cambridge University, to serve as editor in chief.

All that season, while the magazine took shape, the men and their merry band availed themselves of the city's gifts. They gathered at famous literary haunts like La Coupole, Les Deux Magots, and Le Sélect as well as the little boîtes where a *coup de rouge* was cheap and the scent of hashish raised nary an eyebrow. Many of the group's follies took place at the magazine's unofficial headquarters, Le Dôme, on Boulevard Montparnasse. As legend has it, the publishing house from which *The Paris Review* rented its cramped, one-room office would not give out a key to the building. At night, the staff members were often forced to rappel out the second-floor window and then prove to the alerted gendarmes that they were not, in fact, cat burglars. Once sprung, they would head to the café, where they would pass the long night arm wrestling, singing, playing pinball or parlor games. Having advanced the art of fiction by day, the "tall young men" (as Irwin Shaw called them) had no compunction about surrendering to the art of pleasure when the moon rose over the City of Lights.

My father cottoned pretty quickly to this new life, so full of intellectual and corporeal vigor. Enlisted to craft a statement of purpose for *The Paris Review,* Daddy drew up what would, after some contentious editing, become the magazine's essential manifesto. Grounding his ideas in the kind of youthful certitude that pervaded *The Paris Review*'s offices, he proposed a publication emphasizing the best creative work the editors could find. The magazine shouldn't exclude criticism but put it "pretty much where it belongs i.e. somewhere near the back of the book." It was my father's hope, he wrote in the form of a letter to the reader, that *The Paris Review* would concentrate its energies on a simple, if rare, class of people: "the good writers, and the good poets, the non-drumbeaters and the non-axgrinders. So long as they're good." The letter ran at the front of *The Paris Review*'s first issue, published in the spring of 1953.

Remarkably, given the overwhelming recreational lures, my father actually accomplished a lot in Paris. Brief though his service in the Korean War had been, the experience had deeply aroused his writerly conscience. One twenty-four-hour period in particular galvanized his imagination. In June, from his little room in the Hôtel Liberia in Montparnasse, he began to transform the incident into fiction.

It had happened in August, at Camp Lejeune, when my father and his battalion were bivouacking in the woods several miles from their base. Waiting in a chow line beneath a grove of trees, the men had been rocked by twin earth-shaking explosions, centered on a clearing just yards away on their right. They would soon discover the source of the din: in the midst of an adjacent regiment, two mortar rounds had fallen short of their mark. Within an instant, eight young soldiers were blown to smithereens.

"It was not so much they had departed this life," my father wrote, "but as if, sprayed from a hose, they were only shreds of bone, gut, and dangling tissue to which it would have been impossible ever to impute the quality of life, far less the capacity to relinquish it." The soldiers who witnessed the event were, to a man, utterly stunned. Through the late afternoon, ambulances came and went, and, at last, night fell on the encampment. The men in Daddy's battalion were just beginning to settle down and process the events of the day when their commanding officer, Colonel James Masters, rousted them with an unimaginable command. They were to get on their feet and march thirty-six miles back to base camp. Astonished but obedient, the men set off into the dark marshland. Masters, a middle-aged martinet contemptuous of the many older, out-of-shape reservists under his command, wasted no time unleashing the full force of his overweening power. Throughout the endless night, he patrolled the line, coming and going from his chauffeured jeep, prodding, cursing, and berating the exhausted troops. In the end, two thirds of the regiment collapsed and had to be driven back to camp. And though my father, blistered and battered, completed the exercise, it calcified his growing disdain for war, and the theater of the absurd through which it so often finds expression.

Told from the point of view of Lieutenant Thomas Culver, "Like Prisoners, Waking" shows my father grappling for the first time with a motif that would continue to fascinate him the rest of his life. At the center of the narrative is Captain Al Mannix. A powerfully built Brooklyn Jew, Mannix burbles with outspoken contempt for the Marines in general and Templeton (as Masters is called) specifically. Culver is riveted by him, and not a little awed by his rebellious swagger. But ultimately the lieutenant recognizes that Mannix, "born into a generation of conformists," has no hope of forcing any real change. His moral clarity is really a curse, for, like every other man on the long and brutal march, he is trapped by a human compulsion for violence, systematized and sanctified by the U.S. Marine Corps.

The paradigm of a narrator-observer in the thrall of a dynamic and dangerous man would appear again and again in my father's work. Particularly in his war writing, it served as a trope for his relationship to all things martial. The military was a concept that alternately seduced and disgusted him, provoked his outrage and inspired him to flights of poetry and zeal. My father also knew, as his friends Jones and Mailer had proved so ably, that the American soldier's experience was *the* story of his generation. He was bent on having a role in the telling.

To my father's surprise, "Like Prisoners, Waking" spooled out "at white heat," as he would later describe it, and came in at nearly twenty thousand words. A very long short story, the piece would have been hard to place in most established magazines. Fortunately, he had the enthusiastic backing of two editors, Vance Bourjaily and John Aldridge, at a new literary journal called *discovery*. Sold alongside traditional magazines but published in paperback-book format, *discovery* placed no limits on a story's length or format. Bourjaily and Aldridge encouraged my father to play the story out, and, by the middle of July, he had a novella he thought was ready for publication. George Plimpton organized a gathering of friends at Peter and Patsy's so my father could hear the piece read out loud.

In a 1988 essay, written for the *MacDowell Colony News*, George recalled that long-ago afternoon and the tepid enthusiasm with which it had come together. People had shown up out of a sense of obligation, he said. Even the chief organizer admitted to dreading it a bit. ("In Paris there tend to be more compelling ways of spending an evening," he wrote, "than listening to a friend read from his work, especially if described as near-novella length.") At first my father appeared nervous, clearing his throat and struggling to settle into the rhythm of the prose. But eventually he hit his stride, soon captivating the room with the strangely hypnotic quality of the story. Dusk came on. The room grew dark and utterly still. Doc Humes placed a candle by his side. My father continued on, growing hoarse as the hours passed, until finally, "his face as luminous as a light in the moon," he lay the last page facedown on the table.

"Well . . . *Mister* Styron," George remembers someone calling out into the silence.* It was an acknowledgment of my father's primacy, he thought, and also a "benediction." Daddy's new friends, though obviously impressed, were also left to shake their heads in wonder. Amid all the gaiety and carousing, somehow the new guy had managed to craft a work of tremendous force that was also utterly different from the novel for which he had become known. My father, too, knew he'd wrought something exceptional. Four years before his death, in an interview with C-SPAN's Brian Lamb, Daddy would describe that afternoon as among the most satisfying experiences he'd ever had as a writer.

The wave of creativity rolled on. In addition to the novella, my father spent part of his time in Paris exploring an idea that he thought would be his next long work of fiction. It was a subject that had intrigued him ever since a school football trip (too shrimpy to play, my father served as the team's manager) when he was fourteen. On the bus ride from Newport News to Southside Virginia, Daddy had caught sight of a roadside marker and asked the driver to let him get out to take a closer look. The sign memorialized the bloody insurrection of a rebel slave named Nat Turner. Although he had heard of Turner before, my father was shocked to discover that the

---

*James Baldwin, by George's recollection, but my father claims not to have met Jimmy for several more years.

events, which involved the death of more than sixty people, had occurred just a few miles from his home. No one ever talked about it. The facts he read that day had stayed with him and, more than a dozen years later, struck him as the possible subject for a novel. Writing to Grandpop from Paris, with a request for some historical material, my father gave a hint of his aspirations for the project:

> I hope that when I'm through with Nat Turner (and God, I know it's going to be a long, hard job) he will not be either a Great leader of the Masses, as the stupid, vicious jackass of a Communist writer might make him out—or a perfectly satanic demagogue, as the surface historical facts present him, but a living human being of great power and great potential who somewhere, in his struggle for freedom and for immortality, lost his way. And that is the human condition and no one is even half-noble unless he deserves it and no one is all noble, even a saint.

Productive as my father was, he doesn't appear to have missed out on much fun that summer. With August came an exodus from the city, and so he decided to catch a ride south with Doc and his girlfriend, Mary Lee. It was a trip as bumptious as it was madcap. Doc's car, according to my father, "had a terrible odor" and almost no brakes, frequently requiring a person to open the door and drag his foot to bring it to a full stop. This, and the fact that the driver never shut up ("He was a madman," Daddy once laughingly recalled; "I came very close to killing him"), made for an excruciating drive. The two men had "terrible fights," according to Peter, Doc's famously eccentric behavior (which would in later years manifest more clearly as mental illness) colliding with my father's irritable nature. Blessedly, there was much to enjoy beyond the confines of Doc's blue torture-mobile.

Stopping in Saint-Tropez, the travelers were put up by an aging French movie actress who lived in faded splendor in a thirty-five-room estate. There, Daddy swam and fished and got to feeling "as healthy as Tarzan." Then it was on to Saint-Jean-de-Luz to meet up with the Matthiessens at the seaside home of Irwin and Marian Shaw. Back in Paris, Shaw, an expansive figure at the height of his literary success, had taken Daddy and several other young writers under his wing. With a consummate *savoir-vivre*, Shaw introduced his acolytes to good food, good wine, and an altogether higher order of "Rive Droite" living than they were able to get up to on their own. The movie producers Darryl Zanuck and Sam Goldwyn, as well as Artie Shaw, John Huston, Gene Kelly, and "a slew of delectable Hollywood starlets," became a part of Daddy's social scene, adding some glitter to an already festive season. Irwin's generosity included an open invitation to his big country house, which the visitors christened Le Château.

Although the ride home was as nerve-racking as the way down, it had been a delightful holiday for Daddy. He and his friends had taken in the bullfights, laid on savage tans, and dined on a meal that Daddy declared "the best meal of many incredible meals [he'd] eaten in France—frogs legs, coq au vin and a wine that was like drinking liquid velvet." He'd enjoyed afternoons of long conversation with Shaw and had made some new acquaintances, including Art Buchwald and his wife, Ann. Art, a columnist for the *International Herald Tribune* at the time, would in later years become one of my parents' dearest friends. After he'd come home, the jolliness continued, and not even Daddy's hobbled leg ("Your father always claimed I backed over him," Peter says of the mysterious, drunken incident) could dampen the memory of the journey.

But eventually, Paris and its bacchanalian pleasures began to wear on even my sybaritic father. Late August found him at loose ends. He was not due in Rome till October. Awaiting the books on Turner, as well as notes from the *discovery* editors, Daddy did more than his usual share of drinking and smoking, and, underoccupied, began to sense a bogeyman in the room. He grew irritable and got to feeling a melancholy he'd known in fits and starts before. His dyspeptic mood comes through in an interview he gave during his final weeks in Paris, for the fifth issue of *The Paris Review*. The conversation, led by George and Peter, took place at a café on a hot, bright morning, and my father, like his interlocutors, was obviously still wrecked by the boozy night before.

"Do you enjoy writing?"

"I certainly don't."

Later, he is asked when he does his best writing.

"The afternoon," Daddy answers. "I like to stay up late at night and get drunk and sleep late. I wish I could break the habit but I can't. The afternoon is the only time I have left and I try to use it to the best advantage, with a hangover."

Writing with a hangover was a talent my father mastered and skillfully employed for many years. But it was always a black dog, menacing his equilibrium, even when he was young enough to afford a sense of humor about it. And worse perhaps than trying to power through the wreckage of a bender was the wreckage that produced no writing at all. With the characteristic understatement all my father's bluff pals employed, he wrote to John Marquand, "With nothing to do now in Paris, and no project to concentrate on, Paris has become something of a drag."

September came at last, and it was time for my father to move on. He packed up knowing only one thing for sure: his novella, "Like Prisoners, Waking," would run in *discovery* that fall. He wasn't content with the title, but Peter, who saw him off at the Gare de Lyon, soon gave him a better one. *The Long March*, he suggested, and then, reconsidering, advocated for dropping the article. As the two men went back and forth on the subject, they lost track of time. Daddy would have to dash. Not knowing when or if he'd see his new friend again, he made a quick good-bye and headed off to Rome.

*   *   *

PETER AND I talked comfortably and for a long time that day in Sagaponack. Behind us was the dojo where he, a Zen master, has for years taught and practiced. Farther still lay the famous potato fields of Long Island's east end, and a quiet surf lapping the shore. There was, I thought, a peacefulness to Peter and his territory. He was a warrior at rest, eighty-one, with a big new novel that, a couple of months after our meeting, would win him an acknowledgment a long time in coming: the National Book Award for fiction. "Always, all my life, I've been struggling to get my fiction seen," Peter told me. "Your father," he continued, with a flash of urgency, "always encouraged me. He was always, *always* generous. And I was very grateful because writers are famously ungenerous with each other."

I knew Peter's equanimity was hard-won. Sitting there with him, I was struck by a tremendous sadness for Daddy, who, in all his fragility and blindness, had stumbled so far the other way. He must have envied Peter his discipline. Later, Maria would tell me how much Daddy enjoyed the routine of the life in Sagaponack, which was so unlike the craziness he was always up against in Roxbury. Surely Daddy must have wished that, like Peter, he'd found something in which to believe. In 1985, on my father's first-ever night in a psych ward, he put down what he thought would be his last words. He was in the throes of a panic attack at the time and, as he'd been with my sister the night before, felt certain he was dying. So he took two pieces of paper from the bag my mother packed him. First, he wrote a letter to our family lawyer confirming that the recent revisions to his will were indeed his final wishes. And then he wrote a note to his dearest friend.

> *Dear Peter,*
>
> *I've gone through a rough time. I hope you'll remember me with love and tenderness. I wish I'd taken your way to peace and goodness. Please remember me with a little of that Zen goodness, too. I've always loved you and Maria.*
>
> *Love,*
> *Porter*

Peter didn't tell me any secrets that day. We talked some about the contradictions between my father's querulousness, particularly with my mother, and his "social grace and bonhomie" with the people he could not bully. "He became spoiled," Peter said, when I asked him how Daddy had changed. *Spoiled* sounded right, conjuring as it did his often childish nature and at the same time implicating my mother for mollycoddling him. (As a writer friend of my vintage—a man who successfully juggles work and fatherhood—said to me recently, "Those guys of your father's generation, I call them the Big Babies.") But everyone mollycoddled my father. Even his closest friends gave him a pass. Which is why I wasn't surprised when Peter sat up and said with a sudden bright-eyed intensity, "Your father was a *real* writer, a *real* artist. And so, goddamn it, if you have to indulge somebody like that, you do. You do."

Maybe, I thought. *Or maybe not.* Having been born into the system, how would I ever know? The shadows lengthened across Maria's daffodils, and I moved to make my good-byes. It was time to get back to the city. My children were waiting for me.

Eight

At the Campidoglio, just after my parents' wedding ceremony

I WAS IN MY early twenties the first time I saw my parents' wedding album. In the big living room in Connecticut one day, looking for something to read, I idly pulled the latch on a cabinet below the built-in bookcase. A puff of dust hung thick in a shaft of late-afternoon sunlight, and, when it dispersed, I spied two shelves cluttered with photographs, untouched for years. Little black-and-white snapshots with scalloped edging curled up on one another like stacks of seashells. The images—our housekeeper, Ettie, holding a newborn Tommy; Juniper, the cat who drowned in the cistern when I was five—were mundane, but intriguing mostly because they were new to me. Family photographs are an abundant Styron commodity. Thanks to my mother, who fastens on hard to the happy moments in her past, practically every wall in both her houses is papered with photographs. Giant pictorial collages line the halls, Polaroids are nailed to the doorsills, and the refrigerators are completely resurfaced with magnetic plastic picture frames. Mum doesn't take photos herself but avidly collects them from family and friends. Like her cheery disposition, they're handy insulation against the chillier scenes, which have a stubborn way of trying to frost up her atmosphere.

I sat down on the floor, and time breezed by while I peeled apart the piles on the upper shelf. Then, moving some boxes of slides at the bottom of the cabinet, I made a terrific find: a dozen eight-by-tens, bent beyond repair, from a photo shoot on the Vineyard the year my father published *Nat Turner.* The images, if slightly misrepresentative of our family dynamic (Daddy horsing around on the hammock with the lot of us, Daddy walking down the driveway hand in hand with his only son), were nonetheless beautiful. On the back they were stamped with the photographer's credit, and a copyright identifying them as the property of *Life* magazine. Under the last picture, I found a slim album, documenting my parents' wedding in Italy.

Their union was a hastily planned event that came together on May 4, 1953, at the Campidoglio in Rome. The photos in the album, taken by an unknown photographer, are simple and few. And yet they resonate with all the romance I've always attached to that day. The scene was not wholly unfamiliar to me. One or two of the images crop up in my mother's displays and are occasionally reproduced in magazines or books that have chronicled my parents' early life together. But I'd never seen the entire sequence, the afternoon as it unfolded, or the less perfect photos that, taken together, tell the fuller story.

The pictures begin inside the wedding hall. Redesigned in the mid-sixteenth century by Michelangelo, the Campidoglio has been the religious and governmental center of Rome for 2,500 years. Its trapezoidal arrangement of ancient buildings is the modern-day home to a museum, government offices, and, in the grand Palazzo Senatorio, City Hall. Weddings take place in the adjacent Palazzo dei Conservatori. To get there, my parents and their guests would have mounted the Cordonata, an immense staircase leading to the top of Capitoline Hill. Passing the marble statues of Castor and Pollux, they crossed the piazza with its inlaid travertine oval, eventually arriving at the Sala Rossa, an antique, brocade-covered room ornate enough to make New York's City Hall look like the gulag. The guests took their seats on gilt-covered chairs, where they were brought to silence by the judge, Signor Marconi, a stout figure wearing an important-looking medal around his neck and a striped sash. With my mother and father sitting side by side at the front of the room, the short ceremony could begin.

I recognized my mother's dress right away. It had been on a rack in the attic for years, a hole burned along its left flank from decades of direct sunlight streaming through the nearby window. The dress is knee length, silvery blue silk, with capped sleeves and a bit of trim that comes across the breastbone, done in lush black velvet. Looking elegant and modest that day, Mum added a wide-brimmed black hat and matching elbow-length gloves. In the photos I already knew, the skirt of Mum's dress appears merely full. But in the album, I can see it had a hoop. Except for the end, when they affixed their signature to the "contract of marriage," my parents were seated for the entire ceremony. In a few of the pictures, Mum is simultaneously struggling to hold the skirt down and to suppress a fit of giggles. My father and their small entourage soon pick up on Mum's dilemma, and everyone catches the mirthful wave. Smiling away, my father has never, I think, appeared more handsome. His suit, gray gabardine perhaps, fits him like a dream. A white boutonniere blossoms from the lapel. His dark hair is freshly mown, and slicked back from a perfect part. After the necessary protocols and the exchanging of vows, Signor Marconi invites my parents to kiss. My father's face disappears behind the brim of my mother's hat. For the first time in my life, I can imagine her as the sole object of his attention, his affection undiluted by fear, sorrow, or need.

＊　　＊　　＊

THEY USED TO disagree about who fell for whom first. My parents' playful finger-pointing—"she was mad for me," "I most certainly was *not*! *He* pursued *me*!"—was highly unusual for them, and it transformed my father quite suddenly into someone both hapless and utterly benign. His dour mask would fall away, his eyes would crinkle, and then he'd smile resignedly as if to say, "Oh well, can't argue with the boss lady!"

Their first meeting—in Baltimore, shortly after the publication of *Lie Down in Darkness*—was probably a draw. Daddy had been invited to speak to a class of MFA students at Johns Hopkins, and my mother, who was there studying poetry, was part of the small audience. According to her, she'd come only as a favor to Louis Rubin, the professor who invited Daddy. After the talk, Rubin introduced the two. Mum, smart, terrifically pretty, and a couple of years out of Wellesley, made a strong impression on my father, but nothing came of it that day. Then, in October, while traveling through Europe, my mother got a letter from Rubin. Bill Styron had won the Prix de Rome, he told her. She should look him up. While exploring the academy's neoclassical building at the top of the Janiculum, she left a short note in his mailbox. Hoping she was the girl he remembered, Daddy wrote back.

Italy was still fresh for my father in mid-autumn of '52. His first month had been spent getting settled at the academy and taking advantage of some of the institution's cultural offerings. There was a guided car trip through Florence, Ravenna, Siena, and Urbino, during which my father received a healthy dose of "Art (with a capital A)," as he told his father. And he'd broken bread in the academy's dining hall with some of the other artists in residence. But as the only writer on campus, Daddy was a bit of an odd man out. Many nights he went down the hill alone to sample, as he had in Paris, the city's limitless epicurean offerings. Not that he was lonely. He'd already forged a nice friendship with another scholar, a sculptor named Bobby White, who, with his wife, Claire, and two young children, lived in a nearby apartment. He'd also made the acquaintance of his fellow Southerner Truman Capote. At twenty-eight, Truman was already well known for his first novel, *Other Voices, Other Rooms,* and several exceptional short stories. He was also a delightful raconteur, which is likely why Daddy enlisted him as wingman on his first date with Rose Burgunder. They met in the afternoon, at the Excelsior Hotel. According to Mum, Truman came in wearing a sailor suit and a bosun's whistle around his neck. On his shoulder perched a mynah bird with an extensive vocabulary.

My mother tells this part of their story all the time. I never heard my father dispute her description of Truman, looking, I would think, kind of insane. But it has always seemed a little unbelievable to me. I put it in the category, with dozens of other tales, that I think of as Mum's version of things: always more improbable and glamorous, in an antic kind of way, than anything that happens to mere mortals. Not that I question the mynah bird's existence. Truman wrote a thinly veiled story about her, eponymously titled "Lola." And, after Truman's death, my father mentioned the bird in a tribute he wrote for *Vanity Fair.* Evidently, Truman taught Lola to squawk "fuck you" at frequent intervals, sending him into gales of laughter every single time. My mother must have found it pretty amusing, too; she had a wonderful time that day at the Excelsior. In the elegant and storied setting of the hotel's bar, the three Americans passed much of the afternoon discussing politics and literature while my mother and father flirted across the table. Future disagreement aside, it appears the connection between the two was both mutual and immediate. It was also obvious, for before the party had even broken up, Truman looked across the table at the smiling, hazel-eyed young woman and offered my father some unsolicited advice. "You ought to marry that girl, you know," he said.

It wouldn't be long before my father agreed, and complied.

As for Mum, her first order of business seems to have been reading my father's novel, which everyone spoke of so highly. At the U.S. Information Agency library, she put in a request for *Lie Down in Darkness* and went back to her rooms to start reading. But from the very opening pages she thought the book was "terrible." The further into the story she got, the deeper Mum's heart sunk. Just about to throw the book across the room, she turned the cover over and discovered, with relief, that the *Lie Down in Darkness* she was holding was written by someone else the decade before. When she finally got her hands on the right book, a copy of which Daddy lent her after they'd shared a laugh about the mix-up, his reputation—and romantic prospects—were blessedly redeemed.

My father's mood, which had been flagging since he'd finished *The Long March,* began to improve. In a letter to Grandpop, the first in several months, he gave a cheerful report on his state of affairs. The academy was turning out to be a fine place for him. It was, as he told Grandpop, "a real palace," and the commodiousness of his lodgings gave him great hope for the work he planned to do. His quarters were not as grand as the painters' and sculptors' ateliers. But his two high-ceilinged rooms were "huge" and "excellently furnished," with views of the academy's courtyard below. Daddy had been keeping up with the news from home and thought Eisenhower had made a "prime jack-ass" of himself by putting up with Joe McCarthy. He hoped, as he knew his father did, that it would be Adlai Stevenson who took the November election. But there were more urgent things on my father's mind than politics and architecture.

"I have also met an absolutely beautiful girl," he wrote, "American, named Rose, with whom I get along right well." Rose, however, was living on the other side of town, and so my father needed a car *"pronto."* "One thing just leads to another," he declared. "A young man just must have a girl, and that always—even, or I should say <u>especially</u> in Europe—brings up the question of wheels."

Daddy found a cheap Austin convertible, painted green, and, throughout that fall, it conveyed my mother and father on what can only be described as a whirlwind courtship. They spent a good deal of time with Bobby and Claire White, and with the composer Frank Wigglesworth and his wife, Anne. They also saw some of Mum's friend the writer Mary Lee Settle, and Truman and his boyfriend, Jack Dunphy. But just as often they were alone together, happy within the veil of their new love.

I try to imagine my parents back then. By nature, Daddy was a solitary figure. Like so many successful only children, he harbored a rich inner life. But because his mother was constantly sick, there was an edge of fear to his perspective—and no one with whom to share it. A permanent feeling of isolation was hard for him to shake. Daddy's own chronic maladies—he had endless ear infections and chest colds when he was a child—only compounded his separateness, as he was often kept inside and away from the usual childhood scrums. Literature was an ideal getaway. Daddy channeled his diffidence into story writing and, discovering a talent, found a way to connect to the world. By college, following the solitary path of a writer seemed a natural choice. Daddy always had tremendous charm. And having been raised a proper boy in the South, he was naturally a gentleman. But he was never a lighthearted man, nor one for whom uncomplicated happiness came easily.

Mum, then, must have turned his head around. She was beautiful in an utterly natural and self-confident way. Dark and freckled with a big smile and a terrific figure, she'd had lots of beaux back in Baltimore. But for the most part, Rosey Burgunder was much more interested in Yeats and Donne than in the straitlaced boys who came courting. Like me, Mum was the baby of her family. Born eight years after her brother, Bernei, and ten after her sister,

Ann, she was coddled and doted upon by everyone in the family. Her parents, Selma and Bernei Burgunder, Sr. (known as Bernie), were both of wealthy, assimilated Jewish stock, French and German. By World War II, they were already in the second or third generation of their American identity. Nana's family owned Kann's department store, a vast and busy emporium in downtown Washington. My grandfather, who attended Wharton business school, had been a successful D.C. stockbroker before quitting to help run his in-laws' company. Mum grew up in a house full of staff in the leafy Baltimore neighborhood of Windsor Hills and was expected, like her sister, to marry from a local family and settle down nearby. But she had different plans. She wanted to be a poet and to live somewhere other than Baltimore. Mum liked to have fun, and longed for adventure. Mostly, though, she wanted to get free from her parents' loving but emotionally stifled Victorian environment. When her father died of cancer, Mum was nineteen and up north at Wellesley. She didn't learn that he had passed away for several days, because Nana didn't want to trouble her while she was studying for exams.

For a twenty-four-year-old in the early 1950s, my mother was remarkably self-possessed. She had her own money, and when she met my father, she was taking a "European tour" without a chaperone of any kind. Her enormous enthusiasm for life, and almost supernatural energy, must have struck Daddy right off. Not that she was frivolous. She had read a great deal, had strong thoughts about politics, and, like my father, leaned hard to the left on the important issues of the day. She was also self-sufficient, a result of being left alone often when her parents and older siblings went abroad. By the time she was in her teens, she'd honed her talent for exploration and could find the good and the fun wherever life threw her.

For Mum, Daddy must have cut just the sort of romantic figure she'd conjured when studying the lives of her favorite poets. He was scruffy, yes. His clothes weren't much, and his skin was spotty. But he was handsome and sensitive and fascinating to talk to. He was also a fine writer. With her money and looks and his talent, they made a pretty great package. They had all they needed to pursue the ultimate haute bohemian life. They could put their work first and stretch their talent as far as it would go. It's easy to imagine them, in the city that gave romance its name, plotting their unconventional life together. They must have felt filled with promise, and deliciously alone.

Except that they were not. In November, Rose's mother, Selma, arrived in Rome. By 1952, Nana had been a widow for five years. She and my grandfather had traveled through Europe together many times, but now she was on her own. Nana thought it a perfect time to come to Italy. She could check in on her younger daughter and also meet Bill, the new "friend" she'd heard about. My father, apparently, didn't make a very favorable impression.

Mum blamed his suit, the only one Daddy had. It was a kind of light blue, and it fit him badly. Plus he had to borrow a tie from Truman, an unfortunate waffle-knit number, in gray, with some sort of an arrow pattern. This image of Daddy isn't surprising; he was a lousy dresser. There's no question that Nana, from a family of haberdashers and herself always perfectly arrayed, was underwhelmed by Daddy's ensemble. But I expect she also had more pressing concerns.

Who was this young man, and what did he want? My father's profile, a middle-class young man from somewhere in Virginia with literary aspirations but no durable means of support, was both unfamiliar to Nana and inauspicious. He was not a total failure, to be sure. But where the Burgunders dwelt, in the precincts dominated by Jewish gentry—the Hutzlers, the Blausteins, the Guttmachers—women married doctors and bankers and businessmen. Her people were cultured and philanthropic but also modest and prudent. They didn't indulge, nor were they given to overt emotion. My highly intelligent and generous grandmother was also very much a product of her self-consciously refined culture, and of several generations of "Americanization." Daddy, with his tobacco-stained fingers and marginal social skills, his messy artistic passions and all-around tetchiness, no doubt sent a shudder down her Chanel-covered spine.

She played along, for a bit anyway. During Nana's stay, the academy had a trip planned to Ravello, a lovely town high above the Amalfi coast that had been a creative inspiration to Wagner, Gide, D. H. Lawrence, and others. Wanting my mother to join him but conscious of social conventions, Daddy invited both Burgunders to come along. Mother and daughter accepted, and checked into a room together at the Hotel Palumbo. The weekend turned out nicely and introduced my parents to a town to which they would often return. But it's unlikely that Nana failed to notice the pent-up desire distracting the young lovers.

Nana soon left for London, and my parents were able to resume their affair without parental impediment. They were not, however, entirely beyond the bounds of propriety. When one night, in his rooms at the academy, my father awakened my mother and fiendishly rolled his eyes into the back of his head, she screamed loud enough to be heard up and down the hallways. I remember my mother telling me this story. I was, at the time, old enough to understand the implications of the scenario but young enough still to be quietly mortified by it. She must have brought it up in reference to my own experience, the full eye roll being one of my father's weird talents. At one time or another, he stole into all of his children's rooms. Tapping us awake, he would loom over our beds, pupilless, and curl his lips like some remorseless zombie from a B movie. Like a lot of his inappropriate pranks, this one provoked a heart-lurching fright mingling with a secret pleasure that he thought to play a joke on us at all. My father's shenanigans in Rome that night forced his own hand. One of the academy dons, responding to my mother's shrieks, came to my father's door. Faced with the potential consequences of being in breach of residence rules, Daddy introduced my mother as his fiancée. A few weeks later, at the bar at the Hotel Flora, my father proposed and turned the lie into a beautiful truth.

Nana nearly hung up on my mother when she heard of the engagement. This by itself wasn't a deal breaker. Though my mother was very close to her family, and certainly a "good girl," she had always chafed at the restrictiveness of their mores. But she respected my grandmother's taste and must have figured that Nana, being sensible, would come around as soon as she got to know my father better. Certainly she expected her friends to yield, friends who warned her that she was moving too fast, that my father was a dark soul, that his work would always come first. "You leave that Bill Styron alone," Mary Lee Settle had told Mum. "He has mean little hands." But she wouldn't. Disappointed but still hopeful, Mum went with my father to Paris for the holidays.

It began as a happy trip. Daddy's Paris friends were completely taken with Mum. She, meanwhile, got a glimpse of my father's social scene and the charming, urbane gang with which she'd likely be associated if she and Daddy made a life together. The couple took a side journey to London, returning to France in time to ring in the New Year. But when they arrived, Daddy found a letter, from my grandfather, waiting for him. He'd recently been visited by a private investigator, Grandpop wrote, and the man had asked all sorts of strange questions—about Bill Jr., the family's background, their political leanings and social affiliations. Grandpop was very concerned. Was his son in some sort of trouble? He hoped my father knew how much he loved him, and the store he put in his son's good judgment. Whatever it was, they would face it together and find a way to sort the problem out.

It didn't take long for Mum to realize what was going on. Nana had done the same thing, calling on private investigators to conduct background checks, twice before, with people my uncle Bernei and aunt Ann dated. Mortified, Mum confessed what she'd gleaned to my father. And then she broke off their engagement.

As my mother has always told the story, it was not Nana's disapproval that queered the deal but an instinct to protect my father from the world of which this behavior was symptomatic. "I can't let you marry into this family," Mum said to him. Hurt and no doubt angry, my father didn't try to persuade her otherwise. A pall settled over their happy journey, and before it ended, Mum had decided to quit Rome altogether.

I've often wondered how my mother, who claims never to have wavered in her love for my father during this episode, could still have resolved to give him up. I can't imagine that the dissolution of their betrothal could truly have gone off without a fight. In fact, it seems a situation tailor-made for my father to reveal for the first time his legendary and dangerous temper. Whatever the case, the fractured relationship was challenged yet again when they got home to Rome and found another distressing letter. This one also came from Newport News, but it was addressed to Rose Burgunder and it was from Grandpop's wife, Elizabeth. Her low opinion of my father had not been leavened by his efforts or his success. In her letter, Elizabeth warned my mother off her stepson. Though she'd never met Mum, she nevertheless felt certain that the young woman to whom she was writing deserved better than Billy Styron, a no-account boy whose prospects were uncertain at best. Disgusted, Mum destroyed the letter. She'd heard enough about Elizabeth to be highly skeptical of her views on Bill. But even so, the words hung about like heavy stones weighing upon her already careworn heart. In late January, as she'd told my father she would, Mum moved to Florence to get away.

If, occasionally, Elizabeth had the power to mess with my father's mind, she really couldn't begin to compete with Daddy's other constant bugaboo: clinical hypochondria. Mum's departure that winter left him ample time to perseverate on his health, and soon he was deep in a psychosomatic funk. He fretted over a bout of bronchitis, alarming now in its acuity and persistence. There were pains in his leg, which he had reason to believe might be life-threatening blood clots. He was racked by insomnia. His heart was broken. And, to top it all, his creative soul had slipped into a coma. He needed a writing project, a second novel, to lift him from his miasma. But he didn't have one. The Nat Turner project just wasn't ripe yet. And the short story gambit didn't fulfill him. It had been six months since he'd written anything significant. He was miserable, "as inspiration-less as a newt," he wrote the critic Maxwell Geismar.

He was also, quite plainly, still in love. But whether hurt too much to swallow his pride or too shorn of confidence to bother, Daddy had not, in two months, made a single move to try to win my mother back. The Whites, however, were not above taking action. After weeks of listening to my father's lamentations, Bobby took a train to Florence and tracked my mother down. Mum, living with another American girl in an apartment on the Arno, had put Bill Styron out of her head. Or so she thought. But when Bobby came to get her, my mother accompanied him to Rome. She took all of her belongings with her. It was late March 1953. By the beginning of April, my parents' wedding was gleefully, hurriedly, back on.

✳ ✳ ✳

OUTSIDE, AFTER THEIR wedding ceremony, my parents stopped for a picture beneath one of the Campidoglio's colonnaded porticoes. The photographer, judging by the slight awkwardness of his subjects, probably had to shout at them to be still a moment so he could get a proper portrait. *Signor! Signora! Uno momento!* Mum has never been comfortable posing for pictures. In the photo, she gazes up at her new husband with a tight grin, and he gazes back. But you can tell they just want to get on with the celebration.

Together with their friends, standing beneath the statue of Marcus Aurelius, they relax. Their faces come alive again. The group fans out, loose jointed, grinning, for a few more photos. *"L'ultima! Per favore,"* I can hear the photographer shouting. It's not the whole crowd, "the stepchildren of Gertrude Stein, F. Scott Fitzgerald, Henry Miller, and Ezra Pound," as Art Buchwald called them. Patsy Matthiessen is in Paris with her newborn baby and cannot travel. Plimpton couldn't make it. Humes . . . who knows? But it's a nice sampling. And fitting too that my mother and father—whose marriage will last well beyond most of the others—should be at the center of the frame. There's John Marquand—funny, profane, lovable John—who will have a son, James, to whom Daddy will be godfather; Tom Guinzburg, future publisher of Viking Press, with his toothsome smile, for whom my brother is named; Bobby White, Polly's godfather, who will lose his seventeen-year-old daughter Natalie in a car wreck and whom I, an impudent teenager, will one day anger by pointing out that he is drunk (a mother now, I think, *Well, who wouldn't be?*); Bobby's wife, in honor of whom my parents will name me Claire Alexandra; the Wigglesworths, who drift from my parents' life not long after this photo is taken; Bernei and Amelie, my mother's brother and sister-in-law, the aunt and uncle my siblings and I sometimes joke are the "parents we never had"; Peter Matthiessen, in his chunky glasses, looking every bit the CIA operative he will eventually reveal himself to have been but nothing like the Zen priest who someday will don his robes to marry my brother (his godson) and don them again to lay my father in his grave.

In the back of the photo are the novelist Irwin Shaw and his wife, Marian. They're in Rome for the season and are just about to host a bash at their Parioli apartment in honor of the new couple. A crowd is expected, including Lillian Hellman. My mother and father have never met the playwright, but they'll introduce themselves when they ride up in the elevator with her. Later, Lillian will become godmother to my sister Susanna. And when, at last, Daddy publishes *The Confessions of Nat Turner,* she will be one of two people to whom the book is dedicated.

There are no pictures of the reception. But my father penned a hasty description for Grandpop, telling him of the cake and champagne, the big dinner later, and the poem Claire White wrote, "which she sang at the reception to a special tune written by Frank Wigglesworth, who accompanied her on a recorder."

> *Roses bloom in wintertime,*
> *Sweet williams grow in June;*
> *Friends must part in course of time,*
> *But not, but not*
> *But not the bride and groom.*

"This sounds extremely corny," Daddy wrote, "but I assure you it couldn't have been more touching, to be surrounded by so many fine friends."

A year before, my father had not known a single person in that room. Now he was married, and thoroughly aligned in a new galaxy, where he would reside for much of his remaining life.

*   *   *

IN JANUARY 1953, my father received a letter on Ritz Hotel, London, letterhead. It begins:

> *Dearest,*
>   *We were here together once upon a happy time—how many years it seems—and now, without you in this bad time. . . . But perhaps I will come to Rome for a few days, although there is news here from Eden that you are "seeing" a handsome "Jewish" girl, as he put it, in Rome.*

The letter goes on cheekily for another paragraph, and then signs off:

> *My love, my belief in the book, my heart.*
> *L.*

I have no idea who L. was. But, if the continuing stream of love letters my father received is any indication, she was the only one of his paramours who'd been informed that, at last, someone had stolen Bill Styron's heart for good. Daddy's married girlfriend continued to pen letters freighted with longing allusion—"I can't feel too guilty about your statement about enslaving you because making love to you has quite spoiled me for making love to anyone I care less about"—all winter and spring. And even Sigrid de Lima, whose missives are totally dignified in tone and free from expectation, remains entrenched in their former intimacy, still saluting Daddy "Such a dear sweet baby" and signing her letters with the shortened version, SB. In February, Sigrid wrote to tell Daddy that the '53 Prix de Rome was to go to her. Sigrid's last letter to my father, blithely detailing some of her travel plans, was written May 4, 1953. If she wrote to him in the morning, before settling down to work, I figure she might have completed her effort at just the time Mr. and Mrs. William Clark Styron, Jr., disappeared behind that hat for their first connubial kiss.

Forgoing an immediate honeymoon, my parents lingered in Rome for several weeks. In June, they decamped to Ravello for the summer. A hundred dollars a month bought them two floors in a renovated thirteenth-century palazzo with hot running water and a view of the Mediterranean. Another twenty-five dollars paid for a maid and cook. Joined at various times by the Whites, the Matthiessens, the Haydns, William Blackburn, and Daddy's agent, Elizabeth McKee, the newlyweds passed a sublime summer. Afternoons were a lazy swirl of tennis and swimming, napping and walks. At night the friends sat for long dinners, put back a lot of booze, talked and read and played games. *Beat the Devil,* the John Huston movie for which Truman Capote wrote the script, had been shooting in Ravello all that spring. By the time my parents got there, the ancient hill town was crawling with Hollywood types and the atmosphere had turned both kinetic and surreal. In the mornings, my father managed to carve out time to start work on a new piece of fiction, called "Blankenship," about his time as a military guard on Hart Island. But the louche scene that summer intrigued and inspired him. At the margins of his imagination, the seed for a later project began to spread shoots.

In this paradisaical state, my parents' extended honeymoon summer drifted into fall. Letting their plans to return to Rome fall by the wayside, they stayed on in the Palazzo Confalone, hosting friends and enjoying the changing season. Daddy continued work on "Blankenship," expecting, as he told his father, for the finished piece to qualify in length as a novella. But in mid-autumn, with almost nine thousand words on paper, he abandoned the project. It seems his early response to Ravello's beauty—"the panorama . . . couldn't be more conducive to felicitous labor"—hadn't lasted. And, just as in New York and Paris, the nonstop bacchanal acted like a merry thief on his productivity. By October, my parents had decided to move back to the States. Thinking to make their life, at least for a time, in New York, they sailed from Naples on December 13, 1953, and arrived just in time for Christmas in Baltimore.

Nine

A cocktail party at George Plimpton's, New York, 1963.
(My father is seated at the center, in profile, talking to
Truman Capote and Doc Humes.)

NOT LONG AGO, my oldest sister, Susanna, and I were at a restaurant after a meeting about our father's literary estate. The subject, Daddy, had followed us up Third Avenue and lingered through the salad course, where we entertained it as you might a troublesome dog who has, after a lot of wrangling, finally been muzzled and leashed. Safe now, we examined it with fascination and a touch of rue. At Duke I'd seen dozens of letters that Susanna had written to Daddy when she lived abroad. Later, she shared with me the other half of the correspondence. His letters were, as always, terrifically entertaining. But they were also full of paternal affection, and a kind of intimate shorthand. I couldn't help but envy their relationship.

"It must have been different, when you were small," I said, surprised myself that I'd never scoped out this particular angle. "I mean when Mum and Daddy were just married. When they only had one child."

Susanna nodded slowly. "I really got the best of them," she replied. "*Both* of them wanted me. And I was a novelty, for Daddy especially. But after the others were born . . . Polly, then Tommy . . . the situation changed. Everyone was so noisy. I think, in his head, he was saying, *How do I send these toys back?*"

For so many years, the four of us have looked upon the field of our familial experiences as trench mates would. We faced every skirmish in cooperative unison. We stood in the same attitude of mesmerized relief each time the smoke began to clear. But as clannish as we remain, and as reliant on one another, I now realize we are defined as much by where we came into the story as by where we were standing when things turned weird.

Susanna Margaret Styron was born on February 25, 1955. Returning from Italy, my parents had made a swift tour of the Eastern Seaboard, meeting family—given a second chance to make a first impression, my father charmed my mother's mother—before settling into a one-bedroom apartment on East Sixty-sixth Street in Manhattan. My father made preparations to at last begin his second novel, which he would set in Italy. But it wasn't long before he encountered some new distractions entirely less seductive than the ones he'd faced in Ravello. The quotidian noises of the city—car horns, garbage trucks, and fire engines—bothered him immediately. Then, just as the weather heated up, a building project began across the street, completely collapsing Daddy's fragile nerves. Tossed from sleep, he awoke in the mornings often hungover and in a rage. By afternoon, when he would normally settle down to work, he was too tired to think straight. This, of course, led to more drinking. Sometimes he headed down to the White Horse Tavern, where Norman Mailer and Vance Bourjaily held court. He might see Jimmy Baldwin there, or some of the *Paris Review* crowd. But an air of competition hung about these gatherings, compromising the bonhomie. In a miserable loop, my father was made even more anxious and inclined to self-destruction. All summer, his heart raced, his ears rang. He was pretty certain he had a brain tumor. Then, somewhere in the midst of all this, my mother announced that she was pregnant. When Elizabeth McKee and her husband, Ted Purdy, invited my parents to their Connecticut country house, they leapt at the opportunity for escape. Enchanted, my parents asked a real estate broker to show them houses that very weekend. Lone Spruce Farm was the first property they saw. They barely spent another night in their New York City apartment.

By all accounts, my sister was a cheerful baby, smart and pretty, with an easy manner. In short, an ideal firstborn. Daddy was enthralled. "Take a lesson from me and don't get too interested in the child," Irwin Shaw wrote in a congratulatory letter. "Since Adam's first birthday, I've barely written a word, as it is much more interesting to watch all the subtle and terrible currents that run through a complex human being than to sit at a typewriter and battle with the comparatively flat and lifeless material of art. Dole the child out to yourself in small doses, for your career's sake."

Whether my father took Irwin's advice, or was simply responding to the salubrious effects of country life, he was feeling hopeful in the new surroundings. His most recent health hysteria had resolved itself. He had a wife to take care of him, a baby to dandle on his knee, and a new novel, *Set This House on Fire*, which was moving along. My mother was happy in Connecticut, too. Though as the pampered youngest of her family she didn't have much experience with babies, she embraced her new role and learned on the fly. Two new friends with houses in the area, the playwright Jay Presson Allen and the children's book author Sesyle Joslin Hine, also had small children. When Daddy retreated into his work, Mum had companionship and plenty to occupy her time.

Sometimes, my father went into the city to meet with Hiram Haydn, an experience that had become abundantly more exciting since 1954, when Hiram was named editor in chief of Random

House. Driving up to the firm's impressive headquarters at 457 Madison, my father beheld a sight both awesome and strangely familiar. The Italianate structure, known as the Villard Houses, was, after the American Academy, Daddy's second McKim, Mead, and White "home" in as many years. An esteemed guest, he was allowed to pull right up into the circular driveway. If his luck held out, he might run into the firm's famous cofounder Bennett Cerf.

"Boy writer! Boy writer!" Bennett used to call out down the hallway. I remember Daddy telling me this years later, when he was well past the wunderkind stage. The pet name still tickled him. It was part and parcel of Bennett's ineffable charm, which, along with his talents, had a dazzling effect on people. With his partner Donald Klopfer, Cerf had started the company in 1925 with the purchase, from Horace Liveright, of the Modern Library series. As for the name, "we just said we were going to publish a few books on the side at random," Bennett later recalled. His friend Rockwell Kent drew up a little house for the colophon, and Random House was born. Gregarious and funny, Bennett moved deep within New York's haute social circles. He was not only an excellent publisher and a cherished friend but, thanks to his weekly appearances on *What's My Line?*, a bona fide celebrity. In his biography of my father, Jim West quotes from a waggish letter Daddy wrote to John Marquand after signing his new contract: "Being now in the Random House fold I am great pals with not only Ben Cerf but *his* pals too: old Arlene Francis and old Buddy Schulberg and old Mossy Hart and swell old Colesy Porter and Dickie Rogers and sweet, wry-witted bespectacled Stevie Allen. We all get together up at Ben's place in Mt. Kisco and go swimming and play charades and that sort of thing—I have taken to smoking black Brazilian cigars, so that my lips have become wet and lubricious."

Eventually, my father *did* become pals with Bennett. When I was very young, the Cerfs—Bennett's wife, Phyllis, was a powerhouse in her own right—used to drive over from Mt. Kisco for dinner parties. They both made an enormous impression on me, Bennett in particular. Though he wasn't my parents' most famous friend, he was the only one with a *Sesame Street* character—Bennett Snerf—named after him and a knee-slapping book of riddles written for kids just my age. Also, if you asked him nicely, he would turn an ordinary section of *The New York Times* into a palm tree, blooming with newsprint fronds.

Although my parents were pioneers of a sort in northwest Connecticut—transplanted cityfolk—they weren't the first creative people to discover the area. Alexander Calder moved to Roxbury in 1933. The actor Fredric March and his wife, Florence, had a house in New Milford. James Thurber was a little farther north, in Cornwall. Mark Van Doren and his family were up in Falls Village. About a year after my parents settled in Roxbury, the town made its paparazzi debut when Arthur Miller and Marilyn Monroe scheduled a wedding day press conference on the lawn of Arthur's house on Tophet Road. The couple had hoped to quell the frenzy surrounding news of their plans, which, as my father wrote to John Marquand, had delivered "to these tranquil glens and glades a gawking procession of Pontiac-ensconced, yowling cretins such as you would never have imagined." But that afternoon, on the way back from picking up their marriage license, Arthur and Marilyn were tailed by a press car from which they attempted to get away. Misjudging a curve, the driver slammed into a massive oak tree; Mara Scherbatoff, the New York bureau chief for *Paris Match*, died at the scene. Despite such an inauspicious start, the playwright and the movie star carried on with their plans. After the press conference, they were married by a judge across the border in White Plains.

Daddy told me this story in the car on the way home from school one day when I was about ten. If the mood struck him, he liked to pick me up in the afternoon. When I saw the red Mercedes pull into the school driveway, my heart always lurched a bit. But for the most part, those drives were nice. We batted stuff about, made some jokes, and arrived home having inched closer to knowing each other. Whatever quiet affection Daddy and I cultivated for each other got a boost on those twenty-minute drives.

The day he told me of that car crash I remember being moved to turn and look at him full-on. Arthur had long since remarried, and he and Inge Morath were close friends of my parents. Their daughter, Rebecca, was a couple of years behind Tommy at the Rumsey Hall School, a few years ahead of me. We were driving past the Yeldings' pond, where Tophet turns into Gold Mine, and the road winds through a quarter mile of primordial woodland. Daddy liked to drive fast and claimed that a stiff drink, which I sometimes held for him while he downshifted before a turn, made him better at it.

"See that tree?" he said, accelerating out of the tricky hairpin. "A woman, a reporter, died there. A long time ago."

I suppose in twenty years my father hadn't driven that turn without recalling the day, the week, that time in his life, or even where he sat on the night of the accident, mulling such a peculiar occurrence having happened so close to home. I think of the crash, too, and his telling of it, every time I take those roads. Car accidents involving deer, alcohol, ice, or all three are pretty common on those country byways. When I was fourteen and she was sixteen, my best friend drove her mother's car into an equally unyielding tree. Unbelted in the passenger's seat, I took the majority of the impact with my forehead, shattering the windshield and opening a three-inch flap of flesh above my right eyebrow. The darkling night all around us and the sound of laminated glass falling in a light rain on the dashboard are still as clear to me as my babies' first cries.

But at ten years old, I was working purely from imagination. Constructing a coherent reality from the extraordinary facts, I tried to fit this news into the more mundane landscape of which I was certain. *Becky's father was married to Marilyn Monroe?* I considered this, made a picture of it. And then I envisioned the crash. The metal and the glass. A lady's head, which I imagined separated from her body. Blood. And steam rising from the radiator. Up ahead, I pictured Arthur in his car, driving away from the scene. He was wearing the same worn jeans and work boots he always wore, of that I was certain. But Marilyn came less clearly. She appeared in the back window for only an instant. A flash of white, improbable as a unicorn, and then they disappeared into the lightless woods.

A couple of years after this, when I was maybe twelve, Mum told me the story of Daniel.

In early 1966, my mother—thirty-eight and the mother of three school-age children—found herself pregnant. Though family lore has always incorporated the idea that I was "wanted," there's little dispute on one thing: I was not planned. Mum was ready for a little freedom. She wanted to write poetry again, to travel, and above all else to exorcise from her daily life the constant tension created by a house full of noisy kids and a querulous, demanding husband. Besides, Mum's circle of friends was done having babies. So she thought it a happy coincidence when it turned out that Inge, at forty-two, was pregnant as well. Their babies were due within weeks of each other. Mum and Inge would have each other, would raise their "change babies" side by side. Early in the morning of October 28, my mother gave birth to her fourth child without complication at Grace–New Haven Hospital. After several days of convalescence, Mum and I came home to Roxbury, where we were fussed over as all mothers and their newborns ought to be. Two weeks later, Inge gave birth to a boy. Shortly after delivery, the baby, named Daniel, was diagnosed with Down syndrome.

"Arthur couldn't deal with it," said Mum, as I stared at her in dumb wonder. "So he sent him away."

At this point in Mum's revelation, I remember something curious happening. A persistent and nagging memory came into focus, splintered images fitting together into a single picture like one of those mutable, clattering electronic billboards. I had played with Daniel, at least once, when we were three, maybe four years old. What I recall is spare but acute. We're sitting on the floor, just beyond the Millers' kitchen. My mother is there, and so is Inge.

Becky sits on the floor, too, and somewhere in the living room putters Titi, Becky and Daniel's white-haired Austrian grandmother. Something, though, is not right. Something I don't understand. I'm a toddler, and my feelings are no more nuanced than the blocks in front of us, but I know we're not having fun. Daniel cries. Inge lifts him up and carries him away. I want to go home.

For almost a decade, I'd preserved that moment, a quicksilvery idea that glided through my little pool of experience but stubbornly refused my grasp. Now I nabbed it.

Becky has a brother. I knew it.

"Where is he?" I asked Mum, a bit fearful of the answer.

"The Southbury Training School," she replied, with a touch of apology in her voice. My mind reeled as I thought of the institution on the hill, the "retards" and the "spazzes." It was obvious this was one of those times when a grown-up was not offering satisfactory explanations.

"Does anyone ever see him?"

"Oh, Inge visits all the time," said Mum, going suddenly with her arsenal of forced brightness.

"But he doesn't come home?"

Mum paused.

"Not anymore."

In recent years, Daniel's existence has been revealed and scrutinized in magazine essays and newspaper articles, on public radio, and by bloggers whose interests range from celebrity watching through literary criticism to the rights of the disabled. Watching Pedro Almodóvar's film *Broken Embraces* recently, I was startled when the protagonist, a writer, describes the story of "Arthur Miller's secret child" and how he wants to turn it into a screenplay. Of course it isn't Daniel's Down syndrome that's sensational. Nor is it the fact that the Millers institutionalized him. Warehousing children with special needs in places like the Southbury Training School was once upon a time de rigueur for all but the most patient or, some thought, masochistic parents. The explosive and bizarre aspect of Daniel's story was that Arthur never spoke of him. Until 2003, when Martin Gottfried wrote about Daniel in a biography of Arthur, there was no public reference to him anywhere, including Arthur's six-hundred-plus-page autobiography, *Timebends*. That my parents were complicit in the conspiracy of silence troubled me long after I had begun to make some sense of it. It affirmed my suspicion that here, among all these people who traded in great truths, keeping secrets was still the coin of the realm. And that one could spend a lifetime examining the human heart but remain personally, confoundingly, unexamined. If you were good enough at the former, the world would always forgive you the latter.

*   *   *

IN THE FALL of '56, my parents welcomed two more couples to Litchfield County. The first to arrive was Jack Aldridge and his fiancée, who moved to a house that Arthur Miller and Marilyn Monroe had also briefly lived in. Daddy had known Jack since he wrote a nice review of *Lie Down in Darkness* and mutual friends introduced them. More recently, Aldridge had published *The Long March* in *discovery,* the magazine he coedited with Vance Bourjaily. Jack was also the author of *After the Lost Generation: A Critical Study of the Writers of Two Wars,* in which he provided the first cohesive analysis of Mailer, Shaw, Capote, and several more of Daddy's peers. A rising star in the world of literary criticism, Jack was by most accounts an annoyingly self-satisfied fellow. But he was clever and decent company, and my parents were glad enough to hear he was going to be nearby.

Daddy knew his bride to be as well. The last time he saw her, Leslie Blatt Felker was just Leslie Blatt, the audaciously sexy Duke coed who earned an academic suspension for running off with Daddy's classmate Clay Felker. Things with Clay didn't work out, and now Leslie was to become Leslie Blatt Felker Aldridge. Since getting together, Leslie and Jack had been traveling a route curiously similar to my parents' own. They'd been in Paris and in Rome, after which they spent a season in Ravello. Now they were setting up house in Litchfield County, looking for a hospitable place among other writers and artists.

The Aldridges were soon followed by their friends Norman and Adele Mailer. The Mailers had recently been living in Mexico, which Norman found "mildly pleasant, mildly boring." Before that, they had tried Paris for a while. But back in New York, Norman struggled with some of the same issues Daddy had. "The city was not alive for me," he once said about this period of his life. "My wife was pregnant. It seemed abruptly too punishing to live at the pace we had been going for several years." So with encouragement from Jack and Leslie, and from my parents too, the Mailers moved into a large white saltbox in nearby Bridgewater.

By the late fifties, Norman and my father had cultivated a solid, if slightly wary friendship. Linked by age and ambition, the two men were part of a small crew pulling the oars on the Great Novel as it glided through the middle of the century. On the surface, they were of a type. But in truth Norman and Daddy were of vastly different temperaments. The Pugilist and the Brooder. The Brooklyn Kid and the Virginia Boy. The Jazz Lover and the Classicist. They did admire each other, though. And, when on the same continent, they traveled in very much the same circles. Perhaps most crucial to their friendship was a mutual inclination toward melancholy. In a half-dozen years of correspondence, Norman and Daddy never stinted on empathy for each other, or encouragement to keep one step ahead of the demons that were trying to run them down. During my parents' brief, disastrous Manhattan residency in '54, Norman, down in Mexico, wrote: "[This letter is] mainly to give a <u>salud</u> for beginning your novel, and a commiseration to Rose who will learn that your previous depressions were gaiety compared to the GLOOM which is to come."

In the last paragraph of the same letter, Norman tells Daddy of a visit from the writer George Mandel. Mandel had nice things to say about Daddy, according to Norman. But the anecdote Norman shares, and the letter itself, is rounded out by Mandel's final take on their mutual friend.

> *Anyway, he said, "You know Bill's got just one little fault—he's the biggest fucking hypochondriac that ever hit New York." So if he's right, get your tottering liver into a chair, and work, m'bucko, work.*
> *Love to Rose from Adele and me,*
> *Norm*

Over the next year or so, my parents saw a fair amount of the Mailers and the Aldridges, though their fellowship was not without complications. Norman and Adele fought a lot (years later, elsewhere, he would infamously stab her with a penknife). And my mother, for one, didn't care for Leslie's overt flirtatiousness. Both of my parents were bemused by Norman's recreational interests, the invitations to spar in his makeshift ring, the installation in the barn of a makeshift orgone box, meant for the promotion of mind-shattering orgasms. But neither of them had much interest in the Beat poets or jazz, particular passions of Norman's that, late at night and under the influence, often dominated the proceedings. Ultimately, though, it was Jack my parents tired of, with his constant talk about Litchfield County being the "new Athens" and his overweening desire to be the generation's critical spokesman. An incessant pipe smoker with a handsome profile, he also had the habit of admiring himself in the mirror and sitting, awkwardly if necessary, to present to others his best side. One evening, when the three couples were dining together, Jack put a tape recorder on the table and proposed recording the conversation. The group went along, though the evening turned odd, the guests understandably self-conscious. A few weeks later, Jack adjourned another dinner by gathering his friends in the living room and handing out a collection of erotica. It would be fun, he thought, if the wives took turns reading pornographic passages out loud. "I just got the giggles," my mother recalls, and so did the other women. Irritated, Jack called a halt to the game, then reached down to reveal the tape recorder he'd planted, running, beneath the sofa.

By this time, Mum and Daddy had established a nice group of friends in the area. The theater producer Lew Allen and his wife, Jay; Al Hine, a novelist, married to my mother's friend Ses; the editor Henry Carlisle and his wife, the writer Olga Andreyev Carlisle. John and Mary Cheever were just over the border in Ossining. Robert Penn "Red" Warren and Eleanor Clark lived forty-five minutes away in Fairfield. Sometimes, a few of their New York friends came for weekends. My parents enjoyed filling the house with interesting people, and the parties were lively, though things could sometimes get a little out of hand. "The amount of bourbon that went down was beyond belief" is how Peter Matthiessen remembers it. One night, Peter came with his girlfriend (his marriage to Patsy ended in '56) and proceeded to ignore her, swept away as he was by heady conversation with the other big writers in the room. The evening wore on, and everyone, resentful girlfriend included, got pie-eyed. While Peter was seated, deep in dialogue with Norman, his girlfriend poured a glass of champagne directly over his head. "I never even blinked," confessed Peter.

To hear it described, there is something a bit sinister about this era in my parents' life. I've heard these stories over the years, mostly from my mother, who witnessed a lot of craziness and knows the value of juicy historical anecdote. But I always feel like the world she describes is a bit off-kilter. Everyone's so young and gay and arrogant, the mythmaking so intense and so consummate. It was a hell of a party—too bad they didn't notice, till it was over, all fissures opening up underneath them.

Writing continued to come hard for Daddy. *Set This House on Fire* had become an enormous undertaking, a sprawling meditation on the nature of evil—rape, murder, and suicide all figure in the plot— centered on three characters and multiple, shifting points of view.

He had purposely set himself a challenge, wanting the book to reflect an advancement of his skills. But often he got himself backed into a narrative corner that no muse, and certainly no liquor, could ease him out of. Briefly, he tried speed. But it gave him insomnia, so he went back to drinking. In the summer of '57, Daddy delivered to Random House about a hundred thousand words of *Set This House on Fire*. The manuscript was, by his calculation, about halfway finished. "I think I'm writing a good book," he told Leon Edwards in a long letter that betrays a problematic lack of certainty. "At the same time writing a long novel, as I am doing, has an overpowering effect on the psyche. There's so much of it . . . so much that's almost bound to fall short of your lofty aims that, if you're at all serious, you end up existing in a perpetual state of sweat and melancholy and quasi-alcoholism. In effect, it's a perfect symbol of one's own strengths and weaknesses as a human, and I can only console myself with the rather feeble notion that perhaps, after all, that is all a novel is supposed to be."

My mother, meanwhile, had become an indispensable ear for my father's writing. After a busy day overseeing renovations on the main house, taking care of two-year-old Susanna, and tending to other household chores, she would put my sister to bed and then fix a late dinner for herself and my father. Afterward, the couple settled in the living room, where Daddy would read to her the day's pages. Mum often didn't get to bed until 1:00 or 2:00 A.M., only to be up again at dawn. My father usually slept until noon. Sometimes, when the house was quiet, Mum worked on her own poetry, learning to steal little bits of time whenever, and wherever, she could. That time was about to shrink; in the early summer of 1957, Mum was pregnant again.

In anticipation of the new arrival, my parents at last moved into the big house. Perhaps feeling the need to more fully inhabit the larger space, they also acquired a Newfoundland, named Tugwell, the first of many large dogs to dominate our family's life. Working hard, my father had soon completed 850 manuscript pages.

It should have been a happy period. But Daddy, manifesting his anxiety about the novel's complex structure and the troubles he had encountered containing it, didn't feel good at all. Another medical crisis had flared—this time intestinal pain he took to be an ulcer, or cancer—but it did nothing to curtail his hazardous recreations. On the contrary, he doubled down on drinking and smoking and, in the company of friends, often gave himself over to bitter ruminations and loose-tongued talk.

At the end of February, for better or worse, my father was forced to throttle back on his work. His second child was due, and, as my mother was still under the care of her New York obstetrician, the family would have to move into the city to await the big day. The baby, to my father's increasing consternation, was late. But at last, on March 13, following nature's immutable design, Paola Clark Styron was born at Mount Sinai Hospital, just as Susanna had been. An uncommonly perspicacious woman, Polly will tell you her tardiness was no accident. "I did *not* want to come out there. Nuh-uh. No way." And perhaps one shouldn't blame her, given all the Sturm und Drang with which her entrance coincided. After her delivery, Daddy went to Connecticut to take care of some odds and ends. He planned to return to the city the following day. Sifting through the mail at home, he came upon a letter that made his head swim. It read:

Bill,

I've been told by a reliable source—closer to you than one might expect—that you have been passing a few atrocious remarks about Adele. Normally, I would hesitate to believe the story, but my memory of slanderous remarks you've made about other women leaves me not at all in doubt. So I tell you this, Billy-boy. You have got to learn to keep your mouth shut about my wife, for if you do not, and I hear of it again, I will invite you to a fight in which I expect to stomp out of you a fat amount of your yellow and treacherous shit.

Norman

Shaken and perplexed, my father spent the night writing at the bottom of Norman's letter an angry and righteous point-for-point rebuttal of his claims. The next day, he brought the document to the hospital with him. Jim and Gloria Jones, who were about to set sail for Paris, had just then arrived to celebrate the baby's birth. While drinking champagne, the two couples passed the letter back and forth, pondering the reasons for Norman's invective. My father always vehemently denied Norman's accusations. But given the prodigiousness of the drinking, and the persistent air of rivalry . . . who knows? Either way, Jim advised Daddy against the defensive response he'd already penned. My mother got terribly sad about the conflict, and about her friends going overseas. Then the Joneses poured more bubbly and everyone, including my sister, who was latched to our mother's breast, got very drunk.

Two weeks later, my father replied to Norman's letter with a brief caustic note. It began, "Norman: I don't know who your sick and pitiable 'reliable source' is (how _much_ he must hate and envy me, or maybe you, but above all himself) but you might have him or her get in touch with me some day and repeat his allegations to my face." This note Norman returned, appending the parry with another thrust, which suggested my father "recognize [his] reply for what it is—a crock of shit." With that, the correspondence ended. My father, however, continued to be bothered by the accusation and spent many nights mulling the subject with friends. When I was young, it seemed my parents were forever involved in some fierce personal drama that, inevitably, had a public component. Lillian Hellman was mad at my father about something he said on TV (he and Lillian were _always_ fighting), or Daddy was miffed with Ralph Ellison about some symposium or other, nobody was talking to the Podhoretzes anymore, or Daddy was firing off a letter to the editor in defense of some maligned pal or another. Everything got chewed over during dinner parties or drinks on the porch. There was usually some laughter but a lot of swearing too, and a degree of social jujitsu that made me anticipate adult friendships as treacherous, and vaguely dreadful.

After a period of relative quiet, during which time my father nearly completed *Set This House on Fire,* Norman fired the next salvo. In the fall of 1959, G. P. Putnam's Sons published *Advertisements for Myself,* his first collection of nonfiction. Toward the back of the book was an essay entitled "Evaluations—Quick and Expensive Comments on the Talent in the Room." In it, Norman considered—and eviscerated—several of his contemporaries, my father included. Sweeping in with a deceptive bit of praise for *Lie Down in Darkness*—"Styron wrote the prettiest novel of our generation"—the section quickly opens up, revealing a pocket full of verbal cutlery. "It would have been the best novel of our generation," Norman continued, "if it had not lacked three qualities: Styron was not near to creating a man who could move on his feet, his mind was uncorrupted by a new idea, and his book was without evil." This last shiv, leveled as it was at the heart of a serious writer's mission, seemed designed expressly to wound my father rather than to edify Norman's readers.

As for my father's next book, *Set This House on Fire,* Norman predicted success. "The reception will be a study in the art of literary advancement," he crowed. "For Styron has spent years oiling every literary lever and power which could help him on his way, and there are medals waiting for him in the mass-media."

The reaction to Mailer was swift and galvanic. Many fellow writers—the essay went after Jones, Salinger, Vidal, Kerouac, Bellow, and Baldwin—pondered some sort of public rejoinder. Privately, Norman's former friends were shocked, and many felt blindsided. "What he means by having 'sold out' I haven't the slightest idea," Jim Jones wrote my father, referring to his own mention in the piece. "I feel morally obligated to answer him in kind," Jim announced. So did my father. Sprinting to the finish line of *Set This House on Fire,* he made a quick U-turn and sought out a stage for execution.

It was right there, the avatar of Daddy's revenge, in the body of the novel's villain, Mason Flagg. With some tweaking, my father gave Mason just enough of Norman's persona, his interest in jazz and Reichian philosophy, to make his point. Mason also developed some particularities of language that, if Norman were to read the book, he could not miss as his own. Unlike Norman, whose work my father genuinely admired, Mason is a poseur. But he is also a character given to flights of self-importance, a man who is for much of the book faintly ridiculous—until he becomes something entirely more dangerous. Morally bankrupt and increasingly troubled, Mason reveals himself to be capable of great physical violence. He's also a psychological and verbal bully, qualities my father didn't have to go far to flesh out. "You wait right here, Petesy boy," he growls at the narrator in a climactic moment of unhinged aggression, "because when I come back I expect to stomp out of you a fat amount of your yellow and treacherous shit."

Fueled by his devout, if messy, passions, my father at last finished *Set This House on Fire* at the end of 1959. But the achievement left him unsettled. Peter Matthiessen had given him good notes, and some judicious cutting had tightened up the narrative. Still, the manuscript clocked in at close to 300,000 words, and Daddy worried that the thing had gotten away from him a bit. "The novel is so long," he wrote Leon Edwards, "that I have severe doubts anyone will buy it, but it is at last off my chest and I feel totally drained and exhausted, though not without a sense of having accomplished something, no matter how inchoate and no matter how far it falls short of my grand intentions." To John Marquand, he exposed a much darker attitude, shimmering beneath his robust sense of humor. "I am being utterly serious when I tell you that, hefting this mammoth excrescence of mine, I have never been so utterly bereft and depressed in all my life."

My father was also struggling with a more delicate political matter. Hiram Haydn was leaving Random House to form, with Simon Michael Bessie and Alfred Knopf, Jr., his own publishing house,

Atheneum. My father's affection for the man who had essentially discovered him remained strong. Indeed he'd just given his new-born son the middle name Haydn in his honor. But he didn't feel like his editor was paying much attention to him anymore. And it still bugged him the way Hiram had delivered his prudish coup de grâce when Daddy brought in the manuscript of a controversial novel, already published in France, called *Lolita*. "Over my dead body!" Hiram had exclaimed when Bennett suggested they publish an American edition. And then he threatened to resign if Bennett went ahead with it. Bennett, like Daddy, thought the book a masterpiece but decided he couldn't run afoul of his editor in chief. Any lingering negative feelings only deepened when Nabokov's book became a huge success at Putnam. Despite the cooling creative relationship, Hiram had expected my father to come along to Atheneum. But encouraged by Bennett's enthusiasm—"In a single sentence," he wrote at the end of an exhortative letter, "I would like to be your publisher for the rest of my life"—and by the arrival at Random House of his old college friend Bob Loomis, my father had decided to stay. Random House had ordered a first printing of thirty thousand copies. There was nothing left for my father to do but wait.

*   *   *

SET THIS HOUSE ON FIRE arrived in bookstores across the United States in the spring of 1960. Anxious about the book's reception, and not yet tethered to a new project, Daddy had decided to get out of town for a while. In February, with three children under the age of five (my brother Tom's birth followed Polly's by fifteen months), my mother and father sailed for Europe, stopping in Paris to see the Joneses before heading on to Geneva, Milan, and Florence. On May 4, they observed, if not exactly celebrated, the dual occasion of the book's publication date and their seventh wedding anniversary from the apartment where they'd settled the family on the Via San Teodoro in Rome.

"Your new novel is one of the most powerful books I have read in years," Maurice Edgar Coindreau wrote my father. "It is not only beautifully put together, with an uncanny sense of unbearable suspense, but the psychological analysis is as keen as it is fascinating. This book will stand as a masterpiece of modern American fiction."

A professor of French at Princeton and an esteemed translator of Faulkner, Hemingway, and Steinbeck, Coindreau was also the chief literary adviser for Gallimard, the venerable firm that would soon become my father's French publisher. "He is a man of great intelligence and stature," Daddy informed Grandpop in a self-consolatory letter. The Frenchman was in a very small fan club. For though *Set This House on Fire* got a few nice reviews in some of the major literary venues—*The Partisan Review,* the *Saturday Review*—it was skewered in many more (my father lamented melodramatically to Grandpop its having been "lambasted in a way few novels ever have"). *Time* magazine called the book a "507 page crying jag." The *Herald Tribune* deemed it "overdone." Arthur Mizener, in *The New York Times Book Review,* essentially eulogized my father's once promising literary future, and Phoebe Adams, writing in the *Atlantic Monthly,* proclaimed that "Mr. Styron is one of those novelists who assume that serious purpose constitutes a license to bore." Orville Prescott, in his *New York Times* daily review, struck a more chagrined note. "It is my painful duty to report that although much of *Set This House on Fire* is written with great technical brilliance, it is on the whole a hollow and windy book which fails to live up to its own highfalutin manners. . . . It is also a dull and tiresome book that will bore most of its readers into fits of exasperation."

My father was devastated. Although he certainly had had some inkling that the book wasn't a complete home run, he was in no way prepared for the outpouring of antipathy it inspired. The frame of the novel, employing three central characters, a latticework plot, and an industrial-size theme ("the 'decline of values' will do for want of a better book review catch phrase," as Peter put it), had stretched my thirty-four-year-old father to his intellectual limits. But, for many readers, the high-minded drama and experiments in perspective had obscured the simple humanity he'd shown in other work.

Among the book's criticisms, there was one issue that probably didn't surprise him: language. Profane in the extreme, *Set This House on Fire* not only is loaded with *shit*s and *fuck*s and acts of masturbation but also features the kind of sacrilegious language — *Thrice punctured Christ! Triple Bleeding God! I shit on Him because I do not believe!* — that was known to produce waves of agita among the gentle reading public circa 1960. I. Parley, the printer who worked with Hamish Hamilton, my father's British publishers, had refused to typeset the manuscript unexpurgated. And though Random House went ahead with the novel in all its vulgar glory, angry responses came fast, and sometimes furious. Mrs. V. McCartney of West End Avenue in New York City probably summed up the matter best when she wrote to my father her considered opinion. *Set This House on Fire* was, she thought, "beautifully written" but at the same time "filth" and "blasphemy." "I am usually a fast reader, but it was slow going due to my need to dash to the bathroom every few pages to vomit. It speeded up a bit when I decided to keep a basin near my chair which didn't have to be emptied, sometimes, for three whole chapters."

One more sorry footnote to the rollout of *Set This House on Fire* came to my father in the form of a letter forwarded by Bob Loomis. Jack Aldridge, who, along with Norman, had pulled up stakes in Litchfield County the year before, had written to *Commentary* magazine to praise the hatchet job they'd run on my father's novel. Indeed, he liked the writing so much, he requested a subscription to the periodical. From this time forward, Aldridge, loyal friend and fan of Norman's, could be counted on to filet Daddy's work in whatever venue offered him the chance.

Bad reviews aside, *Set This House on Fire* was not a complete disaster. In fact, the negative publicity turned into something of a boon. The novel spent several weeks on the *Times* bestseller list and earned my father more than double his initial advance. He also received dozens of laudatory letters from fellow writers like Truman Capote, William Inge, Wallace Stegner, and Richard Goodwin. What's more, my parents had discovered the pleasures, different but equally rich, of taking their family abroad. My sisters and brother thrived in Europe. Traveling down to Ansedonia for part of the summer and circling back to Paris, my mother kept the carnival rolling. With the help of an Irish nanny borrowed from the Joneses, she also managed to smooth many of the bumps that arose during Daddy's annus horribilis. By the end of August, my father was done licking his wounds and felt fortified enough to return to "real life" stateside.

Ultimately, my parents would find a continuing, reliable outlet in travel. Getting out of Roxbury frequently would become a cure for a whole series of ills, brought on by different conflicts at different times. In the coming decades, they would relocate to Europe several more times. It was, after all, where their love had first begun and, in many ways, suited them better than the States. The French, at least, loved my father, a feeling that was entirely reciprocated. The culture was more attractive and the politics quite often more compatible than the current American regime. But my parents always, without reluctance, came back home. Especially after *Set This House on Fire*, I think my father recognized his strengths as an American writer. If he was not patriotic, there was nonetheless a nativism to his perspective. He felt a strong desire and a responsibility to look upon his country and hold it accountable. The family returned to Connecticut in the fall of 1960. Daddy had his mind again on Nat Turner and that singularly American story he was at last ready to tell.

Ten

*Bill Styron and Bob Loomis, aspiring men of
letters on the Duke Campus, circa 1948*

DID MY FATHER'S depression steal his creative gift? Or was it
the other way around, an estrangement from his muse driving him
down in increments till he hit rock bottom? There's no single answer, no simple trajectory. You *could* say my father's whole life
was one long preamble to personal Armageddon. Hypersensitive,
aloof, unexamined, not to mention hypochondriacal, agnostic, and
alcoholic. Intellectual, passionate, and infantile. It would probably
have required some kind of religious regeneration, or a close encounter of the third kind, to break his inevitable date with madness.
But why, I wondered, did it come upon him so violently at sixty,
and then again terminally at seventy-five? The accepted wisdom—
abstemiousness had unmasked his depression, milestone birthdays
made him blue—wasn't sufficient to me. It didn't factor in my

father's monumental—and, I'd begun to believe, all-consuming—artistic imperative. It didn't consider the truth upon which, like a Catherine wheel, Daddy had been lashed: at the time of his death, it had been twenty-seven years since his last completed novel. Twenty-seven years since he'd felt good about himself.

My father's problem wasn't really writer's block. He wasn't Joe Mitchell, heading into his office every day only to emerge without a word laid upon the page. In the two decades between the completion of *Sophie's Choice* and his 2000 crack-up, Daddy produced a fair amount: a collection of nonfiction entitled *This Quiet Dust*; *Darkness Visible*, the *Vanity Fair* piece as well as the book of the same name; the short story collection *A Tidewater Morning*; more than twenty essays and magazine articles; numerous introductions or afterwords to books by other people; a dozen book reviews; countless speeches, tributes, eulogies, public letters, op-ed pieces, and occasionals. He worked hard at and cared a great deal about all of his writing. But if each creation is, in effect, an artist's offspring, I think Daddy put his nonfiction in the category with his four living, breathing children. There was affection for what he'd made and, frequently, pride. But the Novel owned his heart, and was the one thing about which he really gave a damn. He kept at it, this monument building, the singular love affair. But his extreme perfectionism would not allow him to settle for a dull sentence, a merely competent piece of work. Great fiction was his magnificent obsession.

The monomaniacal (usually male) artist is a familiar image. Even I can see the curious romance in the image of the brilliant writer so consumed with his work he hardly notices his loved ones mooning around in the shadow of his neglect. O'Neill, Melville, Hemingway—their reputations weren't diminished but rather cemented by evidence of messy domestic scenes, as if vice and violence actually produces great work, the dark glamour of it all obscuring the much more banal familial tragedy at the heart of the story. Of course there are also the celebrated soloists—Baudelaire, Flaubert, Proust, Poe, Kerouac, Lowry—who did the world a favor by simply not having families. Who was to scold a fellow for twenty-hour workdays, never mind lying in bed for weeks, full-tilt laudanum benders, or round-the-world brothel tours? This, in my thinking, is all to the good. The bedlam of a sixth-grade slumber party may never have interrupted Thoreau's cogitations on Walden Pond, but we are the better, and more enlightened, for the quiet. And, really, where would the literature of existentialism be had Sartre ever been beckoned, by a child's small hand, to turn cartwheels on the lawn?

Whether or not my father *ought* to have had children is a question upon which, as a chief beneficiary of his largesse, I cannot opine. But I do think that, despite the urgency of his work, he had a deep appreciation for human connectivity. Every temptation he avoided, every crevasse he overtook, was a run at life. It was all part of a constant bid for which good work was his most valuable marker: the bid to be loved. He didn't drink himself to death. He didn't self-destruct. He didn't abandon us, nor, though he often behaved abominably, did he actually drive us all away. He was, for the most part, a domesticated animal. Every one of us felt, though we couldn't always point to any good evidence to support it, loved by him and strangely compelled by his outsize need. At the climax of *Darkness Visible*, Daddy describes the moment when he is pulled back from the third rail over which depression has hung him. Fixated on suicide, he is in the big living room in Connecticut, a video he has put on playing idly in background. Through the fog of his terrible thoughts come the strains of one of his mother's favorite pieces, Brahms's Alto Rhapsody. "In a flood of swift recollection," he writes, "I thought of all the joys the house had known: the children who had rushed through its rooms, the festivals, the love and work, the honestly earned slumber, the voices and the nimble commotion, the perennial tribe of cats and dogs and birds, 'laughter and ability and Sighing, / And Frocks and Curls.' All this I realized was more than I could ever abandon."

I do believe that Daddy's love for all of us, and ours for him, kept him alive. But, especially in his last years, it was a kind of half-life. Those of us who were close to him saw the signs for years, in his reticence to talk about his work, in the set of his shoulders as he approached his study, in the profound privacy and solitude of his experience. His writing must have been, literally, driving him mad. And that, more than any of his other peccadilloes, may have been his greatest secret.

This, anyway, was the idea I was clutching when I arrived for a lunch date with Bob Loomis, my father's editor of forty-seven years. I'd just returned from another trip to Duke, and had been to see Peter Matthiessen only a few weeks earlier. There was a pattern emerging in the carpet, one that my daughterly self found sad but that the writer in me was exalted by. I needed someone with whom to share it.

Entering 1745 Broadway, Random House's sleek new headquarters, I gave the guard at the reception desk my name. Then I turned around to gaze at the floor-to-ceiling bookshelves that line the skyscraper's lobby. Sold in 1965 to RCA and again to S. I. Newhouse's Advance Publications in 1980, Random House has, since 1998, been a subsidiary of Bertelsmann, the German media conglomerate. Advertising itself as the largest English-language trade publisher in the world, the firm now extends across every continent, genre, and major language. But like the Lascaux Caves, the Cerf-Klopfer legacy is easily traceable, preserved along the walls of company headquarters. It's a curated collection, with books lined up row upon row, spines out. The visitor gets an instant sense of volume, and a feel for the firm's varied accomplishments. Here and there, a pretty cover is turned out, preening flirtatiously upon a metal stand. Scanning the shelves, I admired a new Vintage Classics edition of *War and Peace,* done up in an arresting robin's-egg blue; James Joyce's *Ulysses,* which Random House won a landmark court case to publish, unabridged, in 1933; *The Cat in the Hat* and all the other Dr. Seuss books, which have made that little Rockwell Kent "random" house familiar to generations of children; *Butterfield 8; The World Accord-*

ing to Garp. Finally, on an upper shelf, in pride of place, I spied *Lie Down in Darkness.* Reissued not long ago, the edition features the original George Salter cover art, a dilapidated Southern streetscape, reminiscent of Thomas Hart Benton in its palette and eerie light.

A familiar thump of filial pride pulsed beneath my breastbone. Suddenly, I misted up.

"Ma'am?"

The guard, phone dangling on his ear, was connected now to Bob's office. He wanted my name again.

"Stein?"

"*Sty*-ron," I said, straightening my shoulders and giving my nose a pull. "S-T-Y-R-O-N."

He handed me a white card encoded with some mystery data and pointed me toward the turnstiles, which I proceeded to get bollixed up in, just as I had the last time I was there. Standing there fussing with the security card, I remembered Daddy once telling Bob, over lunch on the Vineyard porch, how loathsome he found the new Random House regime. "The woman you have there, answering the phone, is a moron," Daddy said, wincing with irritation, followed by a beery burp. "She can't pronounce my name. Every time I call, she gets it wrong."

"Well, Bill," Bob replied, his soft voice ever flat and Ohio-y, "you know, she's just the receptionist."

"I know that," Daddy snapped. "Still. It's galling."

Fifty years at the same house and the lady at the switchboard doesn't know your goddamn name. Piled on top of his own private self-flagellation, the repeated reminder of his diminished Q rating pained Boy Writer to no end.

After greeting me at the elevator, Bob led me past a warren of cubicles and ushered me into his modest office. Though similar to that of every editor I know—institutional lighting, books and manuscripts everywhere, no real place to sit—Bob's workspace always surprises me a bit. When I am speaking to him on the phone, my mind stubbornly conjures him in a much larger space. Some glass-enclosed aerie, commodious and hushed by a meadow of beige carpeting. I think maybe, when I was a child, book writing seemed like such an unappealing profession—so lonely and bothersome and unrewarding—I glamorized the realm of the editor as compensation. Perhaps, I reasoned, on those rare occasions when Daddy got up in the morning, put on his good blue blazer, and drove to the city for lunch with Bob, it was a Cinder-fella sort of affair. In New York there would be limousines and silver tea services and "Yes, Mr. Styron," "No, Mr. Styron." Where else could that happen but at Random House, the closest thing my father had to a "place of business"?

Bob and my father were a symbiotic pair. Daddy, obsessively writing and rewriting, sentence by sentence, delivered manuscript pages only when they were nearly finished products. Bob then moved in, with a hand Daddy praised for being "very light," and sculpted the pages to their ideal form. Personality-wise, they were a study in opposites. My father, all untidy appetite and noisy id. Bob, a sort of Leslie Howard figure, fair hair always meticulously groomed, his voice as gentle as his demeanor. As with many good teams, their contrasting styles complemented each other, helping their friendship to abide a half century of working together. No one knew my father's artistic voyage as well as Bob, or the shoals he got hung up on along the way.

"I wanted to show you something," Bob said, moving behind his desk.

Fishing through the piles, he pulled up a ream of bound paper that turned out to be proofs of a new book of my father's fiction, one of several planned posthumous volumes of which I was only vaguely aware. I looked at the title, *The Suicide Run,* which struck me as clever, if kind of ironic. As Bob explained it to me, the book (*Five Tales of the Marine Corps* was the subtitle) was a collection of his war narratives, some of which had been only in magazines, others never published at all. Two of the pieces, shaped by Jim West, were from the very different iterations of *The Way of the Warrior.*

"And there's a story from the pages you brought up here," he said, referring to the shopping bag I'd dropped on his desk a few years before.

I riffled the pages, my eye scanning a few of the proper nouns—Saipan, Lacy Dunlop, the Bide-A-Wee Tearoom—that had caught my eye at the library.

"I just came back from Duke," I blurted, anxious to introduce the subject that had been weighing on me. "I went through the boxes of his unfinished manuscripts."

Bob slipped on his jacket, patted his pockets, and gestured for me to precede him out the door to lunch.

"Yes," he replied quietly. "There are a lot of them."

        *   *   *

IN THE CLOSELY autobiographical world of my father's fiction, his narrators are usually defined by the same qualities—Southern orientation, literary bent, sexual longing, deep ambivalence toward the enticements of power—that also preoccupied their creator. Even Nat Turner, Daddy's most dissimilar medium, speaks and thinks more like my father than the original rebel slave probably ever did. But if my father's books gave him an opportunity to explore the man he was, they just as often allowed him to transcend the limits of his identity and become what he was not. With stunning chutzpah, he plunged into alien territory, compelled by experiences antipodal from his own: to be black; to be a Jew, a woman, a Nazi; to be dispossessed, disaffected, condemned to die, unable to fight. Otherness stirred his imagination, his moral conscience, his pathos and his guilt. But, in the end, one archetype seemed constantly to elude his net. It was a quest that drove him ever deeper into the bush.

Or, perhaps I should say, the battlefield.

My father had a cap with the Marine Corps seal—red and black, with a globe and anchor and eagle—which he used to wear when he took the dogs for a walk. He wore it ironically, I think. But he also wore it till it was decrepit from use. Daddy was proud of his time in the service. But he was prouder still of his membership in the select community who wrote with wisdom *about* the service. He was an early and vocal admirer of Jones, Mailer, and Vonnegut, and his friendships with them were predicated as much on his appreciation for their work as on a fondness for their personalities. The bond among the military men of World War II created one of the twentieth century's great cross-cultural fraternities. But only a tiny fraction synthesized the experience into a thematic whole, made it art. Jim Jones had done so to glorious effect in *From Here to Eternity*. It was around a mutual desire to interpret the war experience that my father's unique friendship with Jim was built.

They met for the first time in '51, shortly after my father came home from Camp Lejeune to the excitement of *Lie Down in Darkness*. But it wasn't until several years later, when my father had written *The Long March* and Jim had completed his second war-themed book, *Some Came Running*, that they truly connected. Throughout the fifties and sixties, the Styrons and the Joneses continued to grow closer, even as they drifted apart geographically and their respective responsibilities mounted. Mum and Gloria adored each other. The children were of the same age and companionable. Eventually the Joneses settled in Paris, where they ran their Île St.-Louis apartment like a boozy salon, providing a raucous perch for a constant stream of migratory expats. "The most remarkable group of American no-counts, bums, and hustlers, who would simply turn up on their doorstep" is how Daddy described the scene. My parents visited often, joining in the overnight poker games, caterwauling from Jim's famous Renaissance pulpit–bar, and staying on, with the rest of the louts, for the ritual Sunday night spaghetti dinners. James Baldwin, Allen Ginsberg, Eunice and Sargent Shriver, Lauren Bacall, Betty Comden and Adolph Green, Art and Ann Buchwald, Gore Vidal, and Jerzy Kosinski were just some of the many friends my parents got to know at the house on the Seine with its aerial view of Notre-Dame. The gay nights at Jim and Gloria's were, my father once pointed out, "tough on the liver and the estomac," but I got the feeling these were some of the most mirthful and carefree times in my parents' life together.

By the time I was born, the Joneses had been overseas for more than a decade. My mother and father no longer transplanted across the Atlantic for months at a time, so I didn't get to know Jim and Gloria like the rest of the family did. But on the rare occasions that they came to Roxbury, it was, I remember, a major event. The energy started ramping up days before their arrival. Daddy prepared to cook a big old dinner, scared up his harmonica, laid in the best Scotch, and generally inflated with good cheer. The honored guests would show up sometime in the afternoon and pass before me in the TV room. Gloria was all teeth and blond waves and big boobs. Jim followed behind her, compact and gnarled as a bulldog.

"Give her a twenty," Gloria would say to Jim over her shoulder, flashing her crimson grin at me.

"Huh?" Jim would grunt, cigar gripped at the edge of his mouth.

"Give her a twenty!"

Bemused but obedient, Jim would open his wallet and hand me a crisp bill, then follow Gloria on to the living room, leaving me goggle-eyed. I came to imagine, erroneously, that the Joneses of Paris were epically rich and wonder if my parents' relative penury didn't sometimes cause them, in contrast, some small bit of shame.

I liked to hang around in the living room on nights that the Joneses were there. Like my father, Jim and Gloria were drinkers and swearers. My mother takes only a occasional glass of wine. And when she swears, which is rarely, it never seems to suit her. But still, the couples were a nice fit, and the four of them got up a pretty good time together. Daddy and Jim liked to talk about battles, military and literary (they had both been taken out to the censor's woodpile for the rough language in their early books and been lashed by the critics for their sophomore efforts). They gossiped about current and former friends, decried the state of the world, and dug in deep on the subject of writing. One night, my father made Jim cry by playing a record of General Lee's farewell address to his troops at Appomattox. In his eulogy at Jim's 1977 funeral, he interpreted Jim's reaction. "For you," he said, "and you alone among the writers of your time, war was the inexpressible eternity, the never-ending agony embedded in our human condition."

My father, too, recognized the titanic themes and essential truths tied up in the story of war. And he wanted to paint on that canvas, as Jim and others had done. The only child, steeped in patriotic American lore, continued to try to reconcile his simultaneous attraction to the armed services' marvelous brotherhood and his disgust with war and "its unutterable waste and futility and folly and loss." Men like Jim, macho and sensitive, daring and deep, were the embodiments of this duality. And so he conceived Lieutenant Colonel Paul Marriott, the central character in the first *Way of the Warrior*. Introduced to the novelist-narrator shortly after he arrives for duty at Camp Lejeune, Marriott dazzles the young man as much with his "full panoply of stars and ribbons . . . intimidatingly luminous across [his] robust chest" as with his sparkling intellect. Erudite, worldly, "a Flaubert votary" like the narrator himself, Marriott is an oasis, "a man of formidable experience who had managed to find in the muted and lilac scented province of nineteenth century France harmonies that were compatible with a career in the deafening, bloody universe of modern warfare."

I can't say what was to become of Paul Marriott, or of the narrator. The manuscript pages I found at Duke so hopelessly disorganized were jumbled even further in a seemingly cosmic accident that befell me and my research a week or so after my lunch with Bob. I know from Jim West that Daddy had planned to trouble Marriott's waters with a deepening crisis of faith. As the conflict in Korea wore on, Marriott was to become consumed by doubts, his sensitive mind at odds with his warrior heart. When *Esquire* published "Marriott, the Marine," in 1971, advertising it as "a selection from the forthcoming novel *The Way of the Warrior*," the response to the material was overwhelmingly positive, which gratified Daddy.

But when he lost the next section of the manuscript—his suitcase, containing the only copy, was stolen at New York's Port Authority—my father didn't seem to care. He was having his own crisis. A creative one. He experimented with other forms, writing his play, *In the Clap Shack,* and a screenplay with John Marquand called *Dead! A Love Story.* But neither project was a success. It wasn't until '73, when the idea for *Sophie's Choice* came to him, that he had another big project to burrow into. Daddy would find a way to write about war after all. But his narrator, Stingo, was a medium through which *someone else's* experience is laid bare. My father still hadn't scratched the itch to tell his own story, that of a soldier.

*   *   *

"NO, NO. YOU'VE got it wrong," Bob said, when I presented my idea that Daddy's creative frustrations made him depressed. We were sitting at a table at Trattoria Dell'Arte, the Manhattan institution across from Carnegie Hall. The maître d', nodding to Bob with a familiar deference, had steered us from the main room, hung with amusingly Brobdingnagian plaster of Paris noses, to the windowed front of the restaurant. It was a beautiful June Friday, and it seemed that every suit who hadn't skipped town already was eating lunch in the park or around the open-air plazas that dot midtown. I was glad the place was empty. Even when he's amplified, as he had been at my father's memorial service, you sometimes have to lean in to hear what Bob has to say.

"His illness made it impossible for him to finish anything. Not the other way around."

I was surprised by Bob's conviction, and a bit skeptical. But I wasn't about to contradict him. After all, I felt like I was just getting acquainted with my father. Bob had known him a lifetime.

"The first *Way of the Warrior* was quite good," Bob said. "I liked it a lot. But the theme wouldn't hold up. The thing was, Marriott was gay. Which your father thought was a great idea. At first. But in the end, I think he felt like 'Who cares?' It wasn't big enough."

A decorated soldier in the 1950s who is also a closet homosexual. A great theme, probably, in the right hands. And I imagine my father, always so drawn to writing from perspectives different from his own, saw a potentially interesting opportunity. But he wasn't writing about war to explore human sexuality. I could see this was an imposed conflict, not an organic one. In any case, for the next seven years *Sophie's Choice* swept Daddy off in another direction. By the time my father returned to the Marine material, it was the early 1980s and Daddy was preoccupied with new concerns—particularly Reagan and the conservative fever that now gripped the nation. The "evil empire" baiting, the religious fundamentalism, the passive-aggressive Just Say No sloganeering. All that jingoism felt to my father like a dangerous retread of cold war Eisenhower ideals, and it infuriated him (no doubt this was what he was preoccupied with when he got up on his soapbox at my prep school graduation). Returning to the material, he refashioned *The Way of the Warrior* as a World War II story, introducing Lieutenant Doug Stiles, a comrade of Stingo's he'd carried over from *Sophie's Choice.*

My father made Stiles conservative and patrician, modeling him on a young William F. Buckley. Like Marriott, the lieutenant has a way of inspiring both admiration and enmity. Much of the extant manuscript is crafted in my father's typically excellent prose. And there is great promise in the story as it is set forth—two young second lieutenants of vastly different temperaments and backgrounds, and the unlikely alliance they forge while girding for war in the Pacific. But it also betrays a sort of narrative lassitude, and hints at the difficulty Daddy encountered wrapping a yarn around his Great Idea. Deep within the hundreds of manuscript pages that constitute this version of the novel, I found a note Daddy wrote to himself. It's an unusual sight, the circuits of my father's thinking laid bare. And it hints at a core trouble with his design: the Theme with a capital *T* was overwhelming the forces of a good old-fashioned story:

Creative writing: see flesh,
not bare bones,
But I've wrestled with the
[agenda] so long that I've
decided to show the
schema schematic
dramatic tension

What anxiety and sadness attended my father's work hours during this period I can only speculate. I was then at the peak of adolescence—fourteen, fifteen, sixteen years old. Under any circumstances, I'd probably have been oblivious to the movements of my father's heart. But the discord of my parents' relationship was so epic at that point, I shut down from them with a near-autistic fierceness. When I found out that, because of a clerical error, I would have to be a day student my first year at Taft, I was inconsolable. Through much of tenth grade, I stayed overnight anyway, sleeping in a friend's dorm room closet, where the on-duty monitors wouldn't find me. Among my father's medical records is a snippet of masterful understatement my mother wrote as she was taking notes on the history of her husband's illness. "Often angry, down on world and / or me, pattern over yrs, when not in middle of a book."

Here, then, is where I detect the first signs of Daddy going off the rails. In the winter of 1982, he gave an interview to two college students, the transcript of which I found in the files at Duke.

"What are you writing these days?" one of the young men asked.

"I'm working on a new novel about Nicaragua," Daddy replied. Satisfied, or getting no encouragement, his interlocutors moved on to another subject.

It would take me months of sleuthing, but eventually I figured out it was the memory of *this* project that caused Bob, during our

Italian lunch, to pause. Putting down his fork, he tilted his pate, now heavily dappled with age, toward me and touched his forehead.

"Your father was working on something," he said. "Something else." Looking up, he fixed me with a frank, rueful gaze. "And it just wasn't good. That had never happened before. I told him, and he blew up at me."

Poor Bob, I thought, wincing. I could imagine what Daddy must have sounded like, though with his friends he was usually pretty reasonable. He saved his rage for my mother mostly and, less often, for us kids. "I didn't know that the depression was setting in," Bob continued, "that he just couldn't handle criticism. He told me, much later, that the illness just totally robs you of self-esteem." With his soft blue eyes, now as old as Daddy's when he died, Bob looked at me and shook his head. "I don't think he ever got his self-esteem back. The wounds were open, and they just wouldn't close."

Eleven

William Clark Styron, Sr.,
proud father, 1960

THE PERFECT PEACE my parents found when they moved to Connecticut in 1954 had, by the late seventies, been downgraded to something noticeably less serene. Their house, like a lot of authentic colonials, was no more than twenty feet from the road, a fact of little consequence in the beginning. Rucum Hill was still unpaved then, and the population of Roxbury hovered at around eight hundred, nearly the lowest in its 258-year history. For a long time, the feel of the place remained pretty much the same, though Rucum Road was eventually tarred and citizenship grew at a steady pace. When I was small, only the distant sound of an occasional car on Route 67 interrupted the steady trill of birdcalls around our house and the rustling breeze through the birches. But, in the midseventies, things began to change. The city of Danbury, to the south of us, practically doubled its population; IBM opened a headquarters in nearby Southbury; and the completion of Interstate 84 put the region's charms within an easy two-hour drive from Manhattan. Roxbury was still a tiny town, but everything around us grew. A cul-de-sac of houses sprouted at the top of our hill. Route 67 became a busy thoroughfare. And our little incline turned out to be a good shortcut from neighboring towns to the big world beyond. The whole thing made my father crazy.

"God*damn* it!" he would shout as a construction truck, having lost momentum, ground its gears outside our door. "I can't stand it anymore!"

In the TV room or upstairs, I would hear him and feel my chest tighten as I waited for what came next.

"We're moving to Virginia!"

Moving to Virginia. The words sent a chill down my spine. I couldn't think of the state with any proper geographical parameters. *Moving to Virginia* conjured images of the entire Southeast as I knew it, the podunk town of Goldsboro, North Carolina, where Grandpop and his third wife, Eunice, lived; the unbearably damp vacation house where we visited them in Tallahassee; the old place in Hilton Village I'd been taken once to see; the whole culture from whence Daddy sprung and which he'd long ago fled. I didn't want to move there. And, most important, I didn't want to move *any*where alone with my mother and father.

I'm not sure what was behind my father's Virginia talk. It was probably, like so many other rants of his, an empty threat designed to get a rise out of Mum, much the way my six-year-old baits me with lavish threats when he's looking for validation he doesn't think he's getting. Or maybe Daddy had genuinely begun to feel, in his fifties, the primal lure of his homeland. For no matter how much he assimilated in the North, my father was always a very Southern man. It was a side of him that emerged most clearly when he was at ease. The way the salt draws out flavor in the Smithfield hams he so loved to prepare, there was a certain kind of recreation—cooking, walking his dogs through the piney woods, exercising his flair as a raconteur—that fired up Daddy's good ol' boy persona. With "his people," friends like Willie Morris or James Taylor or Tom Wicker, the transformation was tribal. Feeling utterly understood, he'd slip into a Tidewater drawl, turn loquacious and charming, mind everyone's drinks and encourage them to partake of his cigars, his food, his every resource. Occasionally he'd even pull out the harmonica, an instrument that he'd learned as a child and played quite well but that, like all other pastimes, he'd forsaken in middle age. (It wasn't until I started this book that I discovered he was once an avid chess player, decent on the tennis court, and had a childhood passion for sailing. I can count on one hand the times I saw my father in a bathing suit, and on two fingers when I witnessed him swimming.) The sense of "belonging" can evoke inestimable nostalgia, a reaction to which even my rebellious father was not immune.

Artistically, the late seventies were really good years for my father. Entrenched in *Sophie's Choice,* he was making art, piling up pages every day. But that "zone" in which he operated necessitated complete focus; every minor irritation was a potential threat to production. Daddy enjoyed the pastoral life, required it really, but at some point he must have felt country wasn't country enough. The cosmopolitan nature of his lifestyle with Mum—the fancy parties, political events, the sheer largeness of their social world—was a lure and a curse. "Life outside" had a vampiric seductiveness, for which Daddy's only real apotropaic defense was the Flaubert quotation he kept taped above his desk: "Be orderly in your life, and ordinary like a bourgeois, in order to be violent and original in your works." Living in Virginia would certainly have helped streamline his life. He could, after all, be an orderly bourgeois on the Chesapeake as easily as on the Housatonic. And down there, at least he knew that, no matter how this next book turned out, he'd also be a local hero.

Whatever the case, life conspired to keep us in Connecticut. Daddy had a stone wall built between our house and the road. When that didn't cut the noise, he ordered up a row of evergreen saplings. Then, in a turn of events that would truly challenge the underpinnings of Daddy's identity, my grandfather's health took a sudden downturn. The most expedient solution to his care was for my father to move him north. Virginia, in a manner of speaking, came to us.

*   *   *

NO ONE LOOMED larger in Daddy's experiences, or did more to shape the man he became, than Bill Styron, Sr. My grandfather's quiet iconoclasm, his free-ranging and independent mind, inspired my father when he was young and filled him with awe in middle age. Theirs was also a mutual admiration society. Having observed something special in his only child straight off, Grandpop always encouraged my father to fulfill his potential, and to do so on his own terms. His unstinting generosity personified the best parental instincts. But it also came at a cost that was, at times, more than financial. It couldn't have been easy, when money was tight, for my grandfather to cut Daddy those monthly checks while under the watchful gaze of his second wife. In an essay about her aunt and the young Bill Styron, the writer Mary Wakefield Buxton shares an illuminating memory: "'Billy thinks he's a writer,' she said perhaps a hundred times to her friends and family. I can see her rolling her icy blue eyes and hear the shudder in her voice."

It was a measure of the strength of the father-son bond that Elizabeth's skepticism did little to weaken it. Grandpop's faith was, of course, redeemed in good time. As I've often heard, Grandpop was watching Walter Cronkite when he learned his son had won the Pulitzer Prize for fiction in 1967. "I told you Billy was a writer!" he exclaimed to his wife, running into the kitchen. As for my father, his filial affection was perhaps nowhere more evident than in what he *didn't* say. No matter how poorly she treated him, Daddy remained unflaggingly polite toward the woman to whom his father was conjoined.

But if Grandpop was a role model and a champion, he was also a cautionary tale. There was a quiet desperation to the way his story unspooled, and no one, least of all him, wished to see it repeated. Grandpop, both actively and passively, chose the path of least resistance, avoided risk, and evaded glory in equal measure. His strong convictions rarely translated into self-realizing action. Instead, his thoughts spun into high-minded lectures and homilies, which gave him what my father called "sententiousness," often driving people away with his infernal bombast. Even my father was often frustrated by his speechifying and developed accordingly a short fuse for rhetoric or oratory of any kind. Ultimately it was a lonely place where my grandfather dwelt. In the storybook version, he'd have been Atticus Finch. But on the gritty byways of Newport News, Bill Sr. was essentially a disappointed man. He possessed a poet's heart, a philosopher's soul, and the mind of a thinker, but they were all trapped in the body of a midlevel engineer.

Daddy thought about his father a lot. He appears over and over again in his fiction. Sometimes, as with Milton Loftis in *Lie Down in Darkness,* Grandpop makes a fragmentary contribution to a character my father has pulled together from different sources. But most of the time he is himself, the kind and righteous draftsman who pushes along the plot with a letter, a visit, or by his role in a memorable scene from the narrator's recollected youth. He is Peter Leverett's prolix father in *Set This House on Fire,* "Pop" who comes up from Virginia to visit Stingo in *Sophie's Choice,* he is Jefferson Whitehurst in all three stories in *A Tidewater Morning,* and then appears in that same guise in at least three of Daddy's unfinished works. In the early books, written when Grandpop was still alive, my father maintains a staunchly admiring tone even as he allows for the quirks of personality that give the characters dimension and heft. But in the short stories, and the novels that he struggled to complete later in life, my father digs deep into Jeff Whitehurst's flaws and failures, allowing the narrator's ambivalence to surface. They're raw and poignant portraits, reflecting the melancholy truths my father had come to realize about Grandpop and making him into a kind of metaphor for his complex feelings about the South as a whole.

In September 1940, when my father arrived at Christchurch School, in Christchurch, Virginia, he was fifteen. Small for his age and young for his class, he was totally on his own. He'd been away from home a few times. In fact, just the year before, he'd had an adventurous trip to New York with Leon Edwards and his brother. They'd been out to Flushing to the 1939 World's Fair, where Daddy saw television for the first time, and the boys walked around gaping at the sights of Times Square nearly till sunup. He'd also gone by himself to Pennsylvania, and to visit his father's relatives in the Carolina countryside. But nothing could have prepared him for the lonesome feeling of arriving at boarding school, a motherless boy, without a friend in sight.

"I'm a little homesick (boo hoo)," he wrote to Auntie Elmer on the twenty-third of September, "but do you think I'll get used to the place?"

Daddy, who had a cheeky, bantering tone he used with Elmer, tried to pull up his socks for the next paragraph, putting a hopeful spin on his social prospects. "I do not know many of the boys (there are 50) but hope to, later on, meet and 'git together.'" Not three sentences later, with slipping bravado, he queries Elmer again: "Do you think I'll get used to the place and settle down to routine?"

The emphasis he puts on his sign-off, "<u>Please</u> write me," might as well have run like a thread through the letter's every anxious word.

Christchurch was actually a pretty nice place for Daddy to land. On 125 scenic acres skirting the Rappahannock River, Christchurch maintained a pleasant balance of Episcopal rectitude and relative informality. Classes devoted to a standard boys' school curriculum—English, math, Latin, geography, history—gave way to afternoon recreation on the campus's verdant playing fields and afloat the broad, lazy waterway. It was a small school with a salubrious philosophy, and Daddy was happy there. He made some good friends, ate well, and grew tall. He sailed and played chess, acted in a few plays, and worked on the school newspaper. Outside of English, his grades weren't much to speak of, and he continued an already inglorious streak of abject failure in math. But if not much of a scholar, he nevertheless found a place to pursue his native passion for books. He wrote his first short stories at Christchurch, and was elected president of the Literary Society in the fall of his junior year.

By that time, my grandfather was preparing for his wedding to Miz Buxton. Elizabeth's father, Russell, whom she worshiped and had cared for during his terminal bout with cancer, had passed away. She could now turn her cool and efficient hand to whipping the Styron men into shape. Grandpop was a grateful subject, but my sixteen-year-old father was definitely not playing along. In the previous year and a half, he'd grown to nearly six feet, perfected a withering sarcasm, and learned to drink and smoke with all the confidence of the college-bound young man he was about to be. Christchurch was ushering him from Clever, Lonely Boy to Opinionated Individualist—but not before Daddy had a chance to pause at the eternal adolescent corner of Supercilious and Wisenheimer. Needless to say, Elizabeth was not amused. The previous summer back home had been a disaster. Hopelessly uptight and with virtually no insight into the teenage psyche, Elizabeth spent much of her time riding my father to clean up his room, wash his clothes, mind his manners, and lay off the beer. From a proud and accomplished medical family, Elizabeth considered interest in the arts pure folly. She made my father feel guilty about the money Grandpop was spending on his education, pronounced him lazy, and wondered just when he planned to apply himself to something worthwhile. The sullen adolescent versus the wicked stepmother. Elizabeth and my father were, it seems, locked in a paradigmatic contest of wills.

As for the big event, Daddy was invited, but just.

"I'm going down to Newport News on the 18th of this month

to Pop's wedding," Daddy wrote Elmer in October of '41. "Pop doesn't want me to have the whole week-end, so Mr. Smith, the headmaster, is going to drive me down that Saturday at about 1:00 and bring me back that same afternoon, after the reception. Ain't that something?!"

After the wedding, Grandpop sold the house on Hopkins Street. He and his bride moved to a house overlooking the harbor, furnished with Buxton things. My father didn't feel much welcome there, and so his relationship with Grandpop became largely epistolary. Though Elizabeth wasn't the only cause for his exile, she was a driving force. He would never again spend any significant time in Newport News.

*   *   *

IN THE FALL of '77, with help from Willie Morris, my father went down to Goldsboro to retrieve Grandpop. After eighty-seven years of life along the southern Atlantic, of short winters and long, critter-filled summers, of tobacco fields and kudzu and the briny scents of the intracoastal waterways, Grandpop became a resident of River Glen, a 120-bed nursing home just off the interstate in Southbury, Connecticut. Grandpop's sudden presence in my father's life, and complete dependence on him, really threw Daddy for a loop. Never before or after was Bill Styron so singularly responsible for anybody's welfare, or so unable to escape the strangulating feeling such responsibility conjured.

It was an abrupt end to a particularly happy time for Grandpop. Indeed, during his later years, my grandfather's life had achieved a truly miraculous state of grace. Elizabeth, with whom he had passed companionably from late middle to old age, died of cancer in 1969. Less than a year later, in Florida on business, he got up the courage to call Eunice Edmundson Johnston, the woman with whom he had last communicated by heartbroken epistle—*"I can only hold your friendship in the shrine of memory"*—in 1914. Under pressure from her family, Eunice had turned down Grandpop's proposal in favor of a young and promising lawyer named Greene Johnston III. But, in the fifty-six intervening years, my grandfather never lost track of her. The Johnstons settled in Tallahassee, where Eunice taught high school English and Greene rose to the rank of Florida state comptroller. Together, they had three children and had been quite happy until Greene's death, in 1966. Grandpop and Eunice's 1970 reunion, however, was electric and rejuvenating. For months afterward, the couple rendezvoused in motels and wrote breathless, longing letters to each other when they were apart. Eunice called Grandpop "Darling Dynamite" or "DD." Grandpop gushed to my father about "this girl I've been seeing." In the winter of '71, in a third act worthy of a William Wyler movie, they were at last married. He was eighty-one and she seventy-six. They moved to Eunice's hometown of Goldsboro, where she had inherited a house on a corner lot with a broad front porch, and there they settled into a life of autumnal happiness. My father was touched, and not a little relieved, that his father had found kindness and companionship in the twilight of his years.

This was the grandfather I knew. Elderly and a bit stooped, supremely gentle, a broad, dentured smile playing at all times on his angular face. "Wonnerfuhlwonnerfuhl," he would remark in his high-cotton drawl about everything I did or said, his long, bony fingers wrapped around mine. "Wonnerfuhlwonnerfuhl. You ah the laht of mah life." Eunice was tiny, birdlike, with a head of carefully tended curls, and Grandpop treated her with reverent tenderness. She was a Southern Lady with a capital *L*, always sweet to me, though I cringed at the bristle of chin hair that brushed my cheek when she leaned in for a kiss. In fact, as I recall, no amount of gentleness on their part could ease my impatience with their overwhelming oldness.

As the youngest child on both sides of my extended family, I received plenty of special attention from grandparents, though we didn't see them frequently. In the early seventies, my mother's mother had moved into a brand-new Mies van der Rohe–designed building in Baltimore, where she lived out her dotage in elegant style. I loved visiting her. I would fly down alone, molded gold plastic of my Eastern Airlines wings gleaming proudly on my blouse, and be greeted at the gate by Nana, gloved hands clutching her Hermès purse. With her was her butler, Oscar (imagine *Driving Miss Daisy* and you'll be right on the money), who had worked for the family since my mother was a girl. There were gifts waiting for me on the bed in the blue guest room, peeled orange slices for breakfast, and a bell at my place setting, which would bring, with a simple tinkle, Clara, the uniformed maid bearing a fresh rasher of bacon or pretty much anything else my heart desired.

It was probably with misguided optimism for something similar that at around seven years old I agreed to make a solo trip to Goldsboro. Needless to say, my expectations were quickly dashed. The cabbagey smell of Eunice's house, the dark rooms, and the unrelenting quiet gave me the heebie-jeebies right away (I *had* been there before, but with my parents, who provided an exit hatch by lodging at a downtown hotel). The days went on forever in Goldsboro, punctuated by trips to the nearby Motor Court, where Grandpop convinced the management to let me swim and where for hours I tried to drown my boredom by diving for quarters like some mindless animal in an aquarium act. The rest of the time I sat on the front porch steps, kicking pebbles and listening to the breeze ruffle the elms. Several days in, when my mother called, I broke down sobbing and begged to come home. The bewilderment and hurt that registered on Grandpop's face gutted me, but I'd been unable to stem the homesick tide a minute longer. That night, in their mausolean downstairs bedroom (it was still light when they put me to bed, which compounded my feeling of incarceration), I wept again at the thought of how I'd repaid my grandfather's infinite kindness.

It was a similar kind of guilt and emotional confusion that suffused our house in Connecticut during Grandpop's final year. Daddy was put to a test of sorts, one he seemed destined to fail. The problem began even before Grandpop's arrival. During their last year together, he and Eunice had begun to exhibit natural signs of advanced aging, including a degree of senility that was not alarming or unexpected. But at some point, Eunice had developed a more troublesome dementia that my father, lost in his work and own life, had not picked up on. Paranoid and wishing to keep them safe from the perceived dangers, Eunice put their house in a kind of lockdown, to which her ever passive husband I guess acquiesced. When a neighbor at last grew worried enough to force his way inside, he found the house in shocking disarray and the two old people subsisting on the last of the cans in their larder. Ambulances were called, and both of them were hospitalized immediately. But Eunice, slight and frail to begin with, never recovered. She died a few days later; Grandpop, grief-stricken, disoriented, and half-dead from starvation, waited for his son to come take him away.

Several days a week, Daddy visited Grandpop at River Glen, insisting I come along when school didn't interfere. I'd drag my down jacket along the fluorescent corridors, holding my nose against the odor of decaying funk, made all the more nauseating by a top note of antiseptic. Flopping into a vinyl chair, I swung my legs, blurted a thing or two, brushed the nap of my corduroy skirt. Meanwhile I noticed my father made a pretty poor effort of his own. He would sit beside Grandpop, his face a mild rictus of pain, his irritation mounting every time Grandpop asked the same question twice. But for the most part Daddy remained, uncharacteristically, calm. I can see now I was probably his most effective foil. Just as when seated beside a person truly afraid of flying you can bring out your own bravado, Daddy had no choice but to at least try to act the grown-up with me in the room.

Many years later, in his fiction, my father would capture with lacerating honesty the effect our leave-taking had on Grandpop: "I was more than a little dishonest, I think, in not fully admitting to a perception of the shadows of loneliness that crowded around those frail shoulders as he lifted his hand and with a whisper said goodbye. He feigned bravery. But in a contest for putting up the best mask over desolation he would have come in last."

On weekends, my father looked for other ways to step up to the plate. If I had a horse show nearby, he'd sometimes bring Grandpop, which I loved, since my father showing up for me was such a rare treat. Beleaguered but contained, he would roll Grandpop's wheelchair through the rutted field and push him up to ringside. Each time I circled, Grandpop grinned and waved. Other weekend days, Grandpop came to the house. Daddy would remove him from his walker and, holding him under the armpits, deposit him in the kitchen or TV room. Then he'd split and let Daphne or my mother tend to him while I entertained myself by running Coke and Pepsi experiments ("Ah only drink Pepsi; ahm a Pepsi man") and have a big laugh when he couldn't tell the difference. Grandpop could never get warm in his new, inclement environment. In my memory he is always wearing, indoors and out, the same ugly, pea-colored down parka Daddy had picked up at Deschino's, the local ski shop.

Theoretically, Grandpop could have lived with us. We certainly had the room, though our house wasn't really suited to handicapped living. And, obviously, the means to hire nursing care was not an issue. But I think, for my father, living with Grandpop was out of the question. It would have been an anguishing echo of his childhood experience with his mother's death, which he surely had no interest in revisiting. Caring for his father full-time was simply too much of a sacrifice. He had a book to finish, and nothing took precedence over what my father needed or wanted at any given time. That said, the decision to institutionalize Grandpop weighed heavily on him. His turmoil over it, his needling guilt, was bound to find an outlet somewhere. One night, soon after Grandpop's move, I was awakened by the sound of my father shouting my name and the heavy tread of his feet stomping down the narrow hallway to my room. I sprung upright, terrified, just as he threw open the door.

"*What kind of person are you?*" he thundered. Backlit, he looked like a trembling giant, his finger raised and aimed at me. "I asked

you to do one thing! One *thing*! I asked you to make cookies for
your grandfather, but you *didn't*. You. Are. A. *Creep!* A fucking
princess! You're a hateful girl! It's an outrage, goddamn it. You hear
me? An *OUTRAGE!*"

Eventually he stormed away, as he always did, leaving me shattered and trying to piece together how I had landed myself in the
soup that way. He was probably right. I had said I would make
something for Grandpop, though at eleven years old I wasn't much
of a baker. Anyway, it seems I'd forgotten. Daddy had too until, as
was so often the case, the evening's booze uncorked his thoughts
and dinner with my mother took an unsavory turn. My inconsider-
ate behavior was probably just an itchy thread on some larger hairy
fit he was pitching. That year, with Grandpop around, he seemed
especially unpredictable, his anger ever more molten.

*   *   *

AVOIDING MY FATHER'S wrath was a complicated business. His
moods were so capricious it was hard to know what might set him
off, or when. His rage could be almost laughable—I once saw him
curse, chew apart, and hurl across the room a pencil that had the
gall to lose its point—or it could be unexpectedly frightening. He
might pass between me and the television two hundred times before turning, with no warning, and lighting into me. *Christ, what
sort of hydrocephalic half-wit watches this idiot box all day? Turn it
off! No TV! Ever again!* Or at seven o'clock at night he'd suddenly
haul from the kitchen cabinet all the Fruity Pebbles and Cocoa Puffs
he was never around to see me eat and hold them before me like
he'd found my stash of weed. *What is all this fucking junk? This
CRAP! Are you inSANE? You cannot eat this. I will not have this
in my house!* And then, with a physical concentration of nearly all
his muscle groups, he'd angrily shove the boxes in the trash before
marching the garbage outside. The next day, my mother would au-
thorize Daphne or someone to replace all the junk food and hide it in
the TV room for a little while, until Daddy forgot that he gave a shit.

I was worried about crossing him all the time, but, during those years, I just seemed to have a very hard time keeping my act together. I couldn't fall asleep at night, was always losing stuff, and at school I had become a total mess. It mattered now that I was more than a year younger than the rest of my classmates. Like my father, I'd been an early reader when I started school and so, in a first-grade class with only three or four students, had quickly made a nuisance of myself jumping all over the answers. Since my teacher, Mrs. Ostrander, also taught the second grade at an adjacent table in the same room, skipping a grade meant nothing more than moving my chair. With a birthday in late October, I was, briefly, five years old in second grade. And so I continued for the rest of my school years, always the youngest and smallest kid in the class, a deficit I usually made up for by also being the loudest. For a while the arrangement was fine. I was a good student and, in the very small school I attended, became part of a tight group of girls from my grade and the one above me. But at some point, my friends naturally rose to the next cognitive and developmental level, and no amount of precociousness could lift me along with them. It didn't help matters that I had no study skills whatsoever, was afraid of the silence that engulfed me when I turned off the TV, and never knew if anyone was going to look at my report card anyway. Laura and Tara and Lili grew boobs and matched their argyle socks to the yokes of their Fair Isle sweaters, continued to get A's and arrive with their completed homework arranged neatly in loose-leaf binders. I got teased because my hair was never brushed and provoked the bewildered scorn of teachers for whom my sisters and brother had perpetually been star students.

Rumsey Hall, the school my siblings and I all attended through ninth grade, was certainly a hard place to stay on the straight and narrow. A "pre-prep" school where fully half the students, beginning in the first grade, were boarders, it modeled itself on the spit-and-polish ideals of the traditional English public school. Coats and ties for boys and dresses for girls; "marks" for bad behavior, "points" for good; "blackballs" for missed homework assignments; sequestration, soap eating, mild corporal punishment, and suspension all awaited the shirker, the malingerer, the daringly impudent. Overwhelmingly, the Dickensian punishments—being made to stand outside in the cold and snow for a school day or three, holding the "phantom chair" position in the corner of class, having the gum you were caught chewing pressed into your hair—were meted out to the boarders, who tended to be the troublemakers. There was something bizarre about a school with six- and seven-year-old children living on campus. Many of them suffered terribly; the difference between "them" and "us" was stark. The day kids were children of the local burghers and, in their clean frocks and shiny hair, resembled the country day students down in the tonier towns of Greenwich and Darien. The boarders, however, were something else. They ran the gamut from the offspring of diplomats and potentates to inner-city scholarship kids sponsored by philanthropists with weekend houses in the area. The issue of rock stars, NBA Hall of Famers, consuls general, and prep-for-prep participants mingled not all that successfully with the siblings whose father ran the nearby Chevy dealership, the orthopedist's son, the local estate attorney's blond brood.

What truly set the boarders apart, though, and what made them a symbol of my greatest anxiety, was their lamentable home lives. The divorce rate among the parents of Rumsey's boarders was high, certainly a lot higher than that of the local families. No doubt it was a factor in the circumstances under which some kids were sent away. The boarders seemed broken, angry, and in need of something that for the most part the day students were getting on a daily basis. It's a generalization, but not inaccurate, to say the day students at Rumsey were "good kids," academically on top, well behaved, well groomed, and rarely tardy. The boarders were the ones who got caught smoking pot, or snuck into each other's dorms in the middle of the night; who told the teachers to go screw themselves, failed their courses and didn't care. Day students like myself were intimidated by the swagger and sophistication so many of them pulled off. But they also seemed marked in a way that made any comparison with them undesirable, even dangerous.

With my parents locked in eternal battle mode, I began to play out the potential ramifications for me of their conflicts. Every time my father shouted *I want a divorce!* my mind flashed on the kids I was most frightened of becoming. Like the fat girl who threatened to sit on and suffocate anyone who got near her. Or the shell-shocked boy who repeatedly pooped in the corner of the math classroom at recess. Or the pitiful girl, picked on by everyone, whom I once caught in a stairwell talking to her peanut butter sandwich.* These were, admittedly, the kids on the fringes of sanity, kids I knew in my heart I wasn't likely to turn into. But even the children of more glamorous provenance, boarders who were popular, athletic, and competent, were scary to me because their parents had, undeniably, left them. They came from places like New York and California, where in my mind people's lives played out in public and kids grew up fast and scary. I always pictured the parents in glassy high-rises, screaming at each other and maybe throwing money around. Then they'd pack their kids into a limo and put them out, like a discarded Bloomie's bag, at Rumsey.

It was around this time, 1978, that Leslie Begelman's dad was arrested for embezzling a bunch of money from the studio he ran, Columbia Pictures. The story was in the papers, and all the grown-ups were talking about it. I remember Leslie walking down the aisle in study hall and how the kids—though I doubt one among us knew what *embezzlement* meant—stared at her like she herself might have cut the heart out of a golden retriever puppy. I don't know if Leslie's parents were divorced. I don't even know if Leslie had a mother. I only know that she, like all the boarders with "problems," was in my mind the child of divorce. One more step

---

*Yes, I remember all of their names and, for any contribution I made to their childhood misery, beg forgiveness.

and I'd be living up at Hilltop dorm, menaced in the dark by Saskia Jiskoot and Tanya Mull. Leave me there long enough, and I might become one of them.

Just as Polly was paralyzed by her dilemma when I fell down the basement stairs, I sometimes didn't know which way to turn for my punishment. One day, when I was about eleven, my father picked me up at the barn where I'd gone to ride after school. It was one of those weeks when, wishing to carve out some private time, he had shooed my mother away, telling her he didn't need any help looking after me. We'd been on the road for ten minutes or so when I realized I'd left my book bag at school. Suddenly nauseated, I weighed the consequences of my blunder. Rumsey's system of academic discipline was particularly painful for me. Relying on the power of public humiliation, the headmaster called malefactors up in front of morning assembly every day for a week. One by one, we were issued cards, small white forms, which each of the teachers would sign if we had completed the day's work to their satisfaction. For someone like me, who desperately wished to be thought of as "good," like my siblings, it was a mortifying ritual. In my tenuous state, I could scarcely support the experience emotionally. But I feared my father's reaction even more. I decided to remain silent, and lay awake most of the night cold with dread. The muddiness of my logic became obvious the next week. I was issued the card *and* received a ferocious verbal ass-kicking from Daddy when he got wind of it.

There was always the possibility that life would be *better* if my parents divorced. Maybe Daddy would move to Virginia and I would be left alone, like a countrified Eloise, with my messy hair and my pets and a retinue of staff wandering in and out trying to civilize me. Except that I was deeply attached to my identity as William Styron's daughter. It conferred something special upon me, something I feared he'd take with him if he left, and maybe bestow upon new children if he had them in some other, magically happy home. Irascible as he was, I didn't know what, or who, I'd be without him.

*   *   *

AFTER GRANDPOP DIED, in the summer of '78, the small cache of belongings he'd held on to was moved from River Glen to our house. Boxes of yellowing documents; old, broken briefcases stuffed with thick ledgers; shopping bags filled with paper littered the Ping-Pong table; a lifetime's worth of record keeping relinquished to the punishing damp of our old New England basement. An exuberant genealogist, Grandpop collected and saved all things archival. He took great pride in the Clark-Styron family tree and was forever on the hunt for new information about our ancestry. Of course he liked to talk about it, too. It seems to me that Grandpop was forever explaining, unbidden, which branch of the family had settled North Carolina, how we were related to the explorer William Clark, the adventures his father had in the Confederate army as a teenage courier for General Hoke. Bored by these dusty claims to an unimaginable past, I pretty much tuned him out. But after a time, the papers downstairs, reproaching the family for our neglect, began to intrigue me. Twelve years old and no longer fearful of the basement, I started going down there to poke through stuff.

One of the items, a typed and photostatted letter with no signature, I took and still have today. Dated July 19, 1840, the correspondence came to my great-great-grandfather Clark from one of his sons, who was studying at Harvard. The young man, a passionate Democrat in a hotbed of Whigs, tells his father of campus enthusiasm for William Henry Harrison and decries the "rapacity" of Northerners agitating for protectionism while having "feasted so long on the industry of the South!" At the time of my discovery, the "Tippecanoe and Tyler Too" part of this letter totally passed me by. So did the subtleties of my relative's argument, which prefigure some of the political fury that would soon lead to the War Between the States. Instead, I was riveted by the more mundane passage later in the document that made reference to our family's slave-owning past with an almost technical degree of casualness. Describing to his father the straw cutter he has been asked to scope out, my great-great-uncle analyzes the economics of the purchase. "It certainly would be the cheapest you could possibly obtain for the labor of 6 or 7 Negroes," he reasons, "and as many horses daily saved."

I'll be honest. I didn't lose too much sleep over this evidence. There in the cashmere-covered comfort of my Connecticut upbringing, I'd always thought it was kind of amusing that, as I'd heard a hundred times, my great-grandmother actually had little slave girls, Drusilla and Lucinda, bestowed upon her as playmates by her father, Caleb. It was like growing up knowing you were the indirect issue of a union between the Fat Lady and Wolf Boy. It was too weird to be embarrassed by. If anything, it made me feel exotic. Just months before Grandpop's arrival, *Roots* had made broadcast history, and, like most other kids at my school, I watched the whole thing for eight nights straight. I knew my father had written a book about slavery, but I was as dumbfounded as the rest of my classmates by the barbarities the show hinted at. I was also utterly insensate to the thin membrane that separated me, by just two generations, from such bizarre abominations. Even when I was twenty-two and finally read *The Confessions of Nat Turner*, I didn't think to consider what had compelled Daddy to write it. A Connecticut Yankee come of age under Reagan, I was as untouched by the burden of history as the fresh New England snow.

In Grandpop's last months, his mind deteriorated rapidly. He recognized his family only intermittently, had a hard time following conversation, repeated himself more regularly, slept most of the day. The other curious development—one that horrified the son at the same time it inspired the writer—was his sudden and tumid bigotry.

"Get your black nigger hands off me!" Daddy wrote in a barely fictional monologue Jeff Whitehurst unleashes upon the staff at the Connecticut nursing home to which he's been consigned. "I don't want any stinking niggers messing around with me! Get your black ass out of here, God damn you!"

Like Jeff's son, Daddy was stunned and mortified by this complete inversion of his father's lifelong behavior. But when confronted by the nursing home's administration, he bristled at the notion that his father's "Southernness" was, perhaps even understandably, to blame. Just as Grandpop was stung when subjected to the generalizations of his immigrant colleagues in Newport News, Daddy was always a bit on the defensive culturally. He had tried so hard to transcend his heritage, to bust the monolithic myth of the Southern white racist, in his work and in his politics. *Nat Turner,* an attempt to humanize the issue of race by getting inside it, was the apotheosis of his father's teachings. When the book was excoriated by black people, he was both hurt and compelled to present himself more clearly. But now his father, of all people, was threatening his most cherished identity. For if Grandpop had such foulness at his core, perhaps so did we all.

Grandpop's time with us in Connecticut was short. At eighty-eight, the frail and displaced widower wasn't likely to make some kind of miraculous rebound in the cold clutches of a New England nursing home. By the time we left for the Vineyard in the summer of '78, it was clear he was fading away. My father, working feverishly on the last section of *Sophie's Choice,* came back down to visit with Grandpop in August. Finding his father on the far edge of consciousness, lit by only the faintest glimmer of life, Daddy told him he was dedicating his novel to him.

"It's in honor of you," he said.

"Wonnerfuhl. Wonnerfuhl," his father replied.

They were the last words he spoke to Daddy. Grandpop died on August 10, just shy of his ninetieth birthday. For four more months, my father labored in his grief through the final, heartrending chapters of *Sophie's Choice,* laying down the last sentence on December 17. The book was a fine achievement, one over which its dedicatee would have fairly burst with pride. It was the last novel my father was able to complete.

Twelve

The Vineyard lawn, dusk

NO MATTER HOW tense things got in Connecticut, we always had summer on the Vineyard. The end of spring promised an emotional thaw to follow the literal one, loosening our family's joints and turning the hard ground pliant and forgiving. Happiness loomed on the horizon, just a day's drive and a short ferry ride away.

Daddy usually went up first, on his own. Eager to settle in, and counting on a few weeks of solitude, he would leave Roxbury in mid-May, laying books and manuscript boxes on the backseat of his car, then pushing the dog in behind. "Goddamn it! *Move,* Aquinnah!" he'd growl, slam the doors, and be gone. Mum, who was forbidden to show up before June, eventually took off, too, suitcases stacked under a mountain of summer dresses poised on their hangers for another season's whirl of festivities. Finally, sprung from school in mid-June, we got our turn. Clutching a pillow and muzzy headed from sleep, I'd flop in the way back of our yellow Wagoneer, safe in the knowledge that Terry, who was at the wheel, had checked the "Michigan" (Michelin) tires before he drove us "chilluns" to the house in "Massatooshits." Off we'd career—*we gosts to catch that boat!*—cutting a horizontal line across Connecticut and on through Rhode Island. If Tommy was in the car, he'd have driven me to tears at least twice by the time we hit New Haven. Heel in the small of my back, he would jam me in a corner, against a gerbil cage or maybe a couple of wing nuts on a racquet press. Then he'd command me to invoke the mantra that was, for most of our years together, my daily vocal tithe to him.

"You are superior and I am an ignoramus."

"What? I can't hear you."

"I *said,* You are superior and I am an ignoramus! Ow!"

"Once more. Like you mean it."

"You . . . are . . ."—*urrgh*—"superior . . . Stop it! . . . Terry! . . . And I'm an ignoramus. . . . Get *off* me!"

Crumpled up in the margins of the way back where the dog hair gathered in thick, ruglike clumps, I could usually find some cheer in my unimpeded view of the upslung sky. With each passing hour, I watched the landscape change. Birches and maples, lone warblers, and flocks of starlings gave way as the sun rose higher to scrub oak and pitch pine, to seagulls coasting over marshland, and the gimcrack signs—TAFFY! BASKETS!—that let me know we were overtaking the Bourne Bridge. Two rotaries and twenty more minutes, past the Oceanographic Institution and the Sands of Time Motor Inn, and we were coasting down the hill to the dock at Woods Hole. Pulling into the ferry line, Terry would open the window. A wet burst of brine, the very perfume of summer, settled about the car. With a *thunk-thunk* the car loaded inside the gentle jaws of the *Islander* ferry. In forty-five minutes, we'd be home.

Just off the coast of Cape Cod, Martha's Vineyard is nearly one hundred square miles of terminal moraine ringed by majestic clay cliffs and looping stretches of fine-grain sandy beach. Roughly triangular but with a corrugated coastline, the Vineyard possesses a personality as varied as its terrain. Up-island spreads out in a quilt of hilly farmland, dense woods, and picturesque villages, a kind of Vermont tumbling to the sea. Down-island shelters a hodgepodge of towns, unique in their charms, each clad in a dominant theme—shake shingle, white clapboard, Victorian gingerbread curlicue. Once an agricultural and whaling community, the Vineyard now thrives mostly on a bustling tourist industry and the tax dollars of its wealthy summer residents. Fifteen thousand people live on Martha's Vineyard year-round. In July and August, the number swells to more than 100,000. For our family, the Vineyard has always been a kind of Shangri-la. None of us takes for granted the great fortune that is our small claim to the place. Instead we're always trying to maximize our time there, hoping to forestall reality with another week or month or year in its magical, time-bending little realm. Each of us has at some point in our lives spent the better part of a year or two straight through on the Vineyard. And all of us have sought the healing effects of daily long walks on the beach, in warmth and in bitter chill, to restore our bodies and our minds. Every spring for the last five years of my father's life, we would be in some gray hospital corridor, or makeshift outpatient situation in New York, or rehab center in Connecticut, and Mum would start musing on a plan for Daddy's resurrection. "If I can *just* get him up to the Vineyard . . . ," she'd say. There was no need to finish the sentence. Even when my siblings and I found our mother's hopefulness downright delusional, we were usually willing to line up behind her quixotic agenda. If Daddy was going to get better anywhere, it would surely be on the island we all loved so well.

And she was right. Our father was better on the Vineyard. Or maybe *we* were all better on the Vineyard, anesthetized by the sweet balm of summer so that the edges of Daddy's misery seemed less sharp, his spiral not as consistently downward. Whatever the case, even the inevitable end, when it came, could be lashed to the equanimity the Vineyard bred in us. It was one feeling we could count on and, in the absence of any organized faith, was about the only religion any of us had.

*　　*　　*

MY PARENTS MADE their first visit to Martha's Vineyard in 1957. My father's editor, Hiram Haydn, and his wife had taken a rental on the island that summer and invited my parents to stay with them. Getting off the ferry in Vineyard Haven, they immediately spied Lillian Hellman, whom they had met on their wedding day, as my mother recalled it "chasing a large poodle who'd somehow gotten off her leash." Lillian, as it turned out, had a house on the harbor. She and Dashiell Hammett wrote, drank, and entertained prodigiously during their long summer season, and encouraged my parents to find their own place somewhere nearby. By the following summer, my mother and father, with their two small girls in tow, were renters. Each year they lengthened their stay as their affection for the island grew. John and Sue Marquand were soon coming up from New York. John and Barbara Hersey were nearby, too. In the middle of writing *Set This House on Fire*, Daddy continued to work during island vacations while my mother and the children went off exploring and to the beach. It was a nice change from the relative isolation of Roxbury.

The Vineyard quickly became a treasured destination, a place where momentous things happened and bright memories were made. In August 1959, Mum was climbing the cliffs above a Chilmark beach, blithely unconcerned about her advanced (eight months) state of pregnancy, when she went into labor. My brother, laying enviable claim to native islander status, was born at the Martha's Vineyard Hospital that afternoon. Three summers later, after attending the famous state dinner for Nobel Prize winners, my parents were invited on a day cruise out of Edgartown harbor with President and Mrs. Kennedy on the *Patrick J.* My father and the president talked about *Nat Turner*, which my father had just begun writing, and smoked cigars. There was food and music and Bloody Marys and the couples forged a friendship that, though all too brief with the president himself, would continue to grow when Jackie and my parents all became homeowners on the island.

In the summer of 1964, my parents were renting a pretty yellow Victorian on Vineyard Haven harbor. In order to get to the yacht club, where the kids could swim, they had to cross a dock and seawall that bordered the property of an elderly Ohio couple named Eels. Mr. Eels, suffering from Parkinson's, could often be seen walking in slow circles around the property, aided by a white-uniformed nurse or two. The main house was modest, white clapboard with black shutters, widow's walk above and wide, breezy porch below. At the far end of the lawn sat a little foundationless cottage (built to house Mr. Eels's caregivers), and back behind the main house lay another, small outbuilding. Compared to some of the rambling captains' houses up toward West Chop, the Eels house was nothing grand. But the lawn was magic. Verdant and vast, it unfurled with a prairielike flatness, an acre and a half of velvety bluegrass practically begging to host the idylls of summer. Children needed to streak across that lawn toward the beach, the dock, the cool water beyond. Partygoers were wont to fan out at sunset, lovers to sleep beneath the stars. It was, and remains, a greensward provoking a kind of instant nostalgia, for balmy days of childhood, for romantic moonlit nights—times that, though they'd not yet occurred, would surely happen if you could just stay there long enough to plant your flag. By providence, my mother was in the Realtor's office the day Mrs. Eels called about putting the place on the market. With the consent of my father—and some financial assistance from my grandmother—she made an offer then and there. "I'd never even been inside the house," Mum told me.

It would be hard to overemphasize how joyful the Vineyard made me. Like most children vested with the privilege of summers on the beach, I got a long-lasting, mellow kind of high from the annual pelagic assault on my senses—the feel of warm sand against my cheeks; the brackish air; the view of a lighthouse's brave silhouette; ambient sounds made by boats at anchor, halyards pinkling against their masts. I loved to swim and would surf the chilly New England waters on an inflatable raft until my fingers looked like tips of white asparagus. I rarely got out of my bathing suit, never wore shoes, lived on fried food and Popsicles, and fell asleep each night to the gentle thrum of the ocean lapping our pebbled shore.

Life on the Vineyard was an outdoor arcade of activity, associations, secret pleasures and freedoms unimaginable in the winter months. But, above all else, for me it was a complete hiatus from the anxiety that dogged my every conscious moment in Roxbury. On the Vineyard, I awoke most mornings and, in nearly one fluid motion, rolled out of bed, across the lawn, and through the hedge to the yacht club. Besides the occasional sprint back home for a towel, a tennis racquet, or quarters for the soda machine, I stayed away till nightfall, engaged in every form of recreation (sanctioned and non-) I could scare up. My only other base of operation was Tashmoo Farm, where, as in Connecticut, I devoted a generous amount of time to disappearing through the thick woods on horseback. In the summer, I lived entirely outside my father's range of command. Not only did I not run afoul of him but I rarely even ran past him. Many days it was as if he'd ceased to exist as a person to whom I was even marginally obliged. He went about his business and I went about mine. I was autonomous, without rules—a condition I embraced, and would push to its practical limit when I reached adolescence.

When I was a little girl, my room was in the main house, at the top of the kitchen stairs just above what was then an unfinished laundry room and half bath. With the exposed joists providing a conduit for sound, I was able to plan whole days around overheard phone conversations, or muse on the appearance of visitors who were always plopping themselves down at the breakfast table. The south side of my room furnished me with still more useful intelligence. Peering out these windows, I could watch my father come to and go from the little shack where he worked, though I didn't really need to look. The screen door's screech-and-bang report was always as good as any scout in alerting me to my father's whereabouts. My room featured two other portals to knowledge as well, ones that, though not especially practical, made for countless adventures in voyeurism. A north-facing bedroom window offered a perfect view over the top of the outdoor shower—it was from here that Elizabeth Hackney and I once watched Frank Sinatra lathering up (his chairman of the board status far less amusing to a couple of seven-year-olds than the sight of his body parts). And, under one of the twin beds, you could peer into the downstairs bathroom through a hole in the floor, perfectly and purposely drilled just above the toilet. I couldn't then, still can't, explain that aperture. But lying with friends among the dust bunnies monitoring dinner guests' potty rituals was often as entertaining as any movie playing down at the Capawock.

Summers also meant my sisters came home. Susanna (twelve years my senior) and Polly (nine) are, with the exception of Christmas, virtually absent from my early Connecticut memories. I was two when Susanna went away to boarding school and five when Polly did the same. Both went on to college and lived in Europe for stretches of time. But the Vineyard always lured them back. Joining my brother, who ran a nightly poker game out of the living room, the girls would shack up with their extended friends in the little house and turn the joint into a hippie paradise.

Unlike the Connecticut little house, in my mind a den for lonely labor and tawdry business, the little house, or "kids' house," on the Vineyard was fun central. A crummy, makeshift building with mildew climbing up the walls and a cramped kitchen arrayed with rusty appliances, it became an indestructible hangout for a generation of islanders. My sisters, both of them sexy, down-to-earth, and clever, cast a wide social net across the island's disparate demographic. Carpenters, fishermen, waitresses, cooks. Babysitters and sailing teachers and musicians. Some were year-rounders, others seasonal kids like themselves. But pretty much everybody who was groovy passed through the little house at some time in the seventies. Splayed on the dirty couches, they rolled joints and played beer games. They coupled up. They passed out. When I was two, as legend has it, I toddled in from the driveway and spied a small black comestible on the living room table, sticky looking and delicious. "Licorice," I cooed, a hairsbreadth from popping an ounce of premium-grade hashish into my mouth when Susanna, hearing me from her bedroom, swept in for the save. When I grew older, I would insinuate myself everywhere, scooching into bed with Polly and her boyfriend, cadging shoulder rides across the lawn from one of Susanna's string of paramours, hiding in someone's oversize Army coat to sneak into the Seaview bar in Oak Bluffs. Long haired and sun kissed, my sisters and their friends were, in my mind, bottomlessly glamorous. They were also universally affectionate with me, and I relished my place as their unofficial mascot.

My sisters, it seemed to me, had a great many boyfriends. Susanna especially came home with a lot of different men over the years, most of whom I developed schoolgirl crushes on. Michael, the handsome Chilmark cop who rode me around the lawn on his motorcycle; Paul, the model and aspiring actor; David, the famous jazz saxophonist; "Sluggo," the lefty historian whom Susanna met when they were both involved in the hot-button issue of the day: the antinuclear movement. My mother was expansively welcoming to almost all the guys. Even after things went south in their relationships, my sisters' former flames often worked hard to stay connected to Mum, coming around with a flirtatious smile, hoping to stay for lunch or wangle an invitation to the beach. If they ran into my father, there would be a typical moment of awkward bumbling, Daddy looking clenched and vague, his annoyance at this interruption barely suppressed while our visitor struggled to kindle the Big Man's memory of him. *Hey, Bill! It's Bob Boyfriend! Remember I lived with your daughter in the little house for two years? I just*

*came to show Rose this story on Bosnia. . . . Oh. Sorry. Yes, I totally
understand. Let me just get out of your way here . . .*

Navigating my father's humors was difficult for almost everyone. Thinly veiled hostility toward any person interrupting his daily
flow was his de facto position in the daytime. He might wander
into the kitchen, or pass you while walking his dogs around West
Chop. But he wasn't exactly *there;* you'd be wrong to interpret his
momentary gaze as an opportunity for conversation. In the evening
hours, however, his humanity usually made a swim for the surface.
With my sisters home, we would gather for reunion dinners around
Mum's big white dining table. Pressed in among us were always a
boyfriend or two, a roommate, a friend from some far-off country
where one of the girls had been making a film or studying art or
agitating for social reform. Daddy's response to them, particularly
to my sisters' lovers, was, I always thought, both refreshingly meri-
tocratic and strangely detached. A confounding expression of both
his egalitarian spirit and his raging narcissism. The men who were
smart and engaging made a strong impression on my father. He was
glad for their company, their incisive political and literary ideas. He
encouraged them to another helping, an extra glass, a longer stay in
the relaxed and gracious environment of our Vineyard compound.
But he seemed largely incurious about anyone's essential character,
their integrity or motive. He showed no paternal protectiveness of
my sisters, no fear for their tender hearts. There weren't any pari-
etal rules at the Styron house. A wary beau would get the skinny
soon enough: you could sleep with Bill Styron's daughters as often
as you pleased, just as long as you were amusing and you didn't eat
the last drumstick in the fridge. As a young girl, I took note of the
enhanced status accrued by my sisters when they came home with
men and flopped their bags down together on a little house bed.
They were grown-ups; my father paid attention to them. I longed
to be a grown-up myself.

When I was twelve and my sisters, now fully adult, were coming
home less often, I was allowed to move across the lawn. Tommy, the

little house's Ruler for Life, accepted my presence grudgingly. At nineteen, he was handsome, enterprising, and maddeningly withholding, both emotionally and materially. During the day he and his friends trolled the island for beautiful young women; evenings he waited tables at the Ocean Club, the island's hippest restaurant. The only way I ever got his attention was when I crossed him — using his bike without permission, wearing a sweatshirt of his that I coveted. But every once in a while, he would turn his considerable charm my way — maybe pull an amusing prank on me, or invite me for a ride in his car — and slowly the gulf created by our age difference began to shrink. We discovered in each other a similarly mordant sense of humor and angled to make each other laugh, particularly at our parents' often over-the-top lives. One afternoon in the early eighties, the two of us were sitting on the little house porch when a man whom I swore was Ricardo Montalban climbed up over the seawall accompanied by Senator Kennedy. Both men wore shorts and open-necked denim shirts. The mystery man, his hair a shock of white, accessorized his look with a bandanna around his neck and a captain's hat set at a rakish angle. "Ricardo Montalban. Definitely," I insisted.

"Unhunh," said Tommy, returning to his newspaper as the two men cut across the broad lawn. Our house was Teddy's home base on the Vineyard. He would sail his boat, the *Mya*, over from the Cape often, have dinner with my parents, and spend the night. Once a summer his whole extended family sailed over with him, a veritable Hyannisport boat lift, to camp out on the lawn. Ricardo Montalban was not a far-fetched guess. After all, Rosie Grier came once and did his knitting on the beach. And Maria's boyfriend, Arnold Schwarzenegger, was always showing up in alarmingly small shorts and smoking cigars while playing touch football. Anything that amused him, which was a lot, was "too mucking fuch!"

"Ricardo's taller," said Tommy.

"You'll see," I replied with confidence as the men took a hard right and disappeared into the big house kitchen. Later that night,

Tommy made faces at me across the table while everyone but us got into their cups. The new guest, revealed as our very own senator from Connecticut, Chris Dodd, wanted to go dancing, an idea that Teddy and my parents all thought was grand.

"Come on," said Daddy, cuffing me on the shoulder. Good and tight by then, he was enjoying himself immensely. "We'll go to the Roof. You have some pull there, don't you?"

The Roof, a.k.a. the Hot Tin Roof, was the island's only nightclub, and I did indeed have some pull there. At fifteen years old, I was already a veritable HTR regular, having employed both relentless guile and my freshly minted powers of flirtation to befriend and then stun into submission most of the male staff. The tactic, which my fellow reprobate Alison Fraser and I struck on at the beginning of the summer, resulted in a quasi-VIP status of the sort only two teenage girls could get a true rush from. It also guaranteed us swift entrée so that we no longer had to suffer the frazzle-making scrutiny of our homemade and completely pathetic fake IDs. Many nights after closing, half a dozen bouncers—Howie, Dan, Reggie, Dennis, Tom, Jeff—would show up at the little house, where I'd stocked the fridge with beer from Jim's Package Store bought on my father's house charge account (another ruse designed to avoid being carded and which our family's outsize liquor bill absorbed nicely). We'd all have a few rounds, the guys in their uniform Hawaiian shirts, Alison and I in miniskirts and tight blouses. Eventually, the gang would leave, except for Jeff, whom I would lure into my bedroom and then drive insane by turning away just shy of his intended goal. In his mid-twenties, Jeff—and his mustache and his dog and his truck—was my first romantic obsession. Our relationship, always short on conversation, began under my umbrella of lies (I was eighteen, a freshman at the University of Maryland) and continued on murkily as my credibility folded. I was mad for him and would do anything but surrender my virginity to prove it. How and when he realized I was not a strangely chaste coed but rather a reckless young girl I'm not sure. He soon found other, actual women to take the edge off his desires, and I descended into a pit of hormonal mooning and jealous rages. When I went off to college and promptly got my deflowering over with, I drove up to Stowe, Vermont, where Jeff worked on ski patrol, and exacted my revenge by telling him that, after two years of waiting, he would not be my first.

"What do you say? Albert? Tom, my boy?" Daddy pressed, while the senators finished their dessert and Mum went to get a wrap.

Envisioning certain mortification, Tommy quickly bowed out. But I, though feigning embarrassment, rose to the occasion. An outing like this might, I thought, be good for my profile. Cement my status with the guys, make me more interesting, more something, to Jeff. But walking onto the porch of the club, I was suddenly uneasy. The peculiarity of my posse, and the way being with them alienated me from my new world, was reflected immediately in the bemused look on Dan's face. "Hey, Teddy! Senaddah!" shouted the patrons waiting in the deep line, eliciting amiable waves from both politicians as our group was swiftly led inside. With a sense of happy purpose, Teddy walked straight to the DJ booth. Like nearly everyone who ever knew him, I was enchanted by Senator Kennedy. At our house, he was perennially warm, vibrant, full of fun. And, unlike some of my parents' friends, he always remembered who I was. So it was with red cheeks but a willing spirit that I obeyed the senior senator when he lumbered onto the dance floor and beckoned us all to follow. "*Gloria, Gloria,*" shouted Teddy along with the music. The other dancers let us in and backed away. "Don't you think you're *FALL*in'? If everybody *WANTS* you, why isn't anybody *CALL*in'?" It took me a while to parse the energy in the room, but soon I realized the spectacle we were causing. More than what Jeff or Howie thought, I was attuned suddenly to the bizarre combination of both adoration and scorn Teddy elicited from the crowd. The nearness of his star wattage excited them. But here he was, *partying . . . up to his old tricks . . .*

get a load of him, will ya . . . Watch yer daughters! For the tourists in the room, many of whom first heard of the Vineyard as an adjunct to Chappaquiddick, it was, I'm sure, an astonishing sight. As for me, I was overcome by a confusing welter of embarrassment, defensiveness, and sorrow. The grown-up world was weird. I wished Tommy had come along.

These were my father's prime years as an American writer. After *Sophie's Choice,* his literary stock rose dramatically and he grazed upon a steady banquet of positive attention. The effect, though, at least within our family, was a kind of toxic overload. The same year as the senatorial nightclub escapade, Daddy was the subject of an hour-long documentary by a filmmaker and professor of English named Joel Foreman. I watched the film again recently, for the first time since 1982. In various locales around our house and out in the open air, Daddy talks about his life, work, and ambitions, speaking with typically arresting eloquence and humor. Now and again, his temper flares as he fiddles with something in the kitchen, or grouses at a dog to get out of his way. But although mostly genial, his entire aspect seems suffused with a kind of runaway arrogance that abrogates for me any of his more obvious appeal. Preening and slightly satyric in appearance—hooded eyes, shirts unbuttoned to the navel—he seems almost to be telegraphing his other, more private life, the one that sowed so much unhappiness among those of us who shared his day-to-day. I remember the filming of the documentary and how, at fifteen, I proudly refused to be interviewed. There is only a brief shot of me in the film, walking through the kitchen while Daddy prepares for a dinner party. Sallow complected, badly permed, I look at him, at the food, turn my nose up, and exit the frame. My father returns to his exegesis on ham.

Mum is featured in the documentary, too. It's clearly not a good time in my parents' relationship, and Mum seems unable to talk about her husband without exposing some of their trouble. She speaks with a wistfulness that, to the uninitiated, probably seems purely loving, if a touch nostalgic. Still I can't help but feel her barely suppressed pain, as if, just off camera, someone is standing on her heart. "We had very romantic beginnings in Rome and the south of Italy," she says in a quiet voice, "and our lives were very, very close." The sadness pools in Mum's aqueous hazel eyes. "As I think is true of young people, and people very much in love, we did everything together and for each other."

Watching the film again, I feel a kind of seething anger snake up from inside me. It's the most overwhelmingly negative feeling I've had about my father since he died.

Ugh, goes the voice in my head.

I forgot about THAT guy.

*   *   *

LIKE MY FATHER, I became, long ago, an itinerant island writer. For several years in my late twenties, I spent part of each winter in my parents' house working on my first novel. The book, about a troubled young woman who goes to an island in the Caribbean to attend the funeral of her childhood nanny, was, narratively speaking, pure fiction. But many of the details—warring parents, a child's secret, the hard choices of motherhood—as well as the bigger themes of forgiveness and maturity's apprehension of difficult truths, were taken from experience. This was a very lonely and confusing time in my life, and the book reflected how fragmented I felt. Shuffling around the drafty rooms in search of pockets of heat, I would write most of the day and stay up reading late into the night, absent all other life-forms save the indispensable companionship of my sweet Labrador, Wally. I was, frankly, amazed by my own discipline. After years of the mindless busyness that passes as a life for most actors, I had no idea I could be so singular in my focus, or feel so alive when I felt so alone. Not that I was particularly happy. Uncertain of where this new creative venue would take me, I only knew I was taking a terrific risk in my commitment to it. Nine years after finishing college, I was back in graduate school, looking to reinvent myself. The shadow in which I was suddenly standing did not escape my notice.

I wrote my first stories in near secrecy while I was still in Los Angeles, in 1994 and '95. They were shapeless little things. Spare and awkward as newborn colts, they overreached and under-reached, wobbled and froze, showed a flash of grace and then went splat in a tangle of poetic intentions. I didn't know how to write, but I definitely knew what good writing was, and my stories were not good. But after more than a year under the tutelage of an inci-sive teacher named Judith Taylor, who urged me to "go home and go back to school," I began to allow myself hope. Finally, I wrote a story I thought was pretty all right, and I sent it to my father. I took his long reply by fax, which began, "Dear Al, you really are a very good writer," and concluded, "More! More! Love, Daddy," as both a permission slip and a benediction. He was equally thoughtful, and gave me some excellent notes, on a second story I offered him. But the enthusiasm he showed so freely for these early efforts cooled when I announced my plans to enroll in a creative writing program. What had looked like encouragement curled up rather suddenly into something more familiar—indifference. His incurious, tight-lipped stance wounded me, even as I also sensed from him a notch of anxiety that I was pretty sure he couldn't help. I wondered if he thought I was naïve, that I'd not fully apprehended what a tough slog writing could be (I had). Or maybe he thought I expected the road to literary success to be a smooth coast, through open doors and into the arms of an admiring public (I did not). Or was he just afraid of how he'd feel, or even how it would reflect on him, if I were to publish a bunch of lousy tripe (a legitimate possibility)? I had no intention of measuring myself against him. And I certainly didn't expect our relationship to flower, after so many fallow years, into some sort of marvelous apprenticeship. I had my teachers, my fellow students, and writer friends with whom to commune. And I had my instincts, which, the longer I sat quietly with them, the more I trusted. André Gide wrote that "whoever starts out toward

the unknown must consent to venture alone." Cosseted in the low
light of those Vineyard winters, I crossed over from fear of solitude
to a kind of bleak-embracing pleasure. The words and the pages,
like yeast, began to rise. And so too did my attachment to the island.

In the spring of 1998, I finished my course work at Columbia
University's School of the Arts. For most of my two years in the
MFA program, I'd workshopped sections of the novel. During the
summer break, I left for the Vineyard, where I'd found a cheap
little rental house in Chilmark that suited my new solitary persona.
There I wrote every day, tried to teach myself the guitar, and made
a nice group of new friends who lived on the Vineyard year-round.
Sometimes in the afternoon I'd drive down to Vineyard Haven, but
after an hour or so I'd flee, patting myself on the back for having
had the good sense to extricate myself from the chaos and family mishegas. When I finished graduate school, I had roughly half
the manuscript written, but I was determined to finish the thing
completely before submitting it as my final thesis. I'd come to rely
on my teachers at Columbia. Unlike the tomfoolery of my previous school years, my approach to graduate school was purposeful
and all-embracing. Rather than being the youngest person in the
room, at Columbia I was frequently the eldest. I grew confident in
my knowledge and self-assured with my work. And I took quite
seriously the wisdom of my best teachers as well as their considerable editorial skills. So I saw no reason to graduate until they had
seen me through the entirety of my journey. Besides, I didn't have
any other consistent readers, no true mentors, no like-minded boyfriend to buck me up or egg me on. Other than Wally, and a small
apartment I'd owned for several years, I was tediously, gloomily
unattached.

In June, I went up to the Vineyard again. Buoyed by the fresh
beauty of the season, I decided to look at real estate. (My New York
apartment, bought in the bottom of the eighties market with a little
money from my mother's family, had appreciated considerably. I
could, I was told, sell it for something else and still have a bit of

money left to tide me over.) The first house I saw on the Vineyard was a dumpy seventies cape with two tiny bedrooms, a mildewed bathroom, and a giant and unsightly brick fireplace that rose, like an interior building all its own, right up the middle of the central living space. But through the leaking casement windows in the living room, I could see the place was indeed something special. An ancient stone wall rolled out in a lichen-covered ribbon down the property's western flank. Across the lawn, a great gush of blueberry bushes promised, come August, a bountiful harvest. And then I opened the door and took in a lungful of perfume being diffused by the lilac trees, which, in full bloom, were splashing violet all over the irregular acre. By the end of summer, I'd bought the house and sold my apartment in Manhattan. If I was going to be alone, I wanted to be able to see the stars and to hear the ocean.

Just as I hoped it would, the Vineyard sustained me through my strange but necessary hejira. I was letting go of old things, building anew, and the island held me tight while I worked. A year and a half later, just before Christmas of 2000, I completed the novel (marked in my journal by a sketch of a bottle of champagne and one celebratory glass) and found an enthusiastic publisher. The news, which I delivered in a delirious round of phone calls, was greeted with unfettered joy by everyone in my family—except my father. He hadn't read the manuscript in progress. As far as I knew, he didn't even know what it was about. But no matter, he was distinctly underwhelmed. As my parents alternated on two extensions in Roxbury, I noted Daddy's response ("That's wonderful, Albert," he declared anemically and soon hung up without saying goodbye). But I brushed it off, just as I'd conditioned myself to do so many times before. I was too old to let him steal my happiness.

Thirteen

Styrons and Bernsteins being merry, late seventies

IT FIGURES DADDY would come undone at Christmastime. No man ever hated that holiday more than he did. The first few weeks of December would find him in a simmering stew as my mother mounted a full-scale blitz upon the tristate area's finest shopping emporiums. Stealthy as her operation was—whisking purchases into her basement bivouac, concealing credit card bills—Daddy was on high alert for the coming invasion. *Where are you going?* he'd ask her, with bald suspicion, every time she headed for the door. *Why Danbury? What do you have to get?* Mum deflected his questions, sometimes breezily, or with an ember of irritation, her mission plan largely impervious to his obvious disapproval. With mounting spleen, Daddy monitored the growing stack of catalogs in Mum's study. The mere sight of the UPS man made his blood boil. Any excitement I felt about the Suzy Homemaker oven I asked for, the Crissy doll and the banana-seat bicycle, the new saddle and show boots, Elton John's *Don't Shoot Me I'm Only the Piano Player* and Michael Jackson's *Ben,* the Snoopy quilt and the Dr. Dentons, was cauterized by the looming, glowering pet my father was getting into. *Jesus Christ, Rose!* he would suddenly spew with evanescent rage. *What is all this shit? My GOD. You should all be shot!* (Daddy always thought everybody "should be shot" or "put away.") He'd thunder and threaten, roar and rail. And then after a while, with a slam of the door, he'd disappear.

The way Mum spent money was always a drama with my parents. A lot of it was about control, which, despite his tyranny over us, Daddy didn't really feel he had. During the course of the day, he would sometimes appear, trolling the rooms of his house for no apparent reason except to keep tabs on our whereabouts. My bedroom in the little house on the Vineyard opened directly onto the lawn. At least once a day, without knocking, he'd pass through, mumble hello, glance about the room, and keep moving. He was also an unapologetic telephone eavesdropper. Though he hated the phone, he had a perverse need to answer it, greeting callers with such astonishing rudeness that even his own friends, cowed, sometimes hung up on him. If the call was for one of us, we could be certain he would put down his extension only when the conversation grew too boring for him to bear. Hundreds of times I watched as he called to my mother *Rose! Pick up the phone!* and then stood there, receiver on his ear, registering annoyance or pleasure or mental note-taking, as if he were party to a conference call rather than Mum's private conversation. This was the way he collected raw data, on the connectivity of his territory, the patterns of the tribe, before returning to the wilderness of his study.

But no matter how much information he possessed, Daddy could not gain mastery over an independently wealthy wife. Mum spent her money with an almost aggressive willfulness, fully aware that it was her most powerful weapon against my father's efforts at domination. Even at the peak of his earning power, Daddy couldn't match my mother for net income. Not that he wished to. Daddy appreciated luxury—a great bottle of wine, a deluxe hotel room, the feel of a fancy German automobile. But he loathed wastefulness. And Christmas at our house was nothing if not wasteful. In 1966, shortly after I was born, Daddy wrote a letter to Don Harington, a writer he mentored who was living in southern Vermont. It began:

> *Dear Don,*
>   *Just a brisk brief note on Christmas Eve to wish you all a verrie merrie Xmas and all that bullshit. Our house has turned into a hideous materialistic gang-bang of a Gehenna worthy of the wildest dreams of a Byzantine Santa Claus with tons of junk, candy canes, and all sorts of obscene trash littering the premises from basement to attic. You may read in the* Putney Bugle *of all sorts of wild, demented, violent acts coming out of our Roxbury homestead. My latest ploy is just before bedtime to tell wonderful Yuletide stories to the kiddies about Santa turning at midnight into a hideous man-eating bat and the sugarplum fairies being humped by His reindeer.*

As always, Daddy could manifest his sense of humor about things on the page without ever letting his family in on the joke.

After the epic season of buying and wrapping, our actual Christmases had a familiar pattern. When I was small, we always spent Christmas Eve at Leonard and Felicia Bernstein's. In our velvets and flannels, the six of us piled in the car and drove either an hour to their country house in Fairfield or, more often, the nearly two hours to New York. The maestro, his beautiful Chilean wife, and their children, Jamie, Alexander, and Nina, lived in a grand spread in the Dakota. The night before Christmas it was tricked out in all its *Fanny and Alexander*–esque splendor. The drive would have agitated Daddy into a grim froth, but, parting ways at the door, we'd quickly forget about him for a while. Dinner tables were set up all around the apartment, and soon the amber-lit rooms grew crowded with revelers. We kids—Adam and Amanda Green, Sam Robards, Chris and Eliza Foss, the Bernsteins and their school friends, I and my siblings—would gather in our age-appropriate groups, racing through the grown-ups' legs, sitting in the corner feeling bored and awkward, or disappearing in a back room to get good and high. Late in the evening, Felicia handed out gifts to all the children. And then the entire radiant, largely Jewish crowd would gather around the piano for Christmas carols. While Lenny played and conducted with antic bravado, the grown-ups burst forth with their heartfelt and terrifically silly best. Everyone was drunk by then. But in a room peppered with some of the greatest musical talent in the world—Hal Prince, Betty Comden, Adolph Green, Stephen Sondheim, Lukas Foss, Marin Alsop—even the dopiest Yuletide songs achieved a kind of stirring majesty. By then I was usually sprawled in an overstuffed chair, pie-eyed from exhaustion, dreaming of my own bed and what Santa was on his way to bring me.

Invariably, I slept the whole drive home, stretched out across my sisters. Except for the Christmas I was five, when, nearing home, Daddy became agitated and then frightened by a fellow inebriate who was following too close to us on the dark, narrow country road. Panicking, he swerved into a driveway and ordered us all out of the car. Crowbarred from deep slumber, I was suddenly in Polly's arms as everybody clambered up a snow-massed hillside like some kind of von Trapp family nightmare. Our pursuer weaved off, oblivious to us. But by then the owner of the property we'd rushed was standing on his lawn in pajamas, pointing a shotgun at us. I promptly peed myself, which, more than the firearm, caused me to burst into tears. While my father apologetically identified himself, my sister put me, in my wet party dress, down in an ice-encrusted drift.

Of all the joys of Christmas morning, surely the greatest was that my father was never a part of it. Had he ever seen the full pageantry of my mother's runaway consumerism, I truly think he would have left us entirely or called off future Christmases with a rock-hard ultimatum. Instead, he opted out of the whole celebration. In the wee hours, after our return from the Bernsteins', he pulled the covers over his head and, as was his usual custom, didn't emerge again till well past noon. Mum passed the long night wrapping and tagging and making piles of presents all around the old living room (Christmas was not allowed in Daddy's living room). At dawn, she would go up and rest her eyes until she heard the patter of slippered feet and bounded, "amazingly fresh-faced," as Daddy described her, to greet the kids at the top of the stairs.

For hours we delighted in our bounty. Model trains, cameras, cashmere sweaters, tennis rackets, down jackets, minibikes, putt-putt cars (one year, Polly got a *real* car), jewelry, stereos, Walkmen, CD players. In later years, as we acquired spouses and gave her grandchildren, Mum's production got so out of hand the basement resembled nothing so much as the last days at B. Altman. Every member of her staff put in long hours on gift detail, working frantically and not always with clear direction until they begged off, holiday hats a-droop, to be with their own families. One Christmas, I looked up to see Polly skeptically inspecting a pair of faded, holey black leggings she found under the tree from Santa. "Pol," I called out, recognizing the garment instantly, "those are mine." The day before, after I'd gone for a jog, one of Mum's delirious workshop elves had apparently wrapped my exercise clothes, which had been drying on the overhead laundry line.

By the late eighties, my father had entered his mellow phase. Toothless now, he no longer had the capacity to frighten us. Nor did Christmas provoke in him such fury. He ate breakfast, a meal he'd rarely been awake for during his heavy drinking years. And then he'd quietly pad into the big living room, read the newspaper, and wait for his children to take a walk or make preparations for lunch with just us family. Around sunset, he'd accede to opening a present or two, which set off a stampede, everybody trying to get their gift in front of him before he lost interest or said he'd had enough. He even seemed to look forward to the Christmas party, which Mum took over after Felicia died of cancer in the mid-seventies. My father would light a fire and pour himself a glass of white wine, which was pretty much all he allowed himself anymore. Moving into the kitchen, he'd find my mother and Daphne in a cyclonic frenzy, simultaneously smiling and bickering while battling the smoke alarm and larding the food with various valve-clogging ingredients. Making mild sounds of annoyance, Daddy cleared himself a corner and began tending to his Smithfield ham. The dish, fifteen pounds of smoked, salt-cured meat sliced thin off the bone and served with biscuits and salad, was Daddy's signature fare and his one concession to Christmas ritual. Only S. Wallace Edwards hams from his native Virginia soil would do. For two days, he soaked, glazed, baked, and finally carved the ham, arranging the salty, pink flesh in sheets and pointing out the key elements of the delicacy to anyone who would listen. *You see this? You have to cut along the grain. It is essential, essential.* When guests began to arrive, Daddy turned the carving over to a son-in-law and headed back to mind the bar.

In came the Bernsteins, Lew and Jay Allen, Arthur and Inge Miller, Pete and Molly Gurney, Mia Farrow, our childhood school friends, a recent widower with his hot young girlfriend, someone unexpected—*Who brought Tom Stoppard?*—trailing a little glamour through the familiar crowd. The bigger the party, the happier my mother seemed to be. And, strangely, the more effortless she made the whole affair seem. The food came in great piles, Daphne's famous fried chicken—fought over by generations, coveted by world leaders—squeezed onto plates with heaping blobs of mashed potatoes, overcooked asparagus, Daddy's ham, salad, *leave room for the bûche de Noël!,* and, finally, Lenny would have a seat at my parents' baby grand, signaling us all to order.

Running his fingers up the keys, the maestro would turn to my mother and roll his eyes dramatically. (No matter how hard she tried, Mum could never keep our piano in tune, a failure that never caused her more misery than the day Vladimir Horowitz came to lunch and sat down for an impromptu recital.) *All right! Are we ready?* Lenny cried, fingers poised to pounce. Off we'd race through "Joy to the World" and "Hark! The Herald Angels Sing" and "Good King Wenceslas." Things went a little pear-shaped at "Jingle Bells" with Lenny twisting the song into a barnstorming Russian chastushka, followed by a not too bad "Angels We Have Heard on High," the sublime chorus wringing a maudlin sigh from even my father's existential breast. With the twelve days of Christmas portioned out for maximum zaniness—Alexander Bernstein and my tone-deaf brother's annual murdering of "five gold rings," my father's purposeful profanation of "eight maids a-milking"—we came to the end of the show with a spirited, improvisational crash.

Daddy, though perhaps a bit tipsier than we would have liked, was steadfastly jolly on those nights. Sweet, even. His eyes twinkled, the gentlemanly Tidewater drawl returned, he called you his sweetie pie, offered some younger bard his encouragement or praise. It was hard to remember then, and not worth a try, Christmases past. How the sound of him coming down the stairs signaled that our revels would soon be ended. I didn't consider anymore what strange, cloven-footed madness drove him to behold a scene— vulgar, yes, but nonetheless so innocently joyful—and take such pains to expunge it. I didn't weigh the brutal wisdom that fueled his petty despotism, the harebrained validity of his mind-set when he ordered the mountains of paper and boxes out on the lawn and torched it all upon a field of snow. I saw no point in dredging up his voice: *Who ARE you people? It is incompreHENsible this, this inSANity of materialism! I've never known such raPACiousness! It's . . . an abomiNAtion! You should all be put away!*

Indeed, for years I was swept almost clean of my girlhood memories of him and dwelt instead in a region post-anger, post-grievance. I didn't even have a beachhead on forgiveness. It seemed that in the great, swirling vortex that accompanied Daddy's first depression, my feelings about him had also been sucked into the void. Like Ebenezer Scrooge, my father had been treated to a thorough Christmastime haunting. Anything but gladness for his survival was redundant.

*   *   *

JUST AS SUMMER was about to flower, on June 11, 1985, my father turned sixty years old. A few weeks later, Mum staged a surprise party for him on our Vineyard lawn. A planeload of his oldest friends—Peter and Maria Matthiessen, Kurt Vonnegut and his wife, Jill Krementz, Gloria Jones, her daughter, Kaylie, Willie Morris, and George Plimpton—all flew up from the Easthampton airport. Bob Loomis, piloting his own plane, brought his second wife, Hilary Mills, and their new baby boy, Miles. Jill, in her role as court photographer, took dozens of pictures that day, including one of me, in a pink sundress, bringing an enormous chocolate cake to Daddy's provisional throne. It was a beautiful June day, and the pictures portray a group of happy people in successful late middle age. Everyone, including my father, looks free from care.

In truth, it had been a rotten few months for Daddy. He saw nothing good about turning sixty and had been, quietly, dreading it for some time. Then right on cue, like some cosmic joke about aging, he developed a near-allergic reaction to alcohol. The smallest sip of wine, a tumblerful of beer and he was suddenly beset, as he described it in *Darkness Visible,* by "nausea, a desperate and unpleasant wooziness, a sinking sensation and ultimately a distinct revulsion." What's more, he was having trouble with his prostate; his doctor told him he ought not to drink for a while anyway. My father never considered himself an alcoholic. But he was not so unaware as to overlook the numerous functions drinking had for so long served in his life. As he reflected, "Alcohol was an invaluable senior partner of my intellect, besides being a friend whose ministrations I sought daily." Soon, he would come to realize that drinking served another purpose. It "calmed the anxiety and incipient dread that I had hidden away for so long somewhere in the dungeons of my spirit."

But revelations were for later. "Unhelmed" by abstemiousness, he faced his work with mounting difficulty. A full fourteen years since the magazine first introduced the novel, *The Way of the Warrior*. The new conception of the novel had been coming along, in fits and starts, since 1981. But in the afterglow of *Sophie's Choice,* my father had also allowed himself to indulge in some of the less laborious distractions that his success had brought him. He'd served as the president of the jury at the Cannes Film Festival, attended François Mitterrand's inaugural celebration, taken part in festivities surrounding the film adaptation of *Sophie,* and traveled extensively giving speeches and gathering awards. In 1983, he published his first collection of nonfiction essays, *This Quiet Dust,* bringing together his thoughts on subjects as various as the South, cigarette smoking, F. Scott Fitzgerald, and the river Nile. One piece, a survey of Philip Caputo's Vietnam memoir *A Rumor of War,* originally printed in *The New York Review of Books,* gave my father a springboard to explore his own particular thematic interests. Of his fellow Marine's bracing candor, Daddy writes:

> Some of Caputo's troubled, searching meditations on the love and hate of war, on fear, and the ambivalent discord that warfare can create in the hearts of decent men, are amongst the most eloquent I have read in modern literature. And when in a blunter spirit he states, "Anyone who fought in Vietnam, if he is honest about himself, will have to admit he enjoyed the compelling attractiveness of combat," he is saying something worthy of our concern, explaining as it does—at least in part—the existence of preparatory hellholes like Quantico and Parris Island, and perhaps of war itself.

Once again, Daddy was stalking the big game. He had abandoned his Nicaragua novel, the one of which Bob had been so bluntly critical. And so perhaps he had no choice but to circle back to the subject that persisted to haunt him. The one that, above all others, he knew deep in his core. War was really just the context. It was death, and Daddy's obsessive fear of it, that he kept trying to pin down, to embrace, and, just possibly, to conquer. *All* of his books concerned themselves with suicide. At the heart of every story was a figure at the edge of the abyss, a soul dropping into the void.

"Love Day," a ten-thousand-word story that finds a terrified young Stingo on a troopship steaming toward certain death in the Pacific, appeared in *Esquire* in August. By then, everyone close to him knew something was wrong with Bill.

"I know it's tough and lonely," Willie Morris wrote to my father a few weeks after his birthday party. A fellow Southerner and friend since his days as editor of *Harper's Magazine,* Willie knew that Daddy was feeling very low. All spring he had been writing to his pal from Ole Miss, where he taught, encouraging him in his "lonesome journey." "Stick with it, Stingo," he urged in one letter, and then had "a pretty co-ed" make an addendum. "Mr. Styron," she wrote, "I am a student of WM and I feel that you are the greatest writer in the United States." Now Willie had read "Love Day." "This can't miss," he crowed, "so stick with it and we'll gather at the finish line for one damn good party, as we always have, in some honored place."

Other friends wrote, too, people who had been by to see Daddy that summer and found him more withdrawn than usual, sensed his anxiety, noticed how he fixated only on the negative. Or, if they were not Vineyarders, then they'd heard through the grapevine. "I'm just saying I miss your company," Michael Arlen wrote, tenderly, at the end of an August letter, "and because I admire the difficulty of what you do, and the substance of it, and the sense that these great books of yours don't get any easier in the forging and fashioning." Some of my parents' friends, I suspect, reached out to my father after speaking with Mum. Frightened by his behavior, she began mustering the troops on a daily basis that summer, inviting people onto the porch in a near-constant stream, to "cheer Bill up" while she flitted in and out with coffee or drinks or lunch from the yacht club snack bar. It was a program Mum implemented for Daddy's welfare and her own. Being with him was becoming an increasing challenge, particularly for someone as preternaturally optimistic as my mother. Daddy would sit, his eyes blank as lead slugs, making little pretense about his frame of mind and no effort to mask it.

"How are you, Bill?" his visitors would ask.

"Not well. I'm sick."

"Well, I'm sure you'll feel better in a few weeks."

"No, I don't think I will. I won't."

Oftentimes, he just wandered off while people were talking. After climbing the stairs with slow, deliberate steps, he would lie down on his bed and stare at the ceiling while the whole sunny day carried on outside his window.

This is my first memory of the oncoming storm, Daddy mounting the stairs to his bedroom on a brilliant August day. I was eighteen that summer and had just finished my sophomore year of college. From late June through July, Laura Sherry and I swung in a delirious loop through western Europe on a Wanderjahr that mixed just enough deprivation, alcohol, and hijinks to fulfill our teenage mission; it would be the "Best. Trip. Ever. Waaa!!" Starting in Paris, where we slept on an old schoolmate's floor, we drove badly, in a miniature car, down through Nice, Pisa, and Rome, checking in to flimsy pensiones and then scoping out the loudest and most derelict bars, where we could drink unimpeded until we fell down laughing. After Rome, we motored down the Italian coast, screaming with terror as cars raced up to and around us, got dangerously lost on the mean streets of Naples, and eventually made Ravello, which I'd been hearing about all my life and fancied the metaphoric cradle of my existence. At my mother's instructions, we mounted the stone steps of the majestic Hotel Palumbo and asked for Pasquale, the establishment's venerable padrone. My parents had stayed at the

Palumbo several times during their courtship, and it was Pasquale who had set them up with an apartment, in the Palazzo Confalone, when they returned for their long honeymoon. Several years later, he became the model for Fausto Windgasser, *Set This House on Fire*'s voluble, mercantile-minded innkeeper. The man who greeted Laura and me was, by then, well into his seventies. Snowy haired and slightly stooped, he was still as warmhearted as ever. Delivering us to the outdoor terrace for a look at the breathtaking views of the Mediterranean, he wrapped an arm around each of us, clutched a boob in either hand, and stuck his tongue deep inside my breathless throat.

A week later we arrived in Pamplona during the height of the Festival de San Fermin. With no place to stay, we contrived to "borrow" rooms from a couple of barnacled geezers who were drinking themselves into preparation for the morning's running of the bulls—this time, it was Laura's turn for a geriatric molestation. Like unchaperoned girls the world over, we were giddy and keen and always a hairsbreadth from real, true danger.

Teenage recklessness may have appeared to be my only MO in Europe. But I was also making the trip to put some space between my boyfriend and me. For a year, I had been seeing a man nine years my senior whose affection for me didn't remotely match the feelings I had for him. I was flailing around the deep end of first love; he was in up to his ankles, and even that ambivalently. Already an accomplished writer (two nonfiction books, on the masthead of a couple of magazines) with the discipline of a monk, David was not only old for me but old for him*self*. He was also a friend of both my sisters. Though this may have posed some early awkwardness for the three of them, it delighted me, signaling my first true measure of the adulthood my siblings had so long ago achieved. Our age difference was clearly an issue for David. I sometimes caught his friends, when they thought I wasn't looking, mouthing the words *How old is she?* with comic pantomime. But it wasn't our only impediment. I was a moony and emotional little package—wanting all his time, resentful of his busy life without me—and I'm sure my neediness frightened the bejeezus out of him. After a lot of tearful scenes, and letters written but never sent, it occurred to me finally to go away. It would cure either me of my fever or David of his indifference. So while he went to his family's cabin on the Bay of Fundy to work on his novel and chop wood, I went overseas to have some fun, and act my age without feeling like a fool.

My ingenious ploy worked. Flying up to Nova Scotia after I returned, I found David starved for company and suddenly ecstatic about me. In mid-August we returned to the Vineyard together. David rented a one-room shack where he could write during the day. At night, we lay in my bed in the little house and made plans for moving in together in the fall.

If my parents had an opinion about all this, I didn't know it. There was no reason for me to believe that the permissive attitude about sex they'd always shown my sisters wouldn't extend to me. Besides, regardless of his age, David was any parent's dream boyfriend. Responsible, sober, well mannered, and, big bonus in our family, a professional writer with real chops. In any case, I was fantastically happy. My parents' feelings, about me or anything else, hardly registered that summer. That they apparently had other things on their minds—dire as they might have been—only enforced my sense that David and I were in our own self-sustaining little world. Well into September, we enjoyed our practice run of playing house, largely indifferent to my father's somewhat more than usual display of moodiness playing out across the lawn.

I do remember one thing about the big house that summer— the near-constant presence of a doctor who was then our de facto family physician. A nebbishy internist whose high-class degree and general Jewishness comforted my father, the man had bottomless patience for Daddy's complaints, fears, and medical curiosity. He ate lunch on the porch with my father several times a week. Sometimes he brought his wife. But more often the two men dined à deux, the doctor attending to an hour or two of paranoid ravings in exchange for entrée into the upper echelon of Vineyard society and the confidence of the Great Man. It was obvious how much his new position pleased him. And Daddy came to count on his arrival like Miss Havisham waiting on Pip. Since his twenties, my father had kept a copy of the Merck manual at his elbow at all times. He perused it almost daily, the way a sailor checks the Tide Book, looking to identify every ague and catarrh that advanced on his horizon. It was of course a habit with catastrophic consequences for a hypochondriac. By the summer of '85, Daddy had convinced himself that he was seriously, physically ill. "My body had actually become frail," he wrote of his psychosomatic condition, "hypersensitive and somehow disjointed and clumsy, lacking normal coordination." MS, cancer, Lou Gehrig's disease. *Something* had him, of this Daddy was convinced. Insomnia stalked him every night. And so, in addition to the benefit of his companionship, the good doctor gave my father an unlimited supply of the sleeping aid Halcion.

Since the early 1990s, the potential dangers of triazolam, marketed by Upjohn under the name Halcion, have become widely known. In 1988, a Utah woman shot her elderly mother dead, citing the drug for causing her temporary madness. George Bush, Sr., implicated Halcion in several gaffes—an incoherent speech in New Hampshire, throwing up on the premier of Japan—and stopped taking it despite thinking it "the best sleeping pill in the world." Still many more people—including Daddy's friends Philip Roth, Mike Nichols, and Mike Wallace—reported experiencing profound anxiety and thoughts of suicide while taking Halcion. In 1991, Britain removed the drug, whose potency and short half-life were deemed to induce waking mania, from pharmacy shelves. The FDA, for whatever its many reasons, never did. At the time my father was prescribed Halcion, the paradoxical effects had not been made public. Daddy took Halcion all through that summer but, sensing its contribution to his general malaise, abruptly quit. With no alcohol or drugs in his system, he began to suspect that perhaps withdrawal was the culprit in his unhappiness. It was a theory promoted by several friends with a history of addiction, including the writer Eddie Bunker, who had spent his life in and out of prison and whom Daddy had championed while he was still behind bars. "The only time I was <u>really</u> depressed," Eddie wrote with sympathetic candor, "sufficient to tie some jail pajamas to a ventilator and encircle my neck—was because of withdrawal from drugs." But as his psychic pain grew more intense, Daddy rejected everyone's ministrations and sunk into a frightening despond.

That Vineyard doctor. I still see him around sometimes. It's a small island, and most of the local physicians practice out of what was until recently a shingled, one-story hospital building. I've passed him while taking my son to the pediatrician. I even called him once in a jam, when I knew I needed a course of antibiotics and couldn't reach my New York doctor. When my father was dying, path crossing was inevitable. Every person on the hospital's staff came through the tiny ward while we kept our final vigil. I feel very sorry for him. If you catch his eye, he looks at you, stricken and utterly helpless, before turning quickly and moving away. I believe it would have been his great honor to comfort my father a bit in his last days, to receive some imagined pearls of wisdom from his dying lips. But the Vineyard doctor, along with some psychiatrists at Yale and, later on, others in New York and Boston, was destined to be cast as a villain in the drama of my father's mental illness. Daddy grew increasingly mistrustful of his handlers over the years and contemptuous of their theories when he didn't feel any improvement in his state. To be sure, some of the doctors who treated my father really weren't so good. Incurious, arrogant, overzealous, misguided, careless, fawning. We encountered it all, as well as some exceptionally intelligent, thoughtful, and compassionate practitioners who made Herculean efforts to becalm Daddy's "black tempest." But all his doctors were up against the savagely ironic nature of his illness—depression's hallmark is a refusal to believe in a cure—and the lethality of his pen.

In the end it was a zero-sum game. When Daddy was well enough to write again, he implicated several of his doctors, their useless bromides and their dangerous drugs, in his inability to recover more quickly. Though he always changed their names (my father had taken the scalpel to doctors of his acquaintance before, most memorably with *In the Clap Shack*'s Dr. Glanz), they knew who they were. None of them ever came out from behind their aliases to defend themselves. Nor did they argue the point that, even upon my father's so-called recovery, he flatly refused the two forms of treatment universally acknowledged as beneficial for the maintenance of a mind inclined to melancholia: talk therapy and antidepressants. But had they revealed themselves, I have an idea what they would *like* to have said, and it's something like this: *I told you so.*

*   *   *

Friday, Dec. 13th 1985

Dear Daddy,

Mummy and I just spoke on the phone, she says you may go into the hospital within the next few days. David just looked at me with wide-eyed disbelief when I told him that I have never written you a letter. It never seemed all that surprising, but now that I think of it it's kind of a shame. I guess there's no time like the present. Who knows, with a name like yours and the name I plan to make for myself, a correspondence between you and me could be worth a lot someday.

I found this letter at Duke. It goes on, long and chatty and sequined with false cheer. I remember sitting down to write it, and that I hoped the throat-clearing first paragraph wouldn't betray how completely baffled I was by what was happening to him, and how uncomfortable it made me to talk about it. It seemed important to tell him, probably for the first time in my life, that I loved him, even though we'd probably both agree I was larding it on a bit thick. "I know there's nowhere for you to go but up," reads the penultimate paragraph, "I guess my nervousness stems from the fact that I love you so much. You have been an ogre and a grouch, but you have also been one of the kindest, most generous men, too. I think I can speak for all your offspring in saying that we wouldn't dream of having anyone but you as our father."

With hindsight and age, my Movie of the Week bathos is just embarrassing, even from a teenager. But it *was* a frightful time. All autumn Daddy had continued to lose his grip. The kaleidoscopic events—a disastrous trip to Paris to receive the Prix mondial Cino Del Duca; the meetings with "Dr. Gold" and the beginning of his psychopharmacological odyssey; the night he buried his journal in a raisin bran box, put it in the trash, and planned to blow his brains out—would be exquisitely chronicled by Daddy in *Darkness Visible* five years later. At the time, none of us could have imagined such madness was possible. In September my parents moved back to Connecticut. Wretched and panic-stricken, Daddy began suddenly clinging to my mother as if she were the last raft on the *Titanic*. He'd spent more than twenty years pushing her away. Now he wouldn't let her out of his sight. He followed her to the grocery store, the post office, from their bedroom to the kitchen. If she did manage to sneak away for an hour, a passing rain shower was enough to convince him she and her car were wrapped around a tree.

When my mother wasn't contending with her sudden role as single mother to a colicky, sixty-year-old newborn, she was backed into playing his patient confessor. Of all the demons that plagued my father in the cauldron of his depression, guilt had the longest fangs. He wept and wailed over his shortcomings, his laziness and lack of fortitude. He hadn't written enough, tried hard enough, made enough money, left a sufficient mark. The paranoid aspect of his illness drove him to obsess about all sorts of imaginary calamities—his medical bills would bankrupt us; the Roxbury house was much too small for anyone to live in; a "scandal" would emerge, and, when it did, we would all "hate" him. This last fear remained vague and never exactly bore fruit. But, in his darkest hours, Daddy did try to tell my mother the names of all the women he had slept with over the course of their marriage. (I know this secondhand, through a friend of my mother's—it's not something she would ever share with me—but she did talk freely about my father's rather unbearable "confessions" all that fall.) Though Mum's conduct through Daddy's ordeal was unimpeachable, and her devotion to him almost freakish, I believe she drew the line at that particular indulgence.

I saw my father a handful of times between the beginning of the school year and Christmas. He was all but catatonic most days, mouth frozen at a strange downward pitch, eyes like whirligigs. Following the instructions that must have come with her rose-colored glasses, Mum continued to throw dinner parties and insist that Daddy attend. *I can't, Rose,* he would protest meekly in his curiously diminishing voice. *Well, you have to,* Mum replied, firm as a sergeant, adding another leaf to the table. *Just for a little bit.* On autopilot, my father did as he was told, and soon a dozen people were in his house acting as though nothing at all was out of the ordinary. These evenings were excruciating, at least from my point of view. People would gather around the table, with Daddy at the head, where he always sat. At first, they would try to include him, solicit his opinion or tell a joke tailored to his interests. But after fifteen minutes or so, when the zombie showed no signs of cognition, the group would turn in upon itself and carry on without him. Daddy never made it through the soup without standing up and lurching for the stairs, leaving everyone to talk about him gravely through the meat course. In bed, his "fogbound horror" rarely eased, but at least he was alone with his shame.

Which is where Polly and her husband, Rob, found him on a frosty December night just before Christmas.

Polly kept a record of that night:

When I went upstairs to his room he was lying there, with his long gray hair all tangled and wild. I took his hand, which was trembling. "I'm a goner, darling," he said first thing. His eyes had a startled look, and he seemed to be not *quite there*. His cool, trembling hands kept fumbling over mine. "The agony's too great now, darling. I'm sorry. I'm a goner."

For the next hour he raved about his miserable past and his sins and the waste of his life. Everything was repeated over and over. "I love you so much. And the other children. And your mother. You'll hate me for what I'm going to do to myself. My head is exploding. I can't stand the agony anymore. It's over now. Tell the others how much I love them. I've betrayed my life. All my books have been about suicide. What a miserable waste of life. I'm dying! I'm dying!"

When Mum finally came upstairs, as he held me next to him with his eyes closed, I mouthed the word *hos-pi-tal* to her.

While he slept, Mum, Rob, and I went around the room removing pills, and then throughout the house looking for guns, if you can believe it. After we'd de-implemented the house, the three of us sat in front of the TV with our rented movie, *The King of Comedy*. We laughed and chatted and snacked until 3:00 A.M., our minds flying happily to the mundane, for rest.

The next morning I found Mum dressed and tired looking in her study by the phone. They hadn't slept at all, and the doctor had finally called early with "a bed" at Yale–New Haven. Rob and I went back upstairs to see Dad. He was devastated. Lying on his bed, staring out the window, he was sure that he would never be in his house again, nor sleep in the same bed again with his wife.

At noon, Dad got into the back of the car, asked Mum to get in the back with him, and I drove us to New Haven. We passed a Christmas ad, a huge billboard in front of some outlet or other. IT'S LATER THAN YOU THINK, it warned. *Oh great,* I thought, imagining Daddy taking in the scenery.

I can remember vividly the strange, almost surreal sensation of watching, up ahead of me, my once imposing father shuffle sadly down the sterile hallway, toward the locked door of the mental ward.

*   *   *

OUR FATHER SPENT seven weeks in the psychiatric unit at Yale–New Haven Hospital, from December 1985 to February 1986, getting decidedly worse before he got better. His voice all but disappeared, his gait slowed to a palsied shamble. The fantasies of suicide he'd harbored through much of the fall turned still more lurid—although, institutionalized as he was, he did grow resigned to the fact that that option was probably out of his hands. Meantime the hospital's doctors, like those who had come before them, quickly discovered that Daddy was a uniquely challenging patient. His hyperreactive system—hitched to his chronic hypochondriasis—seemed to be intolerant of any drug protocol; every "possible side effect" tried out its routine on him. Electroconvulsive therapy was suggested as a possible option, having proved to be a particularly efficacious treatment for unresponsive, older patients. But Daddy and Mum both feared that ECT might permanently diminish my father's intellect and rob him of his creative powers. So the idea was scuttled. As the psychiatrists continued to cycle my father through various pharmacological combinations, he teetered on the knife's edge of reality. In his first week at Yale, he got off his letter to the estate lawyer, and his good-bye note to Peter Matthiessen. Then it was Christmas, and we all went to Connecticut so we could gather around him at the hospital.

Those early visits to Yale, I would step out of the elevator and think, every time, *This is the one where I pass out.* Eventually, I became as inured to the loony bin experience as Nurse Ratched herself. But the first time I watched an attendant fish out a key to unlock the ward door, the first inspection of my bags I submitted to, my first apprehension of the plastic butter knife's nefarious potential, the first glimpse I got of the ward's gangrenous fluorescent glow, the turd-colored linoleum-and-vinyl lounge, the television with its twenty-four-hour cycle of *Search for Tomorrow* and *Knots Landing,* the bloated, acne-ridden teenagers, licking their dry lips and staring out the window, the pajama-bottomed girls disconsolate on the pay phone, the elderly women bent permanently sideways in their wheelchairs, I simply couldn't believe we'd put my father in there. Talk about depressing! How would the man ever get better in *that* place? I had a lot still to learn about mental illness.

In 1992, my father was asked to write a short piece for *Time,* part of a series on the family. Daddy, made typically bilious by the first Bush's Republican administration, felt compelled to strike a blow for everyone who didn't fit under the First Lady's moral umbrella. "None of the members of my family is a cheerleader for the values so stridently celebrated at this past summer's convention in Houston," he wrote. "But I want to describe how the rescue team they organized on Christmas Day 1985 helped ensure my survival and, perhaps paradoxically, confirmed a lovely statement made by Barbara Bush at the same event."

He described the holiday, how twelve of us barnstormed the ward that afternoon and, defying the two-visitor limit, brought in a full turkey dinner, cooked by Daphne, "complete with napkins and silver which they laid out on [his] bed." We also brought a television, and a VCR, on which Susanna could play the ten-minute film she'd made out of 8 mm home videos many of us had never seen. She set the whole thing to Daddy's favorite music, Mozart's Sinfonia Concertante. Pushing in the tape, we held our breath, fearful that her effort would elicit a reaction opposite to the one we hoped for. But it didn't. The images whirred by, lifted by the glorious music. My siblings on a fishing boat in the Bahamas; running on the beach in a private tropical cove; playing out a costumed melodrama on our lawn with my sisters in the role of court ladies and my seven-year-old brother the debonair swain; my mother, golden and ravishing; our father, a virile ham. The last flickering image was the only one of me, little more than a baby, sitting on the hall stairs, smiling lopsidedly for the gadget in my face. "How delicious it was," Daddy wrote, "in that chill and laughterless place, to hear the sound of pure hilarity, and feel appetite stir again, and perceive the first glimmer of light in the dungeon of madness."

With its polemical slant, my father's essay went on to describe the "unorthodox profile" of the gathering. "One of my daughters [me] was living in sin with her lover, who was present. Another [Susanna] daughter's stepson—he was also on hand—was born out of wedlock and had been proficiently raised by a single mother who happens to be a lesbian. A favorite godson [Daphne's nephew, whom she had taken under her care and my parents, duly anointed, had taken under theirs] was likewise illegitimate." None of us put much store in the power of prayer, my father averred. We'd all smoked pot. None of us was against homosexuality, abortion, or pornography. "'Family Values?' The phrase would make them hoot. Family, as Barbara Bush said, 'means putting your arms around each other, and being there.' This was the only consideration which had value on that day of the beginning of my own rebirth."

It was, of course, our only consideration, too.

Fourteen

Posing for the photography book Fathers and Daughters:
In Their Own Words, *1994. (I'm on the left, horsing around.
Susanna is on the right. Polly is at our father's knee.)*

WHEN I WAS four or five, I used to go in my father's closet and
take from a hanger his honorary degree hoods. Laying them out
on my parents' bed, I'd rub the silk and velvet along my cheek,
hold them to the light, and size the colors up against one another.
Goldenrod, crimson, azure, emerald. Grabbing at the cowls and li-
ripipes, turning the garments this way and that, I was forever trying
to figure out how they went on the head. Sometimes I wandered
downstairs in one, looking like a very small Obi-Wan Kenobi. My
father didn't seem to mind in the slightest. Though he was often
gratified by awards, he didn't fetishize them. Rather, he took the
piss out of his prizes by displaying most of them in the downstairs
bathroom.

Still, I grew up in a Swiftian dimension. The adults in my world were not just good at what they did but brilliant, and famous for it. Prodigious dramas were to be expected, the collateral effects of an outsize life. When I was old enough to consider what I wished for myself, I found I was genuinely terrified by the idea of obscurity. It wasn't so much that I worried my parents would think less of me, although like most children I did want to shine for their approval. I was afraid I would dematerialize—I would be *nothing*—if I didn't make the transition from the child of "someone" to "someone" in my own right. Which probably has a lot to do with my misguided years as a struggling actress.

At twelve, I was cast in my first school play—Mrs. Ralph Waldo Emerson in *The Night Thoreau Spent in Jail.* The show, mounted on the platform in study hall, was a boffo success, and I was singled out for my precocious stage presence. A couple more solid performances—Grandma in Edward Albee's *The Sandbox,* Kathy (the serious one) in *Vanities*—and I achieved real distinction. My grades were in the crapper, but never mind. I was now the Dame Ellen Terry of eighth grade. Like thousands of other theatrical kids (the casting offices of New York and Los Angeles are lousy with former elementary school stars), I was certain glory was my inevitable path.

For the next fifteen years, acting was central to my persona, even when it wasn't always close to my heart. I hoped performing would be my route to immortality. Perhaps more important, I was relying on it being my ticket to the grown-ups' table. I certainly wasn't qualified for anything else. Writing, in particular, was off the table, my father having set a rather unappealing example of what could be expected day to day. And though I may have been illiterate, I was not stupid. The bar, I knew, had been set well beyond my reach.

With my mind on stardom, it's no wonder *Sophie's Choice,* the film, gave me such a thrill. The premiere was held in December 1982, at Cinema 1 and 2 in Manhattan. I was sixteen and arrived with my parents by limousine wearing a bloodred silk dress and high heels. After the long, starry night, it was more clear than ever that an actress's life was the one for me. I saw the movie another half a dozen times within the first year alone, mesmerized by the performances and moved to tears over and over again by the story's tragic beauty. One weekend, on furlough from boarding school and in New York, I went with four or five friends to an afternoon showing. In front of us a woman sat alone, weeping quietly during the film's most wrenching scene and then openly sobbing as the show ended and the credits rolled. When the houselights came up, one of my schoolmates reached over, tapped the woman on the shoulder, and pointed at me. "Her father wrote that," he said. "He wrote the book." I blushed madly as the woman wiped her eyes and looked at me with astonishment. But the truth was I couldn't have been more proud if I'd written the book myself.

I had a favorite scene. It comes up about a half hour in, when Nathan (Kevin Kline), at a manic zenith, leads Stingo (Peter Mac-Nicol) and Sophie (Meryl Streep) on a giddy night of carousing. They are celebrating Stingo's first novel, the early section of which Nathan has just finished and declared "the most exciting hundred pages by an unknown writer anyone's ever read." The three end up on the Brooklyn Bridge, and Nathan, champagne glass in hand, climbs a light pole. Evoking the borough's great poets, Whitman and Crane, he spins an exultant encomium for his new friend. Standing below with Sophie, the young writer gazes on in admiring, flattered wonder. Finally, Nathan lifts his glass and shouts to the heavens, *"TO STIINGOOO!"*

Marvin Hamlisch's bittersweet theme music swells in a grand crescendo. The camera, shooting presumably from a helicopter, zooms back, taking in the span of John Roebling's noble creation. The lights of the bridge glitter, as does the East River, and the great promising city on the other side. I wouldn't have admitted it then, but that moment always swept me away. I was just about crushed by filial pride. It exhilarates me still, though now it also breaks my heart.

I'm not sure whether my lack of seriousness led me to acting or my pursuit of an acting career made me less serious. Either way, I wasted a lot of time and tuition money chasing my vague fantasy of stardom. This is, of course, not to say that acting is an ignoble profession. Only that I was pretty undisciplined in my approach to it. I majored in theater at Barnard, executing all the requisite obligations such a course of study entailed—costume apprenticeships and scenic design studies, dramaturgical explorations of Shakespeare, Movement for Actors, The Greek Tragedies in a Modern Perspective. I took extracurricular workshops with the late, legendary acting teacher Herbert Berghof at his eponymous HB Studio in the West Village. And, for my senior thesis, I worked for many months with Herbert's help to adapt a Stefan Zweig story into a one-woman show. But, for the most part, my highfalutin ideals were just a lot of talk. I was a starry-eyed flibbertigibbet masquerading as a thespian with a passion for greasepaint and the Bard. After college, when I might have gone to a conservatory like Juilliard, or sought an internship with some hallowed and far-flung repertory company, I hung around New York and hoped to get lucky. I didn't hone my skills, didn't work on my voice or practice the Alexander Technique. Instead I went the hack route: auditioning for little projects advertised in *Back Stage,* blindly sending my head shot to every agent listed in the Ross Reports, taking a scene study class at HB and calling it "working on my art."

HB was, coincidentally, where my father's mistress worked. I discovered this one day when I went up to the office to try to gain entry into a class that was already closed. As I stood by the door explaining my tardy application to the young receptionist, a handsome gray-haired woman walked behind the desk carrying a sheaf of papers. Locking eyes with me for just a moment, she stopped and looked down at the front desk. "It's okay," she told the girl, brusquely, "just let her in the class. I'll sign off on it." And then she walked away.

I froze. For the one second this woman and I had looked upon each other, my life seemed suddenly so much more *dramatic* than anything that ever occurred in acting class. *What should I do?* I wondered. Pull myself up to my full height and stride into her of-fice (Herbert *had* once accused me of behaving like Tallulah Bank-head)? Throw a glass of water in her face, maybe? Tell her to stay away from my family? But then, she looked so *old.* And so . . . what was it? Contrite. Or just sad. Maybe she didn't even speak to Daddy anymore. And really, at twenty, what did it matter to me?

I'd known who she was for several years. One day, when I was in my early teens, I went looking for something in my mother's bedside table. Aspirin, maybe, or a pencil to take a phone message. The drawer I riffled around in was full of stuff, and soon my nosi-ness got the better of me. Toward the bottom, I found a letter that unfolded with the stiffness of paper long forgotten. "Dear Bill," the salutation read, in my mother's rounded hand. I knew in an instant what kind of letter it would be, just as I knew from where I found it that it was a letter never sent. I remember a wave of nausea rolling through me, but I kept on reading. Mum, as it turned out, knew all about my father's infidelities. She knew more than I did; she even had a name. Daddy's lover was a relative, by marriage, of a close family friend. She'd been to our house—*had been my mother's guest*—many times. *Shit,* I said to myself as the pieces began to fall together. The car by the little house door. A certain timbre of voice, carrying across the still night air. The cut of her hair. Larry, the gardener, in the kitchen, complaining to one of my babysitters, *Mr. Styron had me go over there and fix that lady's stereo. It made me goddamn mad, I tell you.* Here I was, all this time, thinking I had a secret! I couldn't have been more shocked if I'd found out I'd been born to a pack of wolves. And yet, this information did nothing to liberate me. If anything, it only made me more confused. My mother's letter was heavy with hurt and betrayal. But it was also forthrightly romantic. Once again, I realized I had no idea what adults were on about.

I didn't say anything that day at HB, or any other day for that matter. Honest confrontation was not a part of my family's skill set. But in that silent communion, the last remnants of a childish wish dissolved. In the same way I'd once maintained my belief, against all evidence to the contrary, that Santa Claus did exist, I'd long persevered in a fantasy that she did not. Now I felt myself shedding another layer of girlhood skin.

In 1987, after four years together, David and I broke up. Alone and, at twenty-one, suddenly on the bridge of true adulthood, I did what everyone else I knew was doing. I went into therapy. For three or four years, I poked around under the hood, pulling out parts and examining them until it felt like everything was laid out around the cold floor. The only problem was I wasn't sure how to put it all together again. Working at a series of part-time jobs—receptionist, personal trainer, SAT tutor, Dukakis campaign volunteer—I sought to leave myself free for "real" acting jobs, which I rarely managed to land. Young and feeling increasingly lost, I was very vulnerable to the psychoanalytic (I talked a lot, the doctor almost not at all) experience. Three mornings a week, I took a cab from my apartment on the Upper West Side across the park to her office. And then I walked home, not wanting even the taxi drivers to see my shuddering tears. Funnily enough, it was on these walks that I kept running into acquaintances who just had to tell me how *Darkness Visible* had changed their lives.

*   *   *

MY FATHER'S EMERGENCE from depression in the winter of '86 was not only miraculous but suffused with grace. Like Scrooge, Daddy had beheld his unreconstructed self and had recoiled in horror. Too late, he had surveyed the beauty of his life, neglected and abused, and watched helplessly as all of it slipped from his grasp. Regretful and despairing, he'd begged for forgiveness and, to his astonishment, received it. Awakening from his nightmare, Daddy found the world much as he'd left it—interested in him, tolerant of his foibles, open to his interpretations, fertile, keen. Grateful, he clutched the fresh chance to his breast. First, he rediscovered his wife. In the months and years that followed Daddy's near-death experience, my parents grew closer than they had been in a very long time. They were unrecognizable, really. My father, gentle and chastened, while Mum suddenly emerged with a sassiness that I could scarcely believe. If my father misbehaved—was short with her or overly demanding—she adamantly and uncharacteristically stood her ground. *I will not,* she'd snap. Or *Just wait a minute, Bill! I'm doing something else!* My Pavlovian response was to cringe, and prepare for my father to start bellowing. But he never did. Their stormy years seemed to be over. Equality came to reign, and with it a measure of calm descended about their union.

For the first time in his life, my father set out to write about himself in an honest and intimate way. He had, in years past, composed many thoughtful essays that relied on the mortar of personal experience for their essential integrity. In "A Voice from the South," for one, Daddy wrote about the bewildering "vanishing act" he witnessed daily as a child, when the Negroes of Newport News—shipyard workers, maids, janitors—returned to their "baleful ghetto" and the nighttime streets became the sole province of Caucasians, "not a single black soul in sight." My father's curiosity about, and discomfort with, what he called "Virginia apartheid" led to some strong opinions about the South and informed much of his most important work. Mining a similar vein, Daddy wrote a series of pieces over the course of twenty years about Benjamin Reid, a young black man sentenced in 1962 to Connecticut's death row for the robbery and murder of a middle-aged woman who was a friend of his mother's. A victim, my father believed, of "foster homes and deprivation" as well as a racist judicial system, Reid and his cause became a minicrusade for my father. His involvement in the case contributed to an eventual commutation of Reid's sentence as well as the alteration of Connecticut's capital punishment laws. In 1970, Reid was scheduled for parole. Pleased with evidence of the man's rehabilitation, my father offered to let him live in our little house while he got on his feet. But just days before his scheduled release,

Reid walked off work detail and escaped into the woods. After crossing the border into Longmeadow, Massachusetts, he broke off a car antenna and sharpened it into a weapon. Then he entered a nearby house, abducted a thirty-seven-year-old woman who was just then preparing breakfast for her children, made her drive to an empty parking area, and raped her. Quickly apprehended, Reid was returned to prison and sentenced to another twelve years.

In 1982, my father reflected on the Reid affair, sifting through his regret and horror: "In my grimmest imaginings I could not help thinking that he might have raped my daughter instead of the Longmeadow housewife." But he refused to feel guilty. He'd been motivated, he said, by deeply ingrained Presbyterian principles that, after years of being "swept by the bleak winds of existentialism," even he was surprised by. With empathy, Daddy also drew an analogy between his own experience and the then recent, and more famous, drama involving Norman Mailer and his protégé Jack Henry Abbott. Abbott was serving an extended sentence for murder and robbery when he struck up a correspondence with Norman, who then assisted in the publication of his prison memoir, *In the Belly of the Beast.* But six weeks after Norman helped him obtain an early release, Abbott killed a twenty-two-year-old aspiring playwright who was, at the time, helping out in his father's bar. Daddy's public support for Norman elicited a grateful letter from his estranged friend and, afterward, a long overdue rapprochement.

Still, before 1985, my father's self-portraits were mostly told with a long lens, observer's stories in which he is secondary to the main show. Like Stingo, like Lieutenant Culver, like Peter Leverett, my father was always reporting from the front lines on someone else's tragedy. After his hospitalization, he was at last ready to write about his own.

Six months after his release from Yale–New Haven Hospital, he wrote "A Tidewater Morning." It is a tender, and quietly devastating, evocation of a mother's last days. The narrator, thirteen-year-old Paul Whitehurst, and his father, Jeff, struggle with despair and anger while in the distance rumbles a war that, like their impending loss, they are helpless to stem. The writing came forth more naturally than any fiction Daddy had produced in years. For a time he considered expanding the story into a novel, and so it was here that he first began to explore Grandpop's romance with Eunice Edmundson. Still, the wound of his depression suppurated, no longer painful but relatively fresh. Perhaps recognizing a more immediate need to heal, he turned his attention to recent affairs.

For several months, my father worked on a fictionalized version of the events leading to his breakdown. Maybe because he was too close to it still, or because he couldn't wrest from the details a thematic whole, the idea just didn't gel. Like several of his later, unfinished novels, the hundred or so pages include a lot of circular, if erudite, pathways. By the time he returns to the plot, he seems to have lost the keys to his narrative engine, or the thing just doesn't want to turn over. I don't know how invested he was in this endeavor. As always, my father's work, particularly fiction, was out of bounds for conversation. He did, however, show his willingness to be public on the subject of depression when, on November 27, 1988, he wrote an op-ed piece for the *Times* entitled "Why Primo Levi Need Not Have Died."

It had been seven months since the eminent Holocaust survivor threw himself down the stairwell of his apartment building in Turin. *The New York Times,* covering a posthumous conference on his life and work, quoted several speakers expressing their surprise that a man of such irrepressible spirit would, after all he'd been through, take his own life. My father pounced on this logic. "The vast majority of those who do away with themselves," Daddy argued, "do not do it because of any frailty, and rarely out of impulse, but because they are in the grip of an illness that causes almost unimaginable pain." My father then confessed to his own near-suicidal episode. He lamented the stigma attached to depression, urging a better understanding of the disease so that sufferers like Levi might be rescued from the wilderness of their ordeal. The op-ed drew a strong response, and led to an invitation to address the American Suicide Foundation at Johns Hopkins. In the audience on the day of my father's lecture was the then editor in chief of *Vanity Fair*, Tina Brown. She approached Daddy immediately and asked him to expand on what he'd written for the magazine.

Every once in a while, a writer touches on a truth that, somehow, has not yet been expressed. Like a magic trick, his ink reveals a panel of human experience felt everywhere but, until illuminated by the writer, never before truly *seen*. Such was the case with *Darkness Visible*. The fifteen-thousand-word essay, which appeared in the December 1989 issue of *Vanity Fair*, was explosive. The slim book, an expansion of the magazine piece published by Random House the following year, rose to the top of the *Times* bestseller list. Grateful responses, pouring in from scores of readers, stunned my father. And though he was very pleased, he was also totally unprepared for his new role. Having written for forty years on man's inhumanity to man, Daddy found himself now the preeminent portraitist of the self-inflicted savagery that was his particular type of mental illness. That he "came forth" — as he quoted Dante — "and once again beheld the stars" offered tremendous hope to fellow sufferers and their families. His insight and powers of articulation gave the mental health community valuable new clues to understand the disease. Suddenly he was in demand at every psychiatric symposium and suicide awareness event the world over. And the mail came in torrents.

"Dear Mr. Styron," wrote a woman from Lenox, Massachusetts,

> *I read your article in* Vanity Fair *last year and I have just watched your interview with Diane Sawyer. I knew the answers to many of her questions before you gave them because I watched my son go through the dark four years ago.*
>
> *In the summer of 1988, when he was feeling well, P— — wrote the following:*

A force unfamiliar to me
Drives a boy to flail the air.
Two clouded eyes must stop to see
A crumbled boy who wants not to care.

On the 25th of January 1989, he jumped to his death
after a night alone in a hotel room. No alcohol or drugs were
involved . . .

Daddy received hundreds and hundreds of letters from people who endured the agony of depression and from the family members who suffered along with them. Some, like my father, had come through the storm. Others had not been so fortunate and, like the young poet, left survivors reaching out blindly in their grief. Still more correspondents were deep inside the struggle, or thoroughly unhinged by some concurrent mental disturbance. Their letters were electric with madness. As always, Daddy responded to almost everyone who wrote him. Meantime, he tried to get on with his life.

This era, the mid-nineties, would turn out to be the autumn of my father's creative journey. The broken branches that remain as evidence of his last work continue to confound me. There is the folder at Duke marked "Grandfather." If Jim West's recollection is correct, it reflects my father's next effort, a brief attempt to make fiction of the Confederate messenger boy turned steamboat captain turned tobacco entrepreneur Alpheus Whitehurst Styron. Daddy had grown up hearing about his grandfather's adventures and trials from his own father. The picture Grandpop painted was of a man of unfulfilled promise, a portrait that matched Grandpop's own—and no doubt struck a personal chord for Daddy, too. Paragraph for paragraph, the "Grandfather" stuff is an engrossing read. But none of it is in order. And though the page count is no more than 50, the handwritten numbers bafflingly go up to 228.

After that dead end, Daddy returned to the subject of his

own father. The story this time is situated in Connecticut, during Grandpop/Jefferson Whitehurst's last year. Jeff is a displaced soul, marooned like the Arctic explorers he's always been fascinated by, on a cold and unforgiving outpost, waiting to die. The narrator, a middle-aged Paul Whitehurst, is, as usual, a thinly veiled version of the writer himself. Using as a device the archival material Grandpop left in our basement, Daddy delves into family history as a way of getting at his father's character. He is also, I think, trying to plumb the tragic, conflicted personality of his entire native region, both its great civic pride and its discomfiting and woebegone shame. In the manuscript, Paul is forced to come to terms with the deeply buried racism his father suddenly unveiled in his senility. While it bewilders Paul, it also inspires a meditation on the tangled roots from whence both men sprung.

Finally, though, my father is looking squarely at himself. His decision to consign Grandpop to a nursing home in his final days haunted my father. Longer than anyone, and with unflinching consistency, "Pop" had adored and admired him, offered his support and his faith. He sacrificed endlessly for his son, but Daddy couldn't do the same in return. And it tormented him. Paul White-hurst describes his visits to the "High Ridge Care Center," delayed often by his own dread, and his father's invariable reaction.

"Where have you been?" he'd say with unmeant reproach, which scarcely bothered me, pleased as I was at this particle of happiness, so cheaply bestowed by a son riddled with guilt. Each visit I would hope for some improvement—foolish notion. There is no sunshine in the forecast for the country of the very old. And so I'd wheel him into the elevator and out to my car, boiling with rage at his helplessness—rage that I sometimes realized, appallingly, was really a secret wish for him to get it over with and die. I say that now, long after he is gone, with a shiver. Eskimos may harbor such thoughts but not college graduates in the low latitudes.

This is a fitting confession. My father could not abide suffering, not his own or anyone else's. His intolerance was no doubt a side effect of his youth, a kind of post-traumatic stress disorder caused by watching his mother slowly die. In his later years, Daddy had a black Lab named Dinah, who was afflicted with a mysterious and unbearable skin condition. For hours at a time, Dinah would rub herself along the floor in a desperate bid to scratch her full-body itch. The hair around her eyes disappeared from constant rubbing; her paws became deformed in the places where she was forever biting at them. The poor thing was just miserable, and Daddy adored her. But much like Salamano, Meursault's dolorous neighbor in *The Stranger,* Daddy was driven to distraction by his mangy mutt's humping and snorfing, by the constant reminder of her terminal pain.

"*Dinah!*" he'd shout, and then for extra measure give her sore, bald hindquarters a swift, sure-footed kick. "Cut it out now!"

Thus reproved, Dinah would throw a backward glance, a true hangdog expression in her rheumy eyes, and then hobble off to another room where she could molest herself in peace. It was when Dinah died, followed quickly thereafter by his retriever Tashmoo, that my father began his precipitous slide into oblivion.

* * *

IN 1993, I gave up on New York City and decided to move to Los Angeles. I was in my mid-twenties, and the time had come for me to admit things were not going the way I planned. I was a decent actress. Competent. On occasion, very good. And over time, I tried hard to be better. But the armor I'd successfully constructed against the chaos of my childhood had made me too tough for the delicate business of real acting. Psychiatry had cut a few notches in my carapace, but I just wasn't willing—or able—to be properly vulnerable. I didn't know that yet when I was twenty-six, so I went out west, where I hoped my seeming bad luck would change. It didn't, or certainly not as I expected it to.

Untethered in the alien moonscape of L.A., I completely lost track of who I was. I spent my days driving through that gussied-up desert, hopeful and anxious, to audition for sitcoms, or waited glumly for my third-rate agent to call me with an appointment. In the evenings, I went to bars or parties, chatting up guys with development deals or "go" movies in which there *might just be a role for me.* What little work I did secure was so frightfully stupid—a nurse on an episode of *Models Inc.,* a ruthless casting agent on *Red Shoe Diaries*—I couldn't mask my contempt no matter how I tried. In truth, I was also downright afraid. Some days, the smog that had been obscuring the horizon would lift and I could see quite clearly that somewhere I'd taken a very wrong turn. After I had utterly wasted my school years, now it was apparent I'd never amount to anything. Still, not content with having shot myself in one foot, I aimed for the other, entering a romance that showcased my genius during that time for complete self-destruction. Two years in, I was whiplashed by heartache. But what truly made my blood run cold was realizing I had absolutely *no direction* in my life. Quietly, just to affix my scrambled self on comfortingly straight lines of paper, I began to write.

There was always, I suppose, a fine line between tacit support and complete indifference where my father was concerned, but I tend to think fondly on the way Daddy was with me in those years. He never questioned my decision to be an actress, never ran down my choices, or suggested I find a more promising line of work. (No one knew better than he the value of a parent's forbearance, or the importance of faith past the point when it might seem prudent or even reasonable.) Like my siblings, I was at last an adult, and he treated me like one. I still opened wine bottles for him, but now we drank from them together. We also both read the newspaper closely, and talked during family dinners on subjects that mattered in the world. He solicited my opinion, but I think he counted on me more to bring a little levity to the proceedings. I did my best to discharge my duties—each child has her role in a family—even when my outlook didn't lend itself to easy patter. Unlike Dinah the dog, I knew better than to expose him to my raw and inconsolable underside.

An equally dark sense of humor would, as ever, be our glue. It was why my father liked me and, very often, the only thing I liked about him. His outrageousness was not for everyone, but it delighted me and he knew it. Which is why, while I was out west, Daddy began sending me his nuttiest *Darkness Visible* mail, stuff he simply couldn't keep to himself.

Some letters he put in an envelope without annotation, like the one from the Grand Rapids man making a claim against Daddy for $15.95 plus tax because the book was, in his opinion, a "rip off." "You couldn't even hold Billy Faulkner's coat," he charged, and suggested my father retitle the book "Philosophical Wimp Made Visible." Or the one from a Florida inmate who probably expected a more enlightened reaction when she asked my father for an autographed photo, made out to "Trisha" but returned to "Dennis," the legal and pretranssexual name under which she was imprisoned. There was the guy from Napa who believed my father—and everyone suffering with AIDS, cancer, or schizophrenia—was being controlled by masers. And the lady from San Francisco who doodled all over her letter random thoughts on "Planetary and personal Perestroika" as well as "global and galactic Glasnost."

And then there were the correspondents who brought out my father's blackest humor, people for whom things were so goddamn awful they gave him the literary equivalent of church laughter. He once sent me a letter from an Ontario woman, married to an admirer whose life had recently taken a turn for the Jobean. After watching helplessly as his mother died of a massive stroke, wrote the woman, her husband had plunged into crippling agoraphobia and depression, had lost his job, and become a virtual shut-in. "Could you send H—— an autograph?" she wished to know. And then she apologized for not including a self-addressed, stamped envelope. "I do not get paid until the 27th," she said. Under her signature, my father scribbled a note to me, saying he'd written back advising the wife she should tell her "stupid husband" to "stop sniveling and face up to life like a <u>man</u>, for Christ sake! I sent up to Canada my autograph for — — — along with the message: <u>Pull up your socks, Creepo!!</u>"

One could hardly blame my father. It was such a grim business, all that mail, a little naughtiness felt like a perfectly acceptable outlet. I pinned a few of the missives to my bulletin board, for laughs, safe in the knowledge—as Daddy seemed to be—that his own days of madness were in the past.

Summers were still times for family reunion. These being the Clinton years, the social scene on the Vineyard was often at a fever pitch. Even Daddy, in all his misanthropy, could not help being swept up by it. Nor, frankly, could I. In the summer of '96, shortly after I'd written my first short stories, my parents invited for a visit the only one of their illustrious friends who ever tongue-tied me, Gabriel García Márquez. Carlos Fuentes, a close friend of both Gabo and Daddy's, came too, with his wife, Sylvia. The timing was hardly happenstance; President Clinton and his family were vacationing on-island, and the writers had a plan to press him on the Cuba issue. After an enormous and impromptu cocktail party on our porch (Mum had cheerfully acquiesced to every lookie-lou in the neighborhood), a dozen of my parents' Latin affairs–minded friends took their seats in the dining room (everyone under forty was consigned to a "children's table" in the living room). Gabo tried to spearhead a discussion on the embargo, but Clinton, a voracious reader, wanted to talk about books. The night went late and turned into an elaborate cultural push me–pull you: the writers parsing UN resolutions and Castro's syntax, the politician reciting Benjy's monologue from *The Sound and the Fury*. As for me, I was alternately transfixed by the Marine in the little house kitchen eating fried chicken with the nuclear "football" at his side and the master of magical realism whose books I adored. Without any Spanish, I was destined that weekend to exchange only a few polite words with Gabo and his translator. But I do have a photo, on the bulletin board just above my computer, of me practically sitting in his lap, grinning like a doofus.

It might have appeared, to the untrained eye, that my father was coasting rather serenely into old age. Enjoying his current popularity, he published a good deal of nonfiction after *Darkness Visible.* There were several essays for *The New Yorker* and *The New York Review of Books,* a piece for *Newsweek* on the death of Vince Foster, a remembrance of a racially tinged childhood incident for *Time,* a piece on JFK for *Cigar Aficionado.* He eulogized Mitterrand for *Le Monde* (the Légion d'Honneur was one of Daddy's proudest honors) and memorialized other friends—Irwin Shaw, James Baldwin, Red Warren, Abbie Hoffman—in more intimate settings. It was during this time that I remember him saying, "You know, anyone who writes a couple of first-rate novels in his lifetime has done all that can be expected of him."

Too bad he hadn't convinced himself. A new idea, or an old idea with new meaning, now seized my father's imagination. The bomb, he decided, had saved his life. Passionately, and with a touch of almost real-time exhilaration, he started talking about this idea: the atomic bomb, which issued a death sentence to more than 200,000 Japanese civilians at Hiroshima and Nagasaki, simultaneously granted clemency to a generation of American boys. Like millions of other people, Daddy had been horrified and frightened by the bomb's impact. But forty-five years on, he was embracing the ugly episode with unconcealed fervor. His line of thinking was provocative. And it was also true. I don't know if he recognized the metaphors, how cheating death at twenty mirrored cheating death at sixty, the way depression had exploded his life and saved it, too. But I'm certain that in the tragic irony he articulated was a theme he thought worthy, at last, of a war novel's grand dimensions.

What survives from Daddy's last stab at *The Way of the Warrior,* his magnetic and elusive white whale, is a story called "My Father's

House." It can be found in the posthumous fiction collection Bob Loomis put together, *The Suicide Run*. The piece, set in August of '46, brings Paul Whitehurst home to the Tidewater after several months of postwar schooling. Still reeling from his experience on Saipan, and his astonishing deliverance from certain death on the Japanese mainland, he endeavors to settle into civilian life. When not coming up against his termagant of a stepmother, Paul disappears into reading, specifically that week's *New Yorker* magazine, devoted entirely to John Hersey's epic war chronicle *Hiroshima*. The story then winds back to the Pacific and Paul's all-encompassing dread of what's to come. In his barracks one night, he is plunged into a ghoulish nightmare. He awakes, pooled in sweat, and busies his mind with a recurring fantasy of going AWOL. But for the tropical flora, it's not hard to imagine the suicidal writer himself on a frosty and more recent Connecticut evening, craving a similar release. My father writes: "The thought of the coming night filled my mind like an ecstatic heartbeat. What night it would be I didn't know, only that there would be such a night for certain, and soon—the night when at last I stole out of the tent into the cricketing darkness, and there amid the hibiscus and flame trees destroyed my fear forever."

Fifteen

My father, circa 2000

DADDY WANTED ELECTROSHOCK, and he wanted it quick. It was the spring of 2000, and there would be no talk therapy or adventures in psychopharmacology this time around. No Ludiomil. No MAO inhibitors, with the frantic signs taped on the fridge reminding him what he couldn't eat. He wasn't going to stand by while Mum consulted with shrinks at the National Institutes of Mental Health and the American Foundation for Suicide Prevention, or conferenced with experts on depression like Kay Jamison and Peter Whybrow. He couldn't endure the weeks of waiting for some other antidepressant to take effect, or the additional months when that drug failed and the doctors tried others . . . and then they tried some more. He'd be dead by then. He was going to have ECT, and fuck the consequences.

With remarkable symmetry, my father succumbed to his second major depression exactly fifteen years after his first breakdown. Both of his dogs had died recently, the old neck injury was causing trouble with his writing hand, and he was just about to turn seventy-five. As for what was going on in his sanctum sanctorum, who knows? Not six months before, Daddy had given an interview in *The Boston Globe Magazine*. Affecting a style more Hemingwayesque than Styronesque, the journalist wrote: "William Styron lives. So many of his contemporaries are gone. There is luck and glory in mere survival. He's writing again, heaving another book out of his seventy-four-year-old soul, something about World War II and the atomic bomb and his own butt possibly being saved because of that savage piece of metal. He doesn't promise but he thinks he'll have the new book finished by year's end."

This thing Daddy told Bob about confidence . . . You can't really write without confidence. And somewhere along the line, my father lost his confidence entirely. The new year had come and gone; the manuscript was upstairs, gathering dust.

It all happened pretty quickly this time. He'd been fine through the winter, capping the season in Cuba on a "cultural tour" with my mother, Arthur and Inge Miller, Bill and Wendy Luers, Mort and Linda Janklow, and Patty Cisneros. García Márquez was there as well, and the group had been treated to several unexpected meals with a voluble, and seemingly indefatigable, Fidel Castro. Daddy came home in good spirits, ready for the long Connecticut winter to come to an end. Soon Mum's daffodils were rioting all over the lawn and Daddy's favorite road at Judds Bridge was clear again for walking. But then Dinah had to be put down, and Tashmoo followed soon after. By the time the lilacs came in, my father knew things weren't right.* After talking it over with Mum, he agreed to meet with a local psychiatrist who prescribed a course of Wellbutrin. But when he couldn't tolerate that drug (it gave him hives, which an allergy to antihistamines prevented him from medicating), he was too anxious to try any others. My mother left for her fiftieth Wellesley reunion, and Daddy totally fell apart.

He always took a dive when my mother went away. In '85, he didn't truly go over the edge until Mum went to Eastern Europe on a trip sponsored by PEN. In Budapest, on her way to Romania and Transylvania (where she would be incommunicado while interviewing dissident writers), Mum spoke with Daddy and heard a new, hollow note of despair. Aware that she was queering many other people's plans, she reluctantly came home. But it rankled her. There was a willful self-indulgence about my father's behavior, a childishness. It was as though he were throwing himself on the pyre of depression rather than trying to resist the flame, and he was pulling her in with him. Daddy had always punished Mum for leaving him. Doing things behind her back, closing off from her when she returned. How galling it must have been, given how often he let *her* down, backing out of trips, dinners, other joint commitments, at the last minute—*I just don't FEEL like it, Rose! Now leave me the fuck alone!*—forcing her to make excuses and go it on her own. Only a few hours after she left for Wellesley, he called her and announced he was cracking up. It was evening already, and Mum was scheduled to speak to her fellow alumnae the following morning, but she promised to come home in the afternoon.

According to the *Diagnostic and Statistical Manual of Mental Disorders,* fourth edition (*DSM-IV*), "Individuals with a Major Depressive Episode frequently present with tearfulness, irritability, brooding, obsessive rumination, anxiety, phobias, excessive worry over physical health, and complaints of pain." My father suffered

---

*According to studies, major depressive episodes occur most often in spring. Suicide rates soar in the (apparently not so merry) month of May.

terrible anxiety in '85, anxiety that to the healthy observer appeared totally irrational. This time, he had plenty to be anxious about. His first depression was hellish, the memory of it sharp and bitter. What's more, because this negative recollection was tied to his health, it conjured terrors of a body out of control and exacerbated the hypochondria ("Preoccupation with fears of having, or the idea that one has, a serious disease based on a misinterpretation of one or more bodily symptoms"), which his neck injury and approaching birthday had already inflamed. The death of his dogs was just piling it on ("Psychosocial stressors, in particular the death of someone close to the individual, are thought to precipitate [hypochondriasis] in some cases"). It was a Gordian knot.

I always thought it was a blessing my father didn't know how to use a computer. Daddy's Merck manual caused him enough trouble. If he'd been savvy enough to wander around the Internet in scary cyberchambers where heartburn is a symptom of stomach cancer and a twitching eyelid is the beginning of ALS, he might never have written a word. He was desperate for a solution and had decided unequivocally that ECT, or electroconvulsive therapy, was it. He didn't want a real, live health professional to talk to him of side effects, contraindications, or warnings. He wanted to be right. So he called up his friend Mia Farrow, who lived not far away, and asked her to come over for lunch.

The NIMH estimates that ten million Americans a year suffer from episodes of severe unipolar depression. Electroconvulsive therapy, a relatively common treatment for the illness in the fifties and sixties, had nearly disappeared by the eighties with the proliferation of Tofranil, Prozac, and other popular antidepressants. But the treatment didn't really hit the skids until films like *The Snake Pit, One Flew over the Cuckoo's Nest,* and *Frances* presented shock treatment as a form of medical torture, its purveyors heartless thieves of the mind. Even without the cinematic drama, the idea of ECT still evokes dread in most people. And understandably so. As Larry Tye writes in his book *Shock,* coauthored with the ECT patient and advocate Kitty Dukakis, "There is no treatment in psychiatry more frightening than electroconvulsive therapy. It works like this: two electrodes are strapped to the patient's skull. The doctor presses a button that unleashes a burst of electricity powerful enough to set off an epileptic-like convulsion. The sheer strength of the seizure shocks the brain back into balance."

Having his brain shocked back into balance was exactly what my father was hoping for. Over the last twenty years, improvements in the administration of ECT—muscle relaxants, anesthesia, and short-acting sleep medication help make it quick and painless—have boosted its popularity again. If circumstances allow, the entire course of treatment can now be done on an outpatient basis. Add to these considerations the numerous statistics supporting ECT's particular efficacy with geriatric patients, and Daddy had his solution. The primary deterrent in 1985—that ECT could rob him of his memories and dampen the creative fire—just didn't signify anymore. Daddy would do *any*thing not to go down that hole again.

Mum returned from Wellesley and found Daddy focused in an intractable manner on shock treatment. She listened, and they both agreed they would need more information. The next day Mum went out for a couple hours. "I can't remember where I'd gone," Mum said, "but I came home and found your father in my office off the kitchen. Mia was at the computer, and he was having her read him everything she could find about ECT. But he only wanted the positive information. He'd already made up his mind. He wasn't going to be talked out of it."

On June 8, three days before his seventy-fifth birthday, my parents drove to Yale–New Haven Hospital for my father's first ECT treatment. Taking into account his extreme sensitivity, and our concerns about his future capacity to create, the initial eight applications would be unilateral, applied to one side of the brain. After that, there would be several bilateral applications, depending on his progress. Each treatment would take only a few minutes, and he would be able to return home within the hour.

That was the plan, anyway.

* * *

BOY, WAS I annoyed by the sudden turn of events in Roxbury. I know this because, on June 7, I produced a rare and particularly hostile entry in my writing journal. In June 2000, I was busily editing my novel, *All the Finest Girls,* for publication the following spring. Virtually the entire hundred-plus pages of that season's black and red Chinese notebook are devoted to work—until this:

> Mum called to say that Daddy's going into the hospital tomorrow, could she bring Wally [my dog, on vacation in the country] back into NY—Good God.

I wish I could report on my virtue, my humble generosity. How I fled to my mad father's side and, in defiance of his past faithlessness, presented myself as an exemplar of filial love. But that's not how it happened. The truth was I felt a lot less like Cordelia in *King Lear* than like Michael Corleone in the third installment of *The Godfather.* After years of itinerancy and lucklessness, I was, just at that very moment, *happy.* I'd finished graduate school, was about to publish my first book, and, a few months before, had met a man with whom I was very much in love. It looked as though, financially and emotionally, I was finally going to break free. I wasn't going to be "the Baby" anymore with nowhere to go at holidays but back to the weirdness on Rucum Road. Except now Daddy was sick again. I was being pulled back in, and I was furious about it.

I had actually done my bit from where I was. Having heard that my father was considering ECT, I also conducted some online research, pulling up a lot of information in support of the treatment as well as some very alarming "my wife had shock treatment and now she's a zombie" testimonials. One of the forums I encountered was moderated by a reputable-seeming physician who had written a textbook on mood disorders. I sent him an e-mail asking for some general advice but failed to disguise my e-mail address (which includes my last name). Inferring the identity of his correspondent's "father," the doctor cautioned me about ECT's known drawbacks. It will very likely impair your father's memory, for days, weeks, or even months, he told me. Sometimes, he said, it can be much worse. Patients have occasionally reported huge swaths, countries of experience, wiped out permanently, though that is rare. But he wanted to be clear. If indeed my father was who he suspected, ECT could make it very difficult for him to create the kind of history- and memory-rich fiction for which he was revered. It seemed to me like a serious red flag. But by the time I called home to relay the information, it was a moot point. My father had made up his mind.

In the last years of my father's life, I performed a lot of tasks not so much for him but for the good of the collective. For three decades, my sisters and brother were the most important people in my life. Even separated by years and miles, I felt indebted to them for my survival. I always knew I would do my part, hold up my corner of our four-legged table. Susanna, a film director with an instinct for governance, was the natural "eldest." She'd e-mail all of us after talking with doctors, meeting with the Visiting Nurse Association, suggest a conference call about important decisions, or delegate when delegation was needed. Tommy, after a prodigal youth, had set off on a course of remarkable humanitarianism, working in New York's homeless services for years before getting a Ph.D. in clinical psychology. On staff at the Yale School of Medicine, not only was he a colleague of many of my father's doctors but he actually understood Daddy's condition and its many byzantine permutations. He was the final word for Mum on all things medical and, in his position as only son, often financial, too. Polly ("rhymes with melancholy," Daddy pointed out in the introduction to the photography book *Fathers and Daughters*) was in many ways Daddy's soul mate. A gifted dancer, sensitive and constant, she tended to his spirit on a level much deeper than any of the rest of us could (or dared to) go. Which left me, the youngest, used to doing party tricks for my father. Not enough to cut it in the current situation.

But I must have suspected in myself another role. For in the last paragraph of this same journal entry, I wrote something that, until I looked back recently, I had no memory of even thinking. "My anger is in direct opposition to my sympathy," I wrote. "And I also know that I, at the last, will have to tell this story. Someday."

*　　*　　*

DADDY'S FIRST ECT treatment went according to plan. But nothing about the experience was simple. In order to mitigate the intense constriction of muscles caused by the ECT seizure, doctors now administer to patients a powerful muscle relaxant. Instead of the writhing and spasming that once made the whole procedure so ghoulish looking, movement is reduced to a mild twitching of the toes or fingers. The drug produces a beneficial paralysis, but, like most pharmaceuticals, it sometimes has mild side effects.

Side effects were my father's specialty.

After coming out of the fog that envelops the post-ECT patient, Daddy found he couldn't pee. He completely flipped out, which more or less negated the positive effects of the treatment. Despite the doctors' assurances that the retention was temporary, Daddy insisted they insert a Foley catheter to circumvent what he now decided was a life-threatening situation. The doctors complied but, because of the risk of infection, told him he'd have to remain at the hospital, where the device could be monitored.

My father was no longer an outpatient. The troops rallied to his side.

"There he was," I wrote of my June 9 visit,

> like a ghost on an unmade bed in the psych ward. His face like an empty gray glove, eyes closed, unshaven, voice soft and halting. Tommy, who has been by his side, a miracle for

<u>both</u> of them, sat on the other bed. I sat down next to him and he apologized for the state he was in. "You shouldn't have to see me like this." Flashes of humor. "This is the World Trade Center of depression." Pacing. Lying on the bed, trying, it seemed, to pull his head off from the pain. Calling Tommy and me "you boys and girls." Saying how he loves us, how we're his favorite people, his kids are. Holding my cell phone away from his head because of the volume when Susanna spoke to him—and smiling!—Thank God.

Daddy's humor—not cheerfulness but his gimlet-eyed gift for irony—died a slower death than his sanity. Even when he was almost unreachable in his anguish, he could appreciate the occasional absurdities of his situation. Most psychiatric wards are wretched places. Even the best of them tend to be completely void of aesthetic pleasures, Dickensian in their grimness and ability to provoke dread in the average civilian. I always thought if you weren't totally depressed when you checked in to a psych facility, you sure as hell would be after a night in one of its prisonlike chambers. My father's room at Yale–New Haven was a study in hideousness. Dirty, dun-colored walls, metal bed and bed stand, swept free from any embellishments—clothing, lamps, framed art—that might conceivably double as instruments of self-harm. A dungeon basically, and for most patients, a perfect external representation of how they are feeling inside. Beyond the windows, though, it was high spring in New England, and Daddy's room had a view of the facility's small park. Perfectly manicured and entirely spotless, it ought to have been a hive for the hospital's high-functioning convalescents, a place to recline with family members, to allow the natural benefits of vitamin D to be soaked up through their sun-deprived pores. But, for reasons we never understood, the park was usually locked. Even when the place was open, it was always empty. We kids called it the Grass Museum, or Marienbad (as in *Last Year at*), which raised a wan smile to Daddy's lips, and we frequently took him for tours around it when we could convince the staff to let us in.

Briefly that June, Daddy went home. But the magnitude of his illness, still largely subterranean, had not been plumbed yet. It was probably too much for my mother to be expected to manage. After she mistakenly allowed him to eat breakfast (a deal breaker) on the morning of one treatment, Daddy was forced to miss an appointment. With the rapidly gathering storm of other conditions—anxiety, mania, hypochondriasis—Daddy became essentially ungovernable. And though the ECT may have been ramping up to work, its effects certainly weren't happening fast enough. Tommy soon discovered that our father had acquired double orders of two prescriptions—the prostate medication Hytrin and Viagra—as well as a book on how to kill yourself (and perhaps have a good time trying). After this bleakly comic revelation, it was determined that Daddy was truly a danger to himself. He was remanded to YNH for the duration of his thrice weekly ECT treatments.

Like most families in a crisis, we found our emotions sometimes spilling out in unexpected and ridiculous ways. June 18, Father's Day, found us at Tommy and his wife Phoebe's house, just outside New Haven. Under my brother's watchful eye, we had been allowed to spring Daddy for a few hours. Phoebe prepared lunch while Daddy lay motionless on a chaise looking out on the meadow behind the house. Meanwhile a scene broke out inside over, of all things, our dead grandmother Burgunder's china. It was probably the first time my father ever heard voices raised in his family when he hadn't been the chief bomb thrower. The altercation eventually died down, but Daddy was hugely agitated by it, stumbling into the kitchen holding his head in his hands. He spent the rest of the visit in the guest room, lying on the bed, whimpering like a child.

Susanna kept a superlative record of this day, as well as the weeks leading up to it and many after. In her notes, she describes a conversation she had with Daddy that evening, after she had driven him back to what he now called the "sick hotel." The inappropriate guilt and agitation that gripped our father are hallmarks of major depression. But underneath his craziness was a wound so personal, so existential as to almost validate his metastasizing anguish. Susanna writes:

> He was getting very paranoid and we sat in his dismal room where he told me there would be a horrible scandal that would humiliate my mother because of the Viagra prescription. He was obviously very ashamed. He said there would be huge scandals when people found out what a bad person he was. I tried to put things in perspective a little, said there was nothing he had done that we didn't know or that would shock us terribly. He kept insisting there was. I finally said, "Are you talking about sex? I mean, you didn't murder anyone or deliberately destroy someone's life, did you?" He said no, but it was pretty bad and it would change how people feel about his work. Then he said the most interesting thing: the worst thing about him is that he'd been unproductive and fallow. He hadn't written a novel in 20 years, hadn't done the work he was supposed to do. I realized how painful that was for him and that there were no reassurances, about his having written three masterpieces which is more than most people ever do, that could possibly soothe him, though I tried. Polly told me that he had said to her that besides the great novels there were many smaller things he wanted to write, that they were like little beasts and he had watched them turn their backs on him and walk away.

By mid-July, our father was totally unhinged. He missed every other ECT treatment, either because he refused to go ("You're sending me to my grave!" he'd moan to whichever one of us appeared to accompany him on the 7:00 A.M. perp walk down to the psych ward basement) or because the doctors said he was too delusional. One day, when Susanna and I were on duty, Daddy announced that he'd acquired a severe vitamin B deficiency from not eating for three days (periodic "hunger strikes," as he called them, were becoming commonplace). "I have beriberi," he said with finality, ignoring us when we burst out laughing. "I can't see anything," he continued, holding his hands up to his face, turning them palm in and palm out. "I'm blind." At the end of the day, when Susanna was instructing him on how to operate the cell phone Mum had gotten him, she asked him if he could see the power button. He nodded. "Guess your beriberi's cured," she said, which got a laugh out of everyone but Daddy, who couldn't seem to make the evident connection.

Treating Daddy pharmacologically was, I suspect, like a very serious game of Whac-A-Mole. Every time the doctors found something to correct his mood, the meds would set off another counterproductive condition. Some, like the hives and the urinary retention, were disagreeable but not overly troublesome. Others, psychological in nature, were much more problematic. Vague delusions turned into hard-core paranoia that summer—"I wonder if any of these hotels has a direct line to the Vatican," "Pioneer audio, old audio company, they're very skeptical about all this," "I have absolutely no clothes; I have nothing to wear"—and a perversion of his lifelong fear for the safety of his family, particularly his wife. At this point in the season, Mum was flying back and forth from the Vineyard, and on her own there, which gave Daddy plenty to worry about. One afternoon, convinced that she had been in a car crash (their cell phone connection died), he went completely berserk and wouldn't rest until our mother's friend Lucy Hackney had gotten assurance from the up-island police that there had been no accidents on the road coming back from the beach.

Watching Daddy go insane was tough on all of us but utterly devastating for my mother. For forty-seven years he had been her razor-sharp, alluring, and formidable husband. Since their early days in Rome, they had always had a companionship of the mind. Even when things were at their worst, they could sit down to dinner together and talk of books and the world beyond their door.

Now he was a total nutcase, helpless, infantile. His obsessions were endless and exhausting. Sit with him all day, placating his fears, answering the same questions over and over again, and *you* started to feel a little bit crazy yourself. We all pitched in, but Daddy wanted Mum most of the time. And it was in the end her job to care for him. She was extraordinary, supernatural in her strength, patience, and kindness. But sometimes I looked at her and it seemed as if she could not breathe, as if the whole unbearable situation would literally suffocate her. I can't pretend to really know her heart. How my father's cruelty over the years, his rank selfishness and intermittent rejection of her, wore her spirit down or bore into the contours of her soul. But I do know that she chose to, she found *a way* to make it work. She carved a fascinating and rewarding life out of the freedom he forced on her. That independence, buttressed by her own willfulness and financial solvency, became her reality. When, as it seemed to me, she was kept outside the fortress, she turned her exile into adventure. Now, at its most foreboding, she was being entombed inside those selfsame walls.

It was time to get him out of the hospital. After much discussion, conferencing, and consultation, Mum decided to take Daddy home to the Vineyard. He was certainly not getting any better in New Haven, and we couldn't really imagine him being any worse. In addition to his despondency, delusions, and paranoia, he had also developed a tremor and halting voice, which the doctors identified as Parkinsonian symptoms either caused or unmasked by the ECT. Whatever Daddy's future fate, we all agreed it would be decided somewhere else, in a different type of facility. Mass General perhaps, where Mum could make an easier commute for however long it was necessary. Besides, Mum *needed* to be on the Vineyard. Her friends were there. *Their* friends were there. After his first depression, Daddy and his fellow depressives Mike Wallace and Art Buchwald formed their own informal club, the Blues Brothers, even traveling together a couple of times to speak on the subject. Art and Mike were on the Vineyard; so were a dozen of their other closest friends.

Mum needed them around to keep her sane, and that way she could help make him sane again, too. After much wrangling with psychiatrists at Yale and on the Vineyard, she devised a plan to fly Daddy to the island on Monday, August 8.

It rained all morning. Even on good days, conditions at the Martha's Vineyard Airport are dicey, affected with surprising abruptness by the weather system, called the Bermuda High, that governs the island. Flights can be operating on or close to schedule one minute and be canceled because of ceiling restrictions five minutes later. What's more, different sections of the island have their own discrete weather patterns. It's very often sunny in Vineyard Haven and at the same time a complete fogbank in Chilmark and Aquinnah. Even the most seasoned island traveler can lose a day sitting around the airport trying to figure out what to tell her boss by reading the faces of the harried Cape Air staff.

We had our own delicate decision-making process that day. Early in the morning, Susanna had left the island by car with Bill Madden, who for several years had been driving for my parents. The plan was that she and Bill would go to Yale, where Susanna would have lunch with Daddy and then tell him at the last possible minute (lest he rebel) that he was going to the Vineyard. Meantime, I was to meet Mum at the airport, where a chartered plane would take us on the forty-five-minute flight to New Haven. Bill would pick us up, take us to the hospital to get Daddy, and we would all return to the airport for the flight home. As I sat in my house in Chilmark that morning, watching the rain and waiting for Mum's call, I worried that weather delays might agitate Daddy. I knew Susanna was going to have to move swiftly and with cunning to get him out of the hospital. Daddy had become increasingly fearful of the outside world, and we had a pretty good suspicion that he wasn't going to leave the hospital easily. Even an extra hour's wait would give him time to worry, and throw off the mission entirely. The weather, we would soon discover, was the least of our problems.

At last, Mum called. The ceiling had lifted. We were scheduled to depart the Martha's Vineyard Airport at 1:30. But when we got there, we found our plane had not arrived. Outside the gates of the general aviation building, a smaller facsimile of Air Force One stretched across the tarmac. Unbeknownst to us, President and Mrs. Clinton were wrapping up their family vacation that day. After weather delays all morning, the airport had closed again while the presidential plane made its landing. All Vineyard-bound flights had been held off or diverted, and now we didn't know when our plane would be able to come in, get us, and get back out. We were then informed that the president and his family would be making their departure at 5:30. At which point the airport would be closed. This meant we had to execute our entire plan in three and a half hours. It was right about this point that Susanna called. She had broken the news to Daddy. Whatever our fears about his reaction, we could multiply them several times, she said. He was refusing to leave. Mum now started frantically calling the charter company. I had half a mind to dig through Mum's address book and track down Hillary's assistant or Vernon Jordan or Dick Friedman, whose house the Clintons had borrowed. *Hey!* I wanted to shout. *Your friend Bill Styron? He's starkers, completely out of his fucking skull. Did you know that? Anyway, we're springing him from the booby hatch, and we need to do it today. Now. Can you just hold off on your flight? Go have a latte at the Black Dog, buy some more T-shirts, SOMEthing, so we can get this done before everybody, including me, falls apart!*

At 3:15 the charter plane arrived at last. Mum had made a new plan. Susanna and Bill would bring Daddy to us at the airport, if Susanna thought she could convince him. We'd put him on the plane and turn the whole thing around in minutes instead of hours. Armed with an Ativan from the nurse, Susanna said she thought she could make it happen. And so we took off, cautiously hopeful that the biggest impediments were now behind us. So imagine our surprise when we arrived at New Haven's very small private airport and saw . . . Air Force Two on the runway. Somehow, swirling in the eddy of our personal family drama, neither Mum nor I had factored in the morning's major news story: in Nashville that afternoon, Al Gore was scheduled to formally introduce his running mate for the 2000 election, Connecticut's junior senator, Joseph I. Lieberman. For whatever cosmically hilarious reason, Lieberman would be departing for Tennessee out of Tweed New Haven airport at just about the same time we hoped to go back to the Vineyard. The entire Connecticut press corps, plus a large national contingent, was corralled beside the two-room terminal. And out in the parking lot, here comes one of the Nutmeg State's most famous residents, stumbling out of his daughter's moving Volvo with his pants around his knees, looking for all the world like Howard Hughes during his last days at the Xanadu.

"I will *not* get on that plane!" Daddy croaked. Thirty or forty pounds lighter than he'd been in May, unshaven, hair long and wild, Daddy was terrifying looking. During those months, he turned a physical corner from which he did not come back—he was not only mad looking but now also ancient. Leaping out of the car after him, Bill and Susanna grabbed Daddy as he wheeled around the parking lot, and I came up beside them. Eventually, we shuffled Daddy into the terminal. Mum consulted with airport brass, while around the corner reporters mingled as they waited for Lieberman. *"I won't go!"* Daddy shouted again. Our pilot, standing at the counter, took one look at him and threatened to honor his refusal. "I'm not flying with a guy acting like that," he said, arms crossed over his epauletted shirt.

Aware of the ticking clock, Susanna and I sat Daddy down and tried to distract him while waiting for the antianxiety medication to take effect. After a few minutes, his demeanor began to change. He started breathing more deeply, and his eyes looked softer, less feral. His shoulders dropped, his mouth relaxed. We made a few jokes, and he smiled in response.

"Well," he sighed, "you've really done it, haven't you?"

We smiled and nodded. Yes we had, we'd saved him.

"You're both just sluts," Daddy hissed.

Susanna and I looked at each other and laughed nervously.

"What do you mean by that, Daddy?" Susanna asked, masking her astonishment with a deliberate calm.

"You're sluts because you lured me here and you deceived me."

It seemed as good a subject as any to keep Daddy's mind off what we were now rather desperately trying to get done. As we discussed the etymology of the word *slut*—which Daddy thought might be Yiddish—we began to move him toward the tarmac. While Mum and the pilot got up front, I climbed in through the small hatch and sat on the floor. Then I pulled Daddy's 120-pound frame onto a seat while Susanna followed behind him, patting him on the back. Defeated and dazed, our shambling wreck of a father at last sat down. I buckled him in, and Susanna gave him a kiss good-bye. As the pilot started up the engines, Daddy leaned forward and touched his shoulder. "Let me tell you something," he said, eyes wide again with fiery intensity. "I've been in a mental hospital in New Haven for two months, and this is the first time in history they've ever let anyone as loony as me get out."

Not about to argue with such evidentiary truth, the pilot nodded and rolled out onto the runway.

＊　　＊　　＊

REMARKABLY, THROUGH ALL of this, Ed stuck by me. The first time he met my family, it was just on the cusp of my father's second downturn. Polly and her husband, Rob, were performing at a theater in Tribeca that spring. After opening night, we all had dinner together, and I brought Ed along. Daddy, preoccupied by the dreadful hoofbeats he was hearing, paid only marginal attention to the person who was at that point simply my new boyfriend. They would meet only two more times before Daddy landed at Yale. In July, just before Ed left for a monthlong job in Los Angeles, he accompanied me to New Haven, where he saw my father in full-blown psychosis. His solicitousness toward the entire family, and his gentle care of me, was a wonder. He sauntered right into the fray, laconic and unflappable, always anticipating how he could help and then quietly, simply making it happen. As I was to learn, support systems need support systems of their own. At last, it seemed I had one. Our nightly transcontinental phone calls buoyed me above the days' crazy and exhausting storms.

The evening my father arrived on the Vineyard, things turned temporarily, freakishly wonderful. For a few hours. It was a gorgeous post-rain sunset. Stretched out on a chaise on his exquisite lawn, watching the lambent water, Daddy seemed blissful. The Ativan, and maybe the sheer beauty and comfort of his surroundings, was doing its trick. Once again he'd been snatched from the jaws of death and was stunned, happy, grateful. That night at dinner he became, in Tommy's description, "hypomanic." He ate three plates of food, had a glass of wine (after which we cut him off), laughed, joked, and stayed up till 1:00 A.M. But by the next morning, he was again a disaster area. Frightened, hysterical (he'd soiled the bed and was certain the house would have to be condemned), he begged Mum to turn him out. An ambulance was called, and it whisked him off to the Martha's Vineyard Hospital.

After three or four days, Daddy was medicated and stabilized enough to come back home. During the weeks of mid-August, practically everybody on the island came around in overlapping shifts to sit with Daddy on the porch, on the lawn, in the living room. They would try to engage him or, at my mother's behest, at least keep up a happy chatter around him. Meantime, in the kitchen, a retinue of pill-wielding nurses from the Martha's Vineyard Visiting Nurse Association had set up a command center. Up and down the stairs they filed, in and out the screen door. With stealth efficiency they came and went, monitoring his mood and his blood pressure, his heart rate and bowel movements, administering meds and changing linens, noting what time he napped and which obsession he was currently fixated on.

Regardless of anyone else's opinion, it was Daphne with whom the nurses truly had to pass muster. Having spent more than thirty years with our family, and devoted beyond all reason to my father, Daphne was gatekeeper, marshal, and the only constant in our household's ever-changing parade. As cook, she fussed over Daddy's every meal. *Here it is, Mr. S!* came her high Jamaican trill. *How that? Goody!* Each bite of toast was a cause for her celebration, and she could talk for an hour about the way she prepared his soup, or how he finished off the milky mashed potatoes. Daphne also took the night shift, turning her long experience as a home health care aide to the patient execution of some of the unpleasant tasks that caring for my father now entailed.

All of this attention certainly sustained Daddy. But sometimes the sheer volume of stimuli threatened to overwhelm him. Mum, however, could not be stopped. For her a populated house was a life-giving one. And having people around also gave her some relief, a relief of which we were all in need. In mid-August, Ed returned from L.A. Having him back was wonderful. I looked forward to introducing him to my Vineyard friends, and to passing the last very social weeks of summer enjoying ourselves and each other.

What happened next is, depending on how you look at it, just another chapter in my father's picaresque journey to the grave or a monumental turn of events, after which nothing would ever again be properly aligned.

August 20 was glorious, one of those halcyon summer days that breaks your heart a little, whispering as it does of the changing season and bittersweet, back-to-school good-byes. It was Susanna's daughter Emma's twelfth birthday. The three-day agricultural fair, one of the island's most delightful annual rites, was in full swing. At my house in Chilmark, Ed and I were entertaining two of our closest friends, the couple through whom we had met. And down in Vineyard Haven, Mum had lined up company throughout the day for Daddy. Jim Hart was coming for tea, after which Bill Luers would arrive to take my father for a sunset drive. Mum was celebrating Emma's birthday by going to see a play Susanna's husband was in, at the island amphitheater, with that branch of the family.

After a day at the beach, my guests and I made a plan to go to the fair. When the sky over West Tisbury glows with particolored carnival lights, and the allée between the food booths turns into a neighborhood social, the fair is, in my mind, at its very best. But first I had to go to my parents' place to bring Emma a birthday present. I would, I told Ed, meet him at the appointed hour, near the ticket booth. I made my trip to the little house in Vineyard Haven and was just getting back in my car when my mother suddenly appeared in the driveway. Bent forward with grim determination, she stopped when she saw me and tried to shake off her fretful mask with a tight smile.

"Your father's on the way to the hospital," she said, resignedly. "He was walking with Bill Luers and he fell."

An ambulance had picked him up, she said, and she was going to the hospital to meet him. More than that she didn't know. Realizing Mum had no one to go with her, I said I'd follow along. I called Ed on his cell and told him I'd catch up with him later.

Daddy was wheeled into the emergency room, badly shaken, his face covered in bandages. As we later learned, Bill and my father had driven to Menemsha, a fishing village at the other end of the island. It's a sweet little town, a great spot for sunsets. Bill had convinced Daddy to take a short stroll on the pier. The two men walked the length of the dock until they came to the end, where the yacht owned by Maurice Tempelsman (Jackie Onassis's longtime companion) was habitually docked. Just as they were turning around, Maurice emerged from belowdecks. Not a word was exchanged among the three men. But my father saw on Maurice's face such a look of shock at the sight of him that his shame impelled him to flee. Catching his toe on an uneven board, he then stumbled and fell, facefirst, onto the dock. Daddy's motor skills were totally shot at this point. He never lifted a finger to break his fall.

Though August 20, 2000, was hardly my father's worst day, it represents what I think was a turning point in his decline. That afternoon, the physical began to rival the psychological, and Daddy's battle was no longer monolithic but strangely internecine. He'd broken his nose in Menemsha. This led, a few days later, to him aspirating on something. The aspiration, in turn, resulted in pneumonia. After having been medevaced to Mass General in extreme respiratory failure, Daddy shuttled back and forth for the next month or so between ICU and rehab. There were more delusions — the white-coated people were members of the Manson family, his room was bugged — and some novel physical problems as well. A bleeding duodenal ulcer, Parkinson's mouth. He lost his ability to swallow and was fitted with his first, of several, feeding tubes.

Back on the Vineyard, Labor Day came and went. It was time for Ed to return to New York. I was starting a new novel and taking turns with my siblings at the hospital in Boston. One night, after failing to pin me down about my plans for the fall — he wanted me to come back to New York, I didn't know what I was coming back to — Ed threw a small black velvet box at me. "Marry me," he said, exasperated, as I opened the box and gazed with utter stupefaction at a beautiful diamond engagement ring.

Ed had been trying to propose to me all month. He'd brought the ring to the beach and to the tennis court, to a poker game, and on a few late-afternoon walks on the beach. On the night of my father's fall, he'd planned a ride on the Ferris wheel and had paid a carny to pull the brake so he could propose to me when we got to the top. Our houseguests had secreted in a bucket of champagne. Other friends were lurking nearby to celebrate. But I never made it to the fair. And every time Ed sought another romantic moment, some further crisis had reared its head. Or I'd dragged us into a crowd looking to maximize the summer's few uncomplicated minutes with activities I thought would be fun for Ed, and make him want to stick around. I was completely oblivious to his intentions, and probably acting more than a little nuts. But, throwing genetic caution to the wind, Ed abided and endured. The next day we drove up to MGH, where Ed asked Daddy for my hand. Feeding tube in his nose but otherwise unencumbered, my father closed his eyes and gave my fiancé a firm nod.

Sixteen

Op-pop and Huck, Thanksgiving 2005

LIKE A MIGRATORY bird, I return home each summer, loading up the car and flying—for I am always running late—for the Woods Hole ferry. In July 2008, along with the suitcases, I'd packed several boxes filled with research material from Duke: photocopied letters, interviews, and five folders from the box marked "WS17. Unfinished Work Subseries, 1970–1990s undated." Also with me were my children, five-year-old William (Huck) and Martha, just three. Daddy had been dead almost two years; they knew their grandfather only a bit. But Huck, who inherited his sweetness from the Beason line, had been attached to my father in a way I found touching and curious.

"Hi, Op-pop!" the boy would shout as he toddled into the living room, using his own diminutive of Grandpop, which was what Huck's cousins called my father.

"Hi, big shot," Daddy would reply, his mouth a bag of marbles.

Two bouts of oral cancer, in 2004 and again in 2006, had made a hash of my father's speech. Talking was painful, and he did so with increasing effort. There wasn't really a mouth smile anymore, but Huck must have picked up a flicker of light in Daddy's eyes that the rest of us didn't detect. Sometimes I would look out the window and see my father being taken to a doctor's appointment. At one elbow was his male nurse, guiding Daddy along with gentle brawn. On the other side, his two-foot-tall assistant would be reaching up to place a chubby hand in the small of his grandfather's back.

Huck liked to get himself right up close. Crawling onto the couch, he'd scooch his bottom along the cushion until the two of them were thigh to thigh. Then he'd take my father's Kleenex box and position it on his small lap. Daddy got pneumonia over and over again. The swallowing problems he developed in 2000 never really resolved, and with them came, inevitably, more aspirations. Even the port implanted in his stomach and the permanent feeding tube didn't completely protect him from fluids going down the wrong pipe and gunk building up in his lungs. It was, truth be told, pretty gross. But Huck didn't seem to mind at all.

Pneumonia was, in the end, my father's "cause of death." *Drowning* would probably have been more appropriate, covered a wider range of truths, but the coroner I suppose doesn't go in for metaphors or for literary double entendres. In the early evening after Daddy's death, my mother and I were in the dining room when Christopher Lehmann-Haupt called. He was very solicitous, expressed his condolences, and wished—if I didn't mind—to check a few facts for the *Times* obituary. "Can you tell me what your father died of?" he asked. Standing on the back stairs landing, looking out over the porch at the first day of November disappearing in the harbor, I stuttered. Below me, my mother was seated at the table, lost in thought.

"Mum," I said, putting my hand over the mouthpiece, "it's *The New York Times*. I'm going to tell them Daddy died of pneumonia ... unless you want me to say something else."

She was looking somewhere in the middle distance.

"Yes," she said vaguely, and then, awakening from her reverie, with sudden firmness, "*No*. Nothing else. Say he died of pneumonia."

His last summer, the summer of 2006, my father gave up sitting on the porch. Like food and reading, the pleasures of an hour or two on that shady promontory had been carnal for him. It was his social nexus, his meditation spot, the place where, after a long day's work, he could kick back and synthesize all the elements of the day. Vineyard Haven, the town and the harbor, reminded him of his Tidewater youth. "I love the soft collision of harbor and shore," he wrote in *The New York Times Magazine* in 1990, "the subtly haunting briny quality that all small towns have when they are situated by the sea." He liked the noises, too, "the blast of the ferry horn—distant, melancholy—and the gentle thrumming of the ferry itself outward bound past the breakwater; the sizzling sound of sailboat hulls as they shear the waves; the luffing of sails and the muffled boom of the yacht club's gun; the eerie wail of the breakwater siren in dense fog; the squabble and cry of gulls." Even the squawking of the PA system next door, and shrieks of children playing rag tag on the dock didn't disturb him, this man who was almost preposterously sensitive to noise.

In the summer of '79, my father and I spent the first hour of every day on the porch together. The Franklin Library was producing a limited, leather-bound edition of *The Confessions of Nat Turner*, part of their Pulitzer Prize Collection "with 22k gold accents." Daddy was being paid "a fortune," he told me, to put his signature on something like five thousand sheets of paper, which would then be bound with the text. Each morning, I sat next to him and pulled the pages while he signed. I got ten cents a sheet. We had a fine time of it.

But all of that was over. The meals, the reading, the light on the water. As Lucy Hackney said to me, "He doesn't want to live. But he doesn't want to die either. He's stuck." Stuck he was.

"Want one?" Huck used to ask, holding up the tissue box before Daddy's cloudy glasses.

My father took one, or he didn't. And there they would sit, the old man and his namesake. Two diapered fellows side by side in the particle-dancing light, while summer wheeled by just beyond the windows.

July of '08 was hot and sticky. My children love staying at their grandmother "Roro's," and, since Ed and I sold the Chilmark house, that's what we do for part of every summer. Luckily, the two-bedroom little house of my childhood is now a five-bedroom affair, and my mother joyously welcomes all of her tribe for as often and as long as we wish to come. My father's old study, its semihumorous Verboten sign still on the door, has become what the little house once was—a den of questionable propriety for the teenagers of the family, (at the time) Susanna's daughters Emma and Lilah. So I had rented a room in a genteel boardinghouse just across Main Street where I could work.

I had a plan to unscramble my father's manuscript pages. It was a big piece of the elaborate puzzle I'd been putting together all winter, ever since my first trip to Duke. Before going down there, I'd suffered a bout of paralyzing panic and decided that I couldn't write about him. Somewhere along the line, my memory had gone haywire. I could recall almost nothing about my father from my early childhood. There were stray bits and pieces—sitting on his lap reading the paper to him, being carried in from the car when I had fallen asleep on the way back from a party, the foghorn sound he used to make for me—*beee-yo beee-yo*—but I had little else. My recollections at eight, and ten, and twelve were not so nice. And then there were his last years. In between was all lacunae, an amnesia so great I wondered whether one of the countless tumbles I'd taken off horses hadn't caused some kind of undiagnosed closed-head injury.

The archives at Duke went a long way toward bringing my father back for me. He came alive in all that paper, the medium in which he lived most purely. I was utterly charmed by the soldier writing home to his father. I communed with the funny and profane young writer abroad. And I ached with maternal sorrow for the grieving boy who couldn't shed well-earned tears. All those words irrigated the arid soil that was my past. Up sprung life in fresh stalks. Voice, flesh, smell. I thought if I could put the pages of his unfinished work in order, maybe the whole landscape would make itself plain.

On the twin beds in my boardinghouse office, I laid out the folders. The heat that day was suffocating, and, though I tugged open the old windows, swollen tight in their frames, not a hint of breeze disturbed the still air. *"Way of the Warrior I," "Way of the Warrior II,"* "Hospital," "Grandfather." A girl in a bathing suit with a towel wrapped around her neck bicycled down Owen Little Way toward the water. I unpacked the rest of my boxes and went to eat lunch with my children.

I should have known the weather would break. It was just too hot and humid not to change. By the time I'd crossed the Hackneys' lawn, a mass of charcoal-colored clouds hung over the harbor. I could see boaters at their moorings hustling sails into bags and tennis players putting their palms up, feeling the drops, trying to gauge if they could finish the set. I jogged back to the little house and slipped inside just as the skies burst open. It poured and blew for fifteen minutes, a benign summer storm with just enough drama to draw small faces to the window. *Look, Mommy!* A branch coming down by the driveway. Some plastic chairs skittering, *Wizard of Oz*–like, across the lawn. I ate a sandwich while Martha unloaded the dress-up box. The rain let up, and I walked back to my office.

The pages were *everywhere*. Not a single folder had escaped the raid. "Felon winds," Milton might have called them. Whatever vestige of order had governed Daddy's manuscripts before was now irretrievably lost. It was chaos. I gave up trying to figure out what went where and put my head in my hands. The obvious thought came to mind.

You stories really don't want to be told, do you?

The next day, I sent a smoke signal to Jim West, in the form of an e-mail.

Can you tell me WHY my father's unfinished manuscripts look like they do? What on earth happened?

Jim's reply left me dumbstruck.

At some point around 1995, your father had all of his MSS for a variety of works-in-progress laid out on the bed in Polly's old room, the room in which he was then writing. He went away for a trip, and left the window open beside the bed. While gone, a severe windstorm came up and picked up the MSS, whirled them in the air, scrambled them up entirely, and then set them down again.

Corny as it may seem, I decided to respect the writing gods on this one. My answers were not in those manuscripts. The answers had not yet been written.

*   *   *

AT THE MARTHA'S Vineyard Hospital, late in the summer of 2000, after my father's fall but before he developed pneumonia, I went to see him in the afternoons. He was bored, recovering from his broken nose and lacerations on his mouth, but he was lucid and very calm. I read to him—articles in the *Times,* Jon Krakauer's *Under the Banner of Heaven*—and he accepted my presence with, if not pleasure, then equanimity. He answered my questions with a nod or a shake, closed his eyes, looked out the window. His eyes revealed a faint trace of gladness when I arrived, but he never made a motion to stop me when I rose to leave. "You must be awfully proud of your dad," he said once, with a bitterness that shocked me. He was, I thought, in a meditative and rueful frame of mind. The time passed slowly with him, and, though the hours were difficult and sometimes awkward, I hoped I was ever so slightly lifting his dismal mood. For the good of the collective, at least, I did what needed to be done.

One day when I was talking with him, the phone rang. It was Polly. She was performing in San Francisco that summer and also, though Daddy didn't know yet, mourning the death of her seventeen-year marriage. At the sound of her dulcet and vulnerable voice, my father came to life. "I'm so glad to talk to you, too, sweetie," he said, his ashen cheeks suddenly abloom. "I'm all right, better, I think. . . . That's wonderful, what else are you doing? . . . When are you coming home?" I'd never before seen my father show favoritism among his children. But now it was quite plain to me that he preferred the company of some of us over others, and it stung me to my core.

Still, I believed I understood. Or maybe I just put it in a context I could safely manage. "He's embarrassed to be depressed in front of me," I wrote the next day, "in front of my 'youth and vigor' as he says about me. My celebration of love and work [is being] marred by him, he thinks."

I was beginning to sound like my mother, crafting myself into an escape artist rather than dwell in the purgatory of his rejection.

My father was released from Mass General in the fall of 2000. Afterward, there followed a period of real recovery. I have photographs of him from the holidays that year, reading aloud "The Night Before Christmas" (a tradition begun in his mellowing years when the first of the grandchildren were born). In them, he looks strong, if aged. The rest of us appear positively giddy. We had a lot to celebrate, not least the miracle of his rebirth.

Through the winter I did a little work on a new novel. But

mostly I was preoccupied with plans for my September wedding and, before that, the spring publication of *All the Finest Girls*. In March, I sent my father the galleys. And then for two weeks I waited to hear from him. Finally, I called home.

"Has Daddy read my book?" I asked my mother. I was trembling with anxiety and riven with hurt.

"I don't know," she said, her voice reedy, strained. "He's not feeling well. He's been going downhill a bit."

I said I was sorry to hear it but didn't ask to speak with him. I was too confused by my welter of emotions. What, exactly, was I to feel?

When Ed and I went home for Easter, my father avoided or ignored me all weekend. On the stands that month was an interview I'd done with *Talk* magazine, in which I'd neither confirmed nor denied the autobiographical elements of my novel. But I had said something like "Nobody's parents are perfect." Stricken by Daddy's coldness, I went up to his room, where he lay on the bed reading, and groveled before him. "I'm really sorry about that piece," I said. "It was all taken out of context. I didn't mean anything by it."

"Okay," he said, gruffly, putting his face back in the book he was reading. "Fine."

But it wasn't fine. With every triumph I had that year, my father sunk a little lower. There was a time I'd worried he wouldn't be alive to walk me down the aisle. Now I wondered if I wanted him to. The *froideur* lasted most of the summer. He took virtually no part in the lead-up to the wedding, and left the room whenever the subject came up. Ed and I had planned a big celebration, much bigger than the weddings of my siblings. I wondered if it was the cost that had my father in such a stew. Or did he resent not being, for a few months, the center of everyone's attention? Whatever the case, the previous concerns I fancied him having had come true, in spades. He *was* marring the celebration, and acting every inch the "royal asshole" I described in my journal. Still, like every happy bride who ever endured a family drama, I tried to stay above the situation. He wasn't the antihero of my story anymore. The narrative was heading in a more pleasing direction.

I have only now recalled that summer not as I gauzily preserved it but as it truly happened. Daddy still had a long fight ahead of him, and for many reasons the drama of his final fight eclipsed a lot of history, both good and bad. Now I see how desperately I was defending myself from him. How untenable it would have been to think he didn't like my book, didn't like my wedding, didn't like *me* (and after so many years of thinking I was one of his favorites!). Of course, any or all of those things may have been true. But it's also true that a generosity of spirit had become one of the many qualities compromised by his illness. I don't think it was the content of my book that chafed at him. It was that I'd written one at all. It wasn't my wedding that offended but my fecundity. It was, indeed, my "youth and vigor." Daddy was drowning, and I, well, I was swimming on.

In the end, he pulled through for me—if not as some idealized version of a father, then as good a man as he could be. Our wedding day, September 8, 2001, was one of unparalleled beauty. Many of our guests remember it still with exaggerated brilliance, the afternoon frozen in time as the last great party before the world we knew changed forever. Good friends turned over their enormous meadow abutting one of the Vineyard's most breathtaking spots, Squibnocket Pond. My father walked me down the aisle (or I walked him, as we joked while gingerly processing over the uneven ground). And after dinner, he stood and delivered what may have been the last composition he ever wrote, a sidesplittingly hilarious and profoundly loving toast to my new husband and me. Three days later, just as thousands of mothers and fathers and husbands and wives began their workday at the World Trade Center, Ed and I were halfway between Amsterdam and Mt. Kilimanjaro.

"I must be the luckiest girl in the world," I wrote in my journal, already swimming on.

*   *   *

THINGS WITH MY father were good for a while. Fragile but steady, he took some enjoyment in simple things. That year, we all traveled down to Newport News for the dedication of Port Warwick, a planned community named after the fictional town in *Lie Down in Darkness*. My brother's second child was born. Another summer passed quietly enough.

In the fall of 2002, I took Daddy as my guest to a screening and party for the season premiere of *The Sopranos*. We had patched up, or over, the previous year's hostilities. He liked Ed enormously, and I was grateful for the calm seas. On a September afternoon, he and I flew down from the Vineyard to New York, looking forward to the night ahead. He loved the show, and it was a sweet, if campy, way for us to do something together. The evening, however, didn't go as I'd hoped. It was a big event, too big, and what should have been a semiexclusive affair turned into a mob scene (no pun intended). We had good seats at the screening, but the party afterward spread all across Rockefeller Center. People jostled for food and drinks and for the little café tables set up all over the complex. I lost my friends in the crowd and grew fearful for Daddy's comfort, as well as his safety. But an ineffable sadness also swept over me that night. For so much of my life, all the real high times I knew were associated in some way with him. The movie openings, the book parties, black-tie events where one could not help but feel a little frisson of excitement. Either by invitation or by implication, I was always Bill Styron's daughter. But now he was so diminished, so frail. No one seemed to know who he was, or care. We enjoyed ourselves at a small table at the perimeter of one of the party's anterooms. Daddy was calm, and perfectly happy. But a shift was happening, a change of alignment. I was a grown woman, time was fleeting, and my father's moment was over.

In January 2003, I gave birth to William Hutchinson Beason. Daddy came to Brooklyn, where Ed and I had recently moved, and held the boy, tentatively, in his arms. He was, I could tell, deeply moved that we'd named our son after him. And he seemed both bemused and amused that we were living in this borough he had so long ago fled. "I lived that way, not too far, near the parade ground," he said, pointing out our parlor windows.

Until I moved there, Brooklyn had always been bound up for me with *Sophie's Choice*. My first visit, and my last for a long time, was June 11, 1979. My father's fifty-fourth birthday and the publication date of *Sophie's Choice*. Random House threw him an enormous party at the River Café, just under the Brooklyn Bridge. I was twelve, wore a white silk blouse with balloon sleeves, and swanned around the great glass atrium high on ginger ale and the supernatural glamour of the night. A birthday cake was wheeled out designed to look just like the book jacket, and the candlelight flickered before the backdrop of the shimmering river. But mostly what I remember of that night was talking to Carly Simon's friend and lyricist, Jake Brackman. He'd just written a movie called *Times Square*. I might be right, he told me, for one of the film's teenage leads (I wasn't). In the first grips of my theater mania, I turned my sights across the river. I wanted to follow my sisters and brother to Manhattan. Never would I have imagined living in Brooklyn, not more than a couple of miles from where I then stood.

In the spring of 2003, Daddy made his next and final break with sanguinity. He submitted to a further round of ECT at Mass General, which mollified him temporarily but eventually devolved into another stretch of paranoid delusions and mania. "They've stolen my brain," he wailed, an accusation it became increasingly hard to dispute. The hunger strikes came back, and so did the unpredictable side effects of various medications. Mum was determined to will Daddy back to health, and part of that effort involved trying to keep up the peripatetic seasonal lifestyle they'd always maintained. For a while he was at the Eye Institute at Columbia-Presbyterian. Then he spent some time at the New Milford Hospital up near our house in Connecticut. For a few weeks he was admitted to a rehab center outside Danbury. In the spring of 2005, he and I narrowly missed a joint internment at NYU: he was released from the Rusk rehabilitation unit just days before I gave birth to Martha in the wing across the way.

One evening, between feedings, I took a paperback of *Sophie's Choice* down from our bookshelves. It was the copy a friend had given to me in college, a jokey birthday present after I admitted that I'd never read it. *If not now, when?* I recall thinking. Sleep deprived and vulnerable, I nestled in. For two weeks I followed my father back in time. But simultaneously I felt the future, hovering. Daddy and his doomed characters became, for me, inextricably linked, and the same incipient sorrow that follows Stingo, Sophie, and Nathan on their tragic summer odyssey dogged my reading. As a writer, I wondered how my father kept giving the narrative over so seamlessly to his heroine. As a new mother, I felt my heart might shatter at the book's climax. And as a once-upon-a-time little girl, I mourned for Eva. "She still had her *mis*"—her teddy bear—"and her flute," Sophie says, describing to Stingo her final, devastating image of her small daughter.

With a catch of my breath, I remembered driving home from school with Daddy one day when I was ten.

"What kind of instrument would a little girl your age play?" he asked.

"Umm . . . a piano?" I answered, my hand out the window, tracing the arc of the power lines.

"No, too big. How about a flute?"

I figured he was asking for his work. I wanted to be a help. My friend Lili had a flute.

"Maybe," I replied, leaping a tree with my fingers.

We dipped into a hollow. The wires disappeared in the trees.

*   *   *

SOME DAYS I just looked at my father and thought: *Are you really going to die of depression?*

Not suicide, which in the end is an act of mercy visited upon oneself. But depression. It was almost unthinkable that he would shuffle off his mortal coil like this, fade so passively to black. But that, of course, is the nature of the beast. Each hospital stay weakened his body further, but his chronic anhedonia made it impossible to work toward recovery when he was released. With great effort, the nurses would get my father to take a single turn around the lawn (a sight that recalled for my mother the house's previous owner, Mr. Eels, taking the exact same turns). But the only action he really had strength for was resistance. No army of medical practitioners, physical therapists, or bossy children could convince him to stretch his legs or work the muscles in his atrophying arms. No delicious repast prepared by Daphne could induce him to practice his swallowing. He couldn't eat anymore, couldn't read, couldn't talk, couldn't write. Perched in the corner of the couch, his cheeks hollowed by malnutrition, his mouth a lopsided *O*, he was almost paralyzed. But he could still clamp his eyelids shut and manage a definitive, head-shaking *no*. He knew he was losing the fight, but he drew the line at being forced to feel better. Not trying was his toehold on personal dignity, his last stand.

On September 21, 2006, our family gathered in Washington, D.C., for the Washington National Opera's presentation of Nicholas Maw's *Sophie's Choice,* the opera. My father had been to the work's premiere at London's Covent Garden in 2002 and been much moved by the experience. It was a long, difficult show and got very mixed reviews, but Daddy was flattered by the grandeur and seriousness of the endeavor. Making it to the opera's American debut had been on both of my parents' minds all summer. My father was by then in extremis. His oral cancer, for which he was receiving only palliative care, had returned, and a recent bout of pneumonia had put him back in the Vineyard hospital for several weeks. Psychologically he was winding down as well, vigorously refusing his meds and making every indication that, after his epic struggle, he was ready to let the tide take him away. "I'm at the end," he told his nurse, Diane. Getting him to Washington seemed almost folly, and yet somehow absolutely necessary.

Accompanied by June Manning, his last attendant, my mother and father flew down to D.C. and checked in to the Hay-Adams hotel. Anxious and weak, Daddy resisted going back out. He said he "couldn't move," according to June's log notes. But with Mum, his great cheerleader, coaxing him on, he finally acquiesced. At the Kennedy Center, he was positioned in his wheelchair at the edge of the stage, where he watched the show, quiet and rapt. After the curtain, the applause for the author was thunderous, and he turned, mouth agape, to take in the scene. It was his last hurrah. "A wonderful night," June noted succinctly.

Six weeks later, on an unusually lovely All Souls' Day in 2006, my father gave up his ambivalent tussle with life and passed away. The five of us sat on the hospital bed. Mum, by his head, stroking his hair. All of his children forming the rest of the circle. While the fluid in his lungs crested, and his breathing halted for up to a minute at a time, we coached him on toward a death that just couldn't be forestalled any longer. *It's okay to go, Daddy. It's okay.* There was no minister. So we talked of heaven, and invented our own last rites. *You'll see Grandpop again. And Jim. Willie. And Dinah the dog. It's okay, Daddy, we love you. Let go.*

On the bridge between here and there, my father lingered for a last hour, raising his eyebrows now and again to let us know he could hear. Someone began to recite the Twenty-third Psalm, a prayer drummed into us in elementary school but that we now, laughingly, struggled to get straight. *The Lord is my shepherd; I shall not want. He leadeth me beside the still waters . . . no . . . He maketh me to lie down in green pastures . . .* Weeping, Mum asked him to say "I love you" just once more. He couldn't speak, but briefly, and for the last time, he opened his eyes.

Each of us pressed our hands to his skin, trying physically to ease his flight into the beyond. But it felt as though we were making room for something else, too. For Judgment Day, Excellent and Fair, perhaps. Or maybe we just wanted to help him write the ending to his story.

It was a great yarn, Daddy. Furiously told. It was urgent and it was grand.

A war story, after all.

Walking each other down the aisle, 2001

Acknowledgments

This book began in a roundabout way, with a phone call from one of my oldest friends, Adam Green. It was March 2007, four months after my father's death, and though I'd returned to work on the novel I'd been writing, my head wasn't really in the game. Adam told me he'd given my name to Valerie Steiker and Chris Knutsen, colleagues of his who were putting together an anthology about my hometown, Brooklyn, New York. Adam's call, and Valerie's subsequent one, were both welcome incursions into my scattered day. Perhaps, I thought, if I could train my sights on something neither dead nor fictional, but firm beneath my feet, I would find my way back to familiar routine.

But all I could think about was Daddy. My earliest context for Brooklyn was in the pages of *Sophie's Choice*. My first visit to King's County was to celebrate that book, and him. Though I'd lived in the borough for half a dozen years already, Brooklyn and my father were, for the purposes of personal essay, thoroughly intertwined. The piece I wrote, "A Sentimental Education," opened the door to a flood of other thoughts and memories. From there, through various stages, came this book. I owe a debt of gratitude to Adam, Valerie, and Chris for midwifing the first phase. I'm also grateful to Cressida Leyshon, Dorothy Wickenden, and David Remnick at *The New Yorker* for teasing a bigger story out of what I initially put down, and helping to realize the project's subsequent iteration.

It's a winding road from magazine piece to full-length memoir, one I would not and could not have traveled without the fierce support and abiding friendship of my agent, Esther Newberg. Among her other good deeds, Esther put me in the incomparable hands of Nan Graham, editor extraordinaire. With exquisite sensitivity, skill, and patience, Nan shepherded me over more crevasses than I care to remember facing. She has my adoration, and my humble gratitude.

Also at Scribner, I was lucky to come under the gentle guidance of copyeditor Susan Brown, who saved me from numerous infelicities. Special thanks as well to Rex Bonomelli for the beautiful cover, and Paul Whitlatch for almost everything else.

At some point, I was finally convinced I would write a book about my father, but I could not have written this particular book without the enormous contributions of James L. W. West III. Jim's astute and informative biography of my father was the single most important source, outside of my own memory, in the creation of this memoir. Jim also put up with three years of tiresome queries from me, doing so not only with forbearance but constant good cheer. He has been a great friend to the whole Styron family—but to me, and *Reading My Father,* most especially.

From my first visit in the spring of 2008 to my last just a few months ago, the superb staff at the Duke University Library kindly accommodated, in so many ways, my quest to "find" my father. I'm particularly thankful to the director of the Rare Book, Manuscript, and Special Collections Library, Robert Byrd, whose door was always open for me. Also helping to make my library visits a productive pleasure were Elizabeth Dunn, Linda McCurdy, Janie Morris, Zachary Elder, Will Hansen, Megan O'Connell, and Kirston Johnson.

Many of my parents' friends went out of their way to encourage me on this journey. Had I sat down to talk with everyone who was willing to give me the benefit of his or her vast insight and experience, I'd be listening still. Of the many generous souls, particular thanks go to Bob Brustein, Mia Farrow, Carlos Fuentes, Lucy Hackney, Sheldon Hackney, Bob Loomis, Maria Matthiessen, Peter Matthiessen, Honor Moore, Mike Nichols, Reynolds Price, and Marcia Smilack.

Brooke Allen and Tony Kiser were early and valuable readers, for which I'm very grateful.

Heartfelt thanks are also due, for reasons large and larger, to Mark Bailey, Michael Barclay, Sydney Barclay, Laura Bickford,

Kate Black, Geraldine Brooks, Jane Butler, Christina Christensen, Mariana Cook, Aleksandra Crapanzano, the gals at Bright City, Gary Ginsberg, Bernard Gotfryd, Tony Horwitz, Edward Kasten-meier, Caroline Kennedy, Judy Kuhn, Jeffrey Leeds, Ilana Levine, Daphne Lewis, George Loening, Jamie Lynton, Annie Malcolm, David Michaelis, Susan Minot, all the terrific folks at Open Road Integrated Media, Annie Otis, Victoria Pearman, Abigail Pogrebin, Priscilla Rattazzi, Catherine Robinson, David Schwab, John Burn-ham Schwartz, Leslie Simitch, Kimbrough Towles, Claire White, and Marilyn Roos White.

Ultimately this is a book about, and for, my family. For their unwavering affection, support, and grandparenting skills, I am enormously thankful to Ann and Ted Beason. Many thanks, too, to Amos Beason, Kimberly Beason, Tavish Graham, Emma Larson, Lilah Larson, and Phoebe Styron.

Susanna Styron, Polly Styron, and Tom Styron—*my* bright shining stars—guided this effort with the light of their love, wisdom, and humor. They are in every line, every word. I am a very lucky and deeply grateful little sister.

As everyone who is acquainted with her knows, Rose Styron is a remarkable woman. Her unflagging enthusiasm for this under-taking, and the license she gave me to tell *my* story as well as my father's, have been a wonder and a gift. She approached the material with the eye of an artist and a mother's heart. I could not have asked for more, nor can I thank her enough.

Finally, I am most fortunate for the family of which I am a part every day: my son (and perhaps my biggest champion), Huck Bea-son; my daughter, the marvelous Martha Beason; and my true love, Ed Beason. I can scarcely imagine having survived this plunge into the past were they not there tethering me, so sweetly, to the here and now.

A Note on Sources

In addition to my father's work, both published and unpublished, I gathered a wealth of useful material from other sources. Chief among them was *William Styron: A Life*, by James L. W. West III, which proved absolutely invaluable. I also collected salient information from *We'll Always Have Paris: American Tourists in France Since 1930*, by Harvey Levenstein (University of Chicago Press, 2004), *Mailer: A Biography*, by Mary V. Dearborn (Houghton Mifflin Harcourt, 2001), and *James Jones: A Friendship*, by Willie Morris (Doubleday & Company, 1978). Paula Heredia's documentary *The Paris Review . . . Early Chapters* was another excellent resource, as was Variety Moszynski's PBS film *Voices and Visions: William Styron*.

Several books on the subject of mental illness proved enormously instructive. I was very glad to have read *Touched with Fire: Manic-Depressive Illness and the Artistic Temperament*, by Kay Redfield Jamison (Simon & Schuster, 1993), *The Midnight Disease: The Drive to Write, Writer's Block, and the Creative Brain*, by Alice W. Flaherty (Houghton Mifflin Company, 2004), and *Shock: The Healing Power of Electroconvulsive Therapy*, by Kitty Dukakis and Larry Tye (Penguin Group, 2007).

Photo Credits

Frontispiece: Photograph by Dominique Nabokov

Chapter 1: Photograph by Susanna Styron

Chapter 2: Photograph by Bernard Gotfryd

Chapter 3: Photograph courtesy of Special Collections, Duke University Library

Chapter 4: Photograph courtesy of Special Collections, Duke University Library

Chapter 5: Photograph courtesy of Rose Styron

Chapter 6: Photograph courtesy of Special Collections, Duke University Library

Chapter 8: Photograph courtesy of Rose Styron

Chapter 9: Photograph by Cornell Capa/Magnum

Chapter 10: Photograph courtesy of Robert Loomis

Chapter 11: Photograph courtesy of Special Collections, Duke University Library

Chapter 12: Photograph by Marilyn Roos White

Chapter 13: Photograph courtesy of Rose Styron

Chapter 14: Photograph by Mariana Cook

Chapter 15: Photograph courtesy of Rose Styron

Chapter 16: Photograph by Susanna Styron

End-piece: Photograph by Priscilla Rattazzi

A Scribner
Reading Group Guide

Reading My Father

QUESTIONS FOR DISCUSSION

1. Consider Alexandra's place in the Styron family as the youngest child. Could any of her older siblings have written this particular memoir? Or do you think Alexandra witnessed a different side of her parents?

2. *Reading My Father* is largely about the way Alexandra gets to know her own father. However, it also details the complex relationship between William Styron and "Grandpop." What did you make of this relationship? How was your reading of their bond affected by Grandpop's lack of correspondence and his remarriage?

3. Discuss Styron's depression. Do you believe it was caused by an inability to write, or was he not able to write because of his mental afflictions?

4. Do you think it is possible to achieve familial closure through an epistolary study? Does Alexandra's reading of her father's letters and papers help her piece together his character?

5. How did you reconcile William Styron's volatile nature with his otherwise warm and peaceful sensibilities? Did

the author's research help bring the two sides into sharper focus?

6. Based on his letters, what do you think was Styron's most formative experience as a young author? Consider his time in Philadelphia, his short service in two wars, his romances, and his integration into the literary intelligentsia following the release of *Lie Down in Darkness.*

7. Discuss Styron's years in Europe, especially the Prix de Rome. How did these years affect his character? Consider his marriage to Rose, meeting Truman Capote, and the many artists he encountered during this time.

8. How did you see the growth of "Albert" into an adult throughout the narrative? Did "reading her father" lend to some form of closure or understanding?

9. Were you surprised to learn of William Styron's infidelities? How did they change or add to your perception of him as both an author and as a character?

10. What did you make of Norman Mailer's vicious attack on William Styron's body of work? In your opinion, was the reaction part of the literary competitive environment of the time or was it more personal? Knowing Styron to have thin skin, do you believe his critics and opponents were part of his psychological demise?

11. Discuss the Styron family's various retreats and vacations. What effect did each of these places seem to have on William Styron's disposition? How do you relate these locales to his writing?

12. Would you characterize William Styron's life as a "war story"?

ENHANCE YOUR BOOK CLUB

1. Perform your own bit of epistolary detective work by rereading the e-mails, letters, and notes from your family members or friends. Are you able to paint a clearer picture of the person whom you're studying? Is there a difference between your perceived memory of the person and the character that is illustrated through these composed articles?

2. Read one of William Styron's numerous books (*Sophie's Choice, The Confessions of Nat Turner, Darkness Visible*) and see how Alexandra's memoir affects your reading of Styron's work.

3. Read another memoir revolving around the writer's relationship with his or her father. Consider Hanif Kureishi's *My Ear at His Heart*, Alison Bechdel's *Fun Home*, or Peter Birkenhead's *Gonville*. How do those paternal memoirs work in comparison to Styron's? What is it about parent-child relationships that make for such ripe material?

A Conversation with
Alexandra Styron

You accessed a very personal part of your father through his letters and correspondence. Was there ever a point you felt like you might be invading his privacy?

One of the nicest, and most surprising, discoveries I made while poring over the William Styron Papers at Duke was just how much courage and generosity my father showed by assisting in the archive's creation. There are thousands of letters there, as well as unfinished manuscripts, first drafts, and almost all of his early prose efforts. By no means does all of it reflect well on him. But I think my father recognized the value of leaving behind his whole, unvarnished story. The collection not only reveals him, but is a fascinating window into twentieth-century culture across the board. He had a great reverence for the power of art, and the power of truth as well. I never felt I was invading his privacy—I wasn't looking in his dresser drawers, after all. He meant for future scholars, biographers, anyone who was interested, really, to have a 360-degree look at him. And that's just what I got.

Who of your father's famous confidants did you most enjoy consulting with?

When I first started this book, I thought I'd go around and interview dozens of people from all different facets of my father's life. But after speaking with a few of his good friends, I realized that it was not as important to get other perspectives, or draw out lots of untold stories and secrets. I wasn't writing a biography. I was writing a memoir. What really mattered was what *I* experienced, and what I thought. I had to trust that my own information was enough to build a strong, truthful narrative. That said, I was very energized by the insights Peter and Maria Matthiessen shared with me. And a conversation with the great film director Mike Nichols on *any* subject, never mind your own father, is always fun and fascinating!

Many writers use the memoir as a form of catharsis or resolution. Do you feel writing about your father's life has been a healing experience?

I tend to think of catharsis, perhaps wrongly, as a kind of wringing-out process. Like the psychotherapy I engaged in in my twenties, where you talk about your childhood feelings till you've cried enough and gotten angry enough that your can put your feelings away and move on. The experience of writing this book was nothing like that. *But,* having finished, I'm definitely more resolved, and possess a certain lightness, vis à vis my feelings about my father. Exploring this material was like being a detective. Or maybe just like being a biographer. I was able to put so many pieces of my father's personality together and to look at the picture detached from my filial self. In the end, I think my empathy is much stronger than any residual anger. I'm glad for that. Carrying grudges, I've discovered, can really wrench your back out.

Which of your father's books is your favorite? Are there any that you have trouble reading?

I like most of my father's work a great deal. *Sophie's Choice* is simply remarkable. It's a true page-turner, devastating but also funny as hell. I guess I'd say it was my favorite. *Set This House on Fire* is, in my opinion, totally underappreciated. And though I think *The Confessions of Nat Turner* is absolutely extraordinary, I'm not sure I could read it again. It's upsetting in a way that just about wrecked me. As a short introduction to my father's work, "A Tidewater Morning" is excellent—charming and transportive.

What advice would you give to someone battling with depression and anxiety?

Well, I'm no doctor. I would never presume to give any real advice on a disease as both amorphous and pernicious as clinical depression. But I guess, if there's one observation I had the misfortune of making, it's that "recovery" is rarely complete and permanent. With the right help, depression can usually be managed. Often, it can be driven off aggressively enough to give sufferers a whole new run at a happy life. But ongoing therapy and medication are really important. My father was very old school. After his first depression, he believed he was cured and didn't want any more help. So he didn't do much in the way of maintenance. Eventually, of course, the disease came back. With a vengeance.

Having read *Sophie's Choice*, how do you view the modern environment of Brooklyn?

The Brooklyn my father describes in *Sophie's Choice* is a vanished place. In 1947, he lived in what is now known as the Prospect Park South neighborhood (the realtors who eventually gave it that name probably weren't even born yet). The whole country, the planet, was still recovering from World War II; Brooklyn was the nexus of the European diaspora. I imagine for my father, a Southern boy whose ancestors had settled North Carolina, Brooklyn must have felt as alien as the streets of Minsk or Kraków. Now that neighborhood is home to another wave—Jamaicans, Dominicans, Puerto Ricans. The change would have stunned my father. But probably not as much as the transformation of the part of Brooklyn *I* live in, a mere fifteen-minute walk from his old corner. It's pretty and quiet and safe, and everyone is either a writer or a documentary filmmaker. Had it been that like this sixty years ago, I bet he'd never have left. And I'd be a Brooklyn native!

Your father seemed to be a tremendously political man. Do you believe there are strong ties between politics and art? Were your father's leftist leanings an important aspect of his authorship?

I grew up with a very strong sense that art and politics were sort of cultural Siamese twins. They share some of the same organs, rely on and enhance one another with their expressive power. During my childhood, my mother's human rights work focused largely on prisoners of conscience, i.e., people living under oppressive regimes whose writings had led to their imprisonment. And, more often than not, my father's work was propelled by his political and moral convictions. Artists, I learned, are often exceptionally brave and truly important people. With their grab bag of tools—words, paint, musical instruments—they can circumvent even the most authoritarian regimes, galvanize whole nations, and all with the trick of metaphor. I think my father's devotion to the novel was also a devotion to politics; he wanted to wake people up, make them think, remind them of their history so they would not be condemned to repeat it. It's probably what I admired about him above all else.

You have devoted an entire book to examining your relationship with your father. If you were limited to describing him in just one word, what would it be?

I might have to go to the thesaurus for this one. "Unquiet," perhaps.

Do you plan on writing another novel now that this memoir is complete? Do you feel you've inherited your interest in writing from your father?

I would like to return to the novel I was working on when I began this memoir. I put a lot of time into it, and believe I have a strong theme, the kind that would hold up to my father's scrutiny. But I'm taking a breather right now and focusing on some shorter, less-intense projects. I learned a lot by observing my father. Not only the value of a well-turned sentence, but that truly good work takes time and faith.